Resource Guide:
Cases, Exercises, and Study Options
to Accompany

Human Resource Management
Eight Edition

Robert L. Mathis
University of Nebraska at Omaha

John H. Jackson
University of Wyoming

Prepared By

Sally A. Coltrin
University of North Florida

Roger A. Dean
Washington and Lee University

WEST PUBLISHING COMPANY

Minneapolis/St. Paul   New York   Los Angeles   San Francisco

WEST'S COMMITMENT TO THE ENVIRONMENT

In 1906, West Publishing Company began recycling materials left over from the production of books. This began a tradition of efficient and responsible use of resources. Today, 100% of our legal bound volumes are printed on acid-free, recycled paper consisting of 50% new fibers. West recycles nearly 27,700,000 pounds of scrap paper annually—the equivalent of 229,300 trees. Since the 1960s, West has devised ways to capture and recycle waste inks, solvents, oils, and vapors created in the printing process. We also recycle plastics of all kinds, wood, glass, corrugated cardboard, and batteries, and have eliminated the use of polystyrene book packaging. We at West are proud of the longevity and the scope of our commitment to the environment.

West pocket parts and advance sheets are printed on recyclable paper and can be collected and recycled with newspapers. Staples do not have to be removed. Bound volumes can be recycled after removing the cover.

Production, Prepress, Printing and Binding by West Publishing Company.

 TEXT IS PRINTED ON 10% POST CONSUMER RECYCLED PAPER

Contents

Human Resource Management Resource Guide

Preface

In the study of human resource (HR) management, it is essential to integrate theory and practice. This resource guide, to be used in conjunction with *Human Resource Management, Eighth Edition*, by Robert L. Mathis and John H. Jackson, is designed to supplement your knowledge of HR management theory and to enhance your ability to apply theory to practice.

CONTENTS OF THE RESOURCE GUIDE

The chapters of this resource guide follow the sequence of chapters in the Mathis and Jackson textbook. Each chapter begins with a set of *Chapter Objectives*. To provide continuity and reinforcement, the objectives are stated exactly as they are in the Mathis and Jackson text. The objectives are followed by a *Summary of the Chapter*, which briefly reviews the essential elements of the chapter, highlighting major topics around which your learning should focus.

Next, a set of *Study Questions* is provided. These consist of matching key terms with their appropriate definitions, true false, completion, and multiple choice questions which review your general knowledge of the factual material, and essay questions which provide you with an opportunity to conceptualize major ideas presented in the text. An *Answer Key*, following the questions in each chapter, provides you with immediate feedback.

Each chapter includes two *Cases* and/or *Exercises* which have been written to encourage you to think of real world HR issues. Most of the cases are based on true events, although the names and places are usually changed.

SUGGESTIONS FOR USING THE RESOURCE GUIDE

This resource guide should be used as a supplement to, not a substitute for, your textbook. Therefore, you should develop a pattern for using the book to facilitate your learning of HR theory and practice. Some students may find that scanning the objectives and summary, before reading the corresponding text chapter, provides a helpful preview and overview of what to expect in the chapter. Others may feel these sections provide an appropriate synthesis and review after reading the text.

The study questions may be similar to those used by your professor for examination purposes. Since the correct answers are provided, you can check your own work to determine if further study of the text material is necessary.

The cases and exercises provide a variety of approaches for understanding the theory and its application to real world situations. Even if your professor does not specifically assign a case or exercise, you will find that studying and working through them will enhance your ability to apply theory to practice.

NOTE TO INSTRUCTORS

This resource guide provides instructors with a composite of ancillary materials. Most of the cases and exercises conclude with a series of questions, and thus may be used as a basis for class discussion and/or they may be used as homework assignments. Comments and possible solutions for each case and exercise are found in the *Instructor's Manual* which accompanies *Human Resource Management, Eighth Edition*.

Sally A. Coltrin
Jacksonville, Florida

Roger A. Dean
Lexington, Virginia

Chapter 1

The Strategic Nature of Human Resource Management

CHAPTER OBJECTIVES

1. Discuss the goals of HR management and tell how they link with the two roles of HR management.

2. Define organizational culture and discuss its link to HR strategy.

3. Identify four major HR challenges currently facing organizations and managers.

4. List and define each of the six major categories of HR activities.

5. Explain why HR professionals and operating managers must view HR management as an interface.

6. Discuss why ethical issues and professionalism affect HR management.

SUMMARY OF THE CHAPTER

The management of people at work is one of the primary keys to organizational success. Changes facing organizations require that employees be viewed as *human resources* whose value can be managed, and not just seen as labor costs.Employers have found that better management of human resources can enhance productivity, quality, and service.

The field of human resource (HR) management is in the midst of a transitional period where some of the traditional roles are being replaced by a variety of new responsibilities. Two types of roles are associated with the management of human resources in organizations. The *strategic* role of HR management emphasizes that the people in an organization are valuable resources representing a significant investment of organizational efforts. The focus is on the planning and attainment of organizational objectives with a longer-time horizon. Thus human resources must be viewed in the same context as the financial, technological, and other resources that are managed in organizations.

The *operational* role involves activities that are tactical and administrative in nature. These activities, typically associated with the day-to-day management of people, have often been referred to as "the personnel function." Operational activities include such functions as equal employment compliance, interviewing job applicants, orientation of new employees, training, and wage and salary administration.

Two factors, organizational life cycles and organizational culture, affect HR strategies. Organizations typically evolve through four life cycle stages: Introduction, growth, maturity, and decline. HR strategies differ across the various stages and the focus of HR activities shifts as well. The culture of organizations also affects HR strategy. Organizational culture is a pattern of shared values and beliefs giving members of an organization meaning and providing them with rules for behavior. Thus, it is important that organizational strategies in general and HR strategies in particular be compatible with the organizational culture.

As the environment in which HR management changes it requires changes in HR strategies to meet a number of challenges. Five areas in particular present new challenges for HR management. These include economic and employment shifts, education and training, organizational restructuring, demographic diversity, and balancing work and family.

HR management is composed of several groups of interrelated activities. Legal, political, economic, social, cultural, and technological forces affect the following groupings of HR activities:

* HR Planning and Analysis
* Equal Employment Opportunity Compliance
* Staffing
* HR Development
* Compensation and Benefits
* Employee and Labor/Management Relations

Cooperation between people who specialize in HR management and other managers is critical to organizational success. This cooperation requires contact, or interface, between the two groups. HR management is a concern of both the managers and the HR unit in an organization.

As an organization grows, so does the need for a separate HR department. In a growing number of organizations, some specialty HR activities are being contracted to outside providers and consultants.

Ethical issues in HR management have proliferated, and must be faced in all types and sizes of organizations. Ethical issues are ones that pose fundamental questions about fairness, justice, truthfulness, and social responsibility.

The effective management of human resources requires professionals. There are several levels of HR jobs ranging from executive to clerical in nature. Preparation for a career in HR includes broad and specialized education, experience, professional involvement, and certification.

STUDY QUESTIONS

Matching Questions

Match the key term from the list below with its most appropriate definition.

a.	Operational activities	h.	HR Planning and analysis
b.	Organizational Culture	i.	Business Process Reengineering
c.	HR Specialist	j.	HR Generalist
d.	Outsourcing	k.	Downsizing
e.	Compensation	l.	Human Capital
f.	Strategic role	m.	Ethics
g.	Human Resource Management	n.	Interfaces

____   1.   Managers attempt to anticipate forces that will impact the future supply of and demand for employees.

____   2.   The design of formal systems to ensure the effective and efficient use of human talent to accomplish organizational goals.

____   3.   Areas of contact between the HR unit and managers within the organization.

____   4.   Rewards people for performing organizational work through pay, incentives, and benefits.

____   5.   The total value of organizational human resources.

____   6.   The fundamental rethinking and redesign or work to improve cost, service, and speed.

____   7.   A pattern of shared values and beliefs giving members of an organization meaning and providing them with rules for behavior.

____   8.   Someone with responsibility for performing a variety of activities.

___   9.   Someone with in-depth knowledge and expertise in a limited area.

___   10.   Emphasizes that the people in an organization are valuable resources representing a significant investment of organizational efforts.

___   11.   Activities that are tactical and administrative in nature.

___   12.   A strategy to reduce costs, most often through a reduction in payroll.

___   13.   Deals with what "ought" to be done.

___   14.   Contracting with another organization to provide operations that were previously handled internally.

True/False Questions

___   1.   HR strategies and activities remain about the same regardless of the organization's life cycle stage.

___   2.   Preparation for a career in HR includes broad and specialized education, experience, professional involvement, and accreditation.

___   3.   Staffing emphasizes the recruitment and selection of the human resources for an organization.

___   4.   Unit labor costs have risen dramatically since the advent of downsizing.

___   5.   Concern about employee rights and privacy protection must be incorporated into HR policies and practices.

___   6.   The area of ethics is not a major concern of HR Managers.

___   7.   Cost savings associated with outsourcing often are over estimate.

___   8.   Equal employment compliance affects all HR activities.

___   9.   HR specialists are more often found in small organizations.

___   10.   "Outplacement" is the concept whereby small organizations contract out their HR activities to a firm of consultants.

___   11.   Enlightened managers do not regard employees as "human resources" because this would dehumanize people.

___   12.   Organizational culture has little impact of HR strategies.

___   13.   Increased legal requirements and constraints have had very little impact on HR departments.

___   14.   "Liking to work with people" is the major qualification necessary for success in HR.

___   15.   Human resource management is primarily seen as concerned with administrative and operational activities.

___   16.   HR management is a concern of both the managers and the HR unit in an organization.

Idea Completion Questions

1.   There are two major roles that are associated with the management of human resources in organizations. These roles are _____ and _____.

2.   The interface concept recognizes that HR management is a concern of both the _____ and the _____ in an organization.

3.   As a response to ethical situations, many organizations have established a _____, and conduct _____ for all employees.

4.   HR management is composed of six groups of interrelated activities. These groupings are: _____, _____, _____, _____, _____, and _____.

5.   The stages in an organizational life-cycle which affect the choice of HR strategies and activities are: _____, _____, _____, and _____.

Multiple Choice Questions

___   1.   Compensation and HR planning become a major focus for HR efforts in the _____ stage of the organizational life cycle.
   a.   introduction
   b.   growth
   c.   maturity
   d.   decline

___   2.   A point of contact on HR activities between the HR unit and the managers within the organization is a(n)
   a.   dualism.
   b.   definition of personnel management.
   c.   interface.
   d.   idea.

___   3.   _____ is the design of formal systems to ensure the effective and efficient use of human talent to accomplish organizational goals.
   a.   Employee relations
   b.   Personnel management
   c.   Human resource management
   d.   both a and b
   e.   all of the above

___   4.   _____ is the fundamental rethinking and redesign of work processes to improve cost, service, and speed.
   a.   Downsizing
   b.   Outsourcing
   c.   Restructuring
   d.   Reengineering

___   5.   Someone with responsibility for performing a variety of human resource activities is a
   a.   personnel manager.
   b.   personnel consultant.
   c.   HR specialist.
   d.   HR generalist.
   e.   all of the above.

___   6.   HR management as a specialized function in organizations really began its growth about
             a.   1900.
             b.   1920.
             c.   1940.
             d.   1960.
             e.   1980.

___   7.   The strategic role of HR began to emerge about
             a.   1920.
             b.   1940.
             c.   1960.
             d.   1980.
             e.   1990.

___   8.   Projections on workforce diversity suggest that by the year 2000 about _____ percent
             of the workforce will be members of a racial minority.
             a.   10
             b.   25
             c.   33
             d.   50

___   9.   In the decade leading up to the year 2000, which of the following industries are declining?

             a.   health care
             b.   computer processing
             c.   manufacturing
             d.   service
             e.   all of the above

___   10.   In order to develop more "family friendly" policies and support systems for their employees,
             organizations are
             a.   assisting with child and elder care arrangements.
             b.   permitting work-at-home options.
             c.   adopting flexible work schedules.
             d.   both a and c.
             e.   all of the above.

___   11.   Viewing human resources in the same context as the financial, technological, and other resources that are managed by organizations, is an example of the _____ of HR management.
    a.   operational role
    b.   personnel function
    c.   global nature
    d.   strategic role
    e.   traditional role

___   12.   The most frequently outsourced HR activity is
    a.   recruiting.
    b.   selection.
    c.   401(k) plan administration.
    d.   labor relations.
    e.   payroll administration.

___   13.   Ethical issues in HR management are important because
    a.   such decisions often affect the personal lives of employees, and their families.
    b.   they have an immediate, short term impact.
    c.   the consequences of making decisions with ethical dimensions often are not known.
    d.   both a and c.
    e.   all of the above.

___   14.   Recruiting and selecting employees for current openings is an example of the _____ role of human resource management activities.
    a.   operational
    b.   personnel
    c.   global
    d.   strategic

Essay Questions

1.   Discuss some of the major ethical issues to be faced by HR management in the 1990s. What are the possible consequences of making unethical HR decisions? How can an organization encourage ethical HR decision making?

2.   Describe some of the external forces that will challenge an organization in the decade leading up to the year 2000. How will some of these forces influence HR management?

3.   Distinguish between the operational role and the strategic role of HR management. Why are they both important in today's organizations?

4.   Define the interface concept, and explain its use as it applies to HR management.

5.   List and describe the six HR management activities. Discuss how these activities may be performed differently in settings other than large private-sector organizations.

ANSWER KEY

Matching

1. h	2. g	3. n	4. e	5. l
6. i	7. b	8. j	9. c	10. f
11. a	12. k	13. m	14. d	

True/False

1. F	2. T	3. T	4. F	5. T
6. F	7. T	8. T	9. F	10. F
11. F	12. F	13. F	14. F	15. F
16. T				

Idea Completion

1. strategic;   operational

2. operating managers;   HR unit.

3. code of ethics;   training programs

4. HR planning and analysis
    equal employment opportunity compliance
    staffing
    HR development
    compensation and benefits
    employee and labor/management relations

5. introduction
    growth
    maturity
    decline

Multiple Choice

1.	c	2.	c	3.	c	4.	d	5.	d
6.	a	7.	d	8.	c	9.	c	10.	e
11.	d	12.	c	13.	d	14.	a		

ERIKKSEN MANUFACTURING

Erikksen Manufacturing is a mid-size manufacturer of automobile parts. Their customers are primarily the discount chains and the auto parts stores. They have a reputation for quality products that are as good as, and sometime better than, those sold by the automobile companies.

Miriam Jennings, human resource manager at Erikksen, has just learned that one of the big three automobile firms has placed a very large order for brake parts. The firm acknowledged that it can purchase better brakes at a lower price than they can be manufactured in its Michigan plant. John Erikksen, a major shareholder and CEO of Erikksen, informed Miriam that success in filling this order will probably lead to more business in the future from the automobile industry.

Miriam's immediate concern is in finding and hiring two hundred and fifty new, qualified employees to work on this brake contract, which needs to be filled progressively over the next twelve months.

In the past, Erikksen's growth rate required adding twenty to thirty new employees a year. With Memphis nearby, Miriam never found it difficult to find enough people to fill job openings, although inevitably some new employees quit or failed to perform adequately. Never had the company needed to hire so many people so quickly, and never had the company been so concerned about meeting the high standards of a major customer. In addition, most of the new jobs had to be filled with semiskilled and skilled employees. Previously, most new hires were unskilled workers who filled jobs that simply involved a six-step assembly process. Consequently, when Miriam needed job applicants, she just filed a request with the Tennessee State Employment Commission and selected workers on a "first-come, first-served" basis.

Miriam realizes that she must abandon her previous selection practice. She knows it will be necessary to find out the skills of the job applicants and place them in the jobs they are qualified to perform. But performing the job is not Miriam's only concern. She realizes that other behaviors such as attendance, team work, loyalty, concern for quality, flexibility, availability to work overtime, and willingness to retrain will affect the successful fulfillment of the auto-firm contract. She sees this as an opportunity to systematically develop an entire set of human resource practices and get the line managers more involved in the process. First things first, however: she needs to hire two hundred and fifty new, qualified applicants.

Questions

1. What are all the activities Miriam Jennings must do to be successful here?

2. Where should Miriam Jennings begin? What should she do first? What goals should she set to accomplish within the next year?

HR MANAGEMENT IN THE NEWS

The text identifies four major HR challenges currently facing organizations and management: economic and employment shifts, education and training, organizational restructuring, demographic diversity, balancing work and family.

Throughout the semester, subscribe to the *Wall Street Journal* and your local newspaper. As you read these newspapers daily, take special note of stories that may impact human resource management. These stories may include legislative proposals, governmental policies, civil rights issues, affirmative action, court decisions, employee discipline, employer liability issues, substance abuse on the job, labor union activities, and tax reform. Cut out the relevant stories, and prepare a journal.

At the end of the semester, re-read chapter 1 and update the material based on what you have read and compiled in your journal. A class discussion on the last day of term will indicate how the field of human resource management is rapidly changing.

Chapter 2

Strategic Human Resource Planning

CHAPTER OBJECTIVES

1. Identify HR practices associated with two strategic business approaches.

2. Define HR planning and discuss management and HR-unit responsibilities for it.

3. Outline the HR planning process.

4. Discuss why external environmental scanning is an important part of HR planning.

5. Explain how auditing current jobs and skills relates to HR planning.

6. Identify factors to be considered in forecasting the supply and demand for human resources in an organization.

7. Discuss several ways to manage a surplus of human resources.

SUMMARY OF THE CHAPTER

Human resource planning begins with the overall strategic plan of the organization. Organizations typically choose one of two basic business strategies: defender or prospector. The defender strategy, appropriate in relatively stable business environments, approaches competition on the basis of low prices and high quality product or service. The prospector strategy requires finding new products and markets and is more appropriate in rapidly changing, unstable markets. Human Resource strategy then varies as a function of the organization's strategic plan.

Human resource planning is the process of analyzing and identifying the need for and availability of the human resources required for an organization to meet its objectives. While top management is responsible for overall strategic planning, the HR unit usually plans the necessary human resource support to implement overall organizational goals. Once compiled and approved the HR plan is monitored by managers and the HR unit.

The strategic HR planning process involves five steps:

1. *Organizational philosophy and mission* defines the values of the company, promotes the essence of why the organization exists, and identifies the unique contribution it makes.

2. *External environmental scanning* affects HR planning because an organization must draw from the same labor market that supplies all employers. The composition of the workforce is changing with a reduction in the rate of growth in the total labor force, women and minorities accounting for an increased proportion of the labor force, and a decline in the number of younger workers. Other environmental influences on HR planning include government rules and restrictions that have a tremendous impact on HR activities, economic trends, and geographic and competitive conditions.

3. *Internal strengths and weaknesses* of the organization must be identified by the strategists. This involves a comprehensive analysis of all current jobs and an audit of current employees. Individual employee data included in the audit would be employee demographics, career progression, and performance records. Once the jobs and employees have been audited, a profile can be developed which addresses the strengths and weaknesses of the current workforce. The profile may identify skill shortages, turnover statistics, anticipated retirements, mobility restrictions of current workers, and specialization of workers by group.

4. *Forecasting* uses information on the past and present to identify expected future conditions. Models for forecasting human resource needs range from a manager's best guess to a rigorous and complex computer simulation. Human resource forecasting should be done over three planning periods: short-range, intermediate, and long-range. The forecast should identify the supply of human resources, and the demand for human resources.

5. *A human resource plan* is compiled to enable managers in the organization to match the available supply of labor with the forecasted demands in light of the strategies of the firm. If the plan identifies a human resource surplus, workforce reductions or "downsizing" may be necessary. Attrition, early retirement buy-outs, layoffs, and outplacement are the most easily devised ways of downsizing an organization. If forecasts identify a shortage of workers with particular skills, the HR plan should address how to close the gap between supply and demand.

A final aspect of strategic HR planning is the evaluation of the effectiveness of the process.

STUDY QUESTIONS

Matching Questions

Match the key term from the list below with its most appropriate definition.

a.	Demand-pull forecasting	g.	Employee skills inventory
b.	Downsizing	h.	Human resource planning
c.	Strategic planning	i.	Environmental scanning
d.	Outplacement	j.	Transition Matrix
e.	Workforce profile	k.	Philosophy and mission
f.	Forecasting		

___ 1. The process of identifying organizational objectives and actions needed to achieve those objectives.

___ 2. The process of studying the environment in which the organization exists to pinpoint opportunities and threats.

___ 3. Analyzing and identifying the need for and availability of human resources required so that the organization can meet its objectives.

___   4.   Define the values of the company and promote the essence of why the organization exists.

___   5.   The average rate of historical movement from one job to another shown in probabilities.

___   6.   A group of services provided for displaced employees to give them support and assistance.

___   7.   Considers specific openings that are likely to occur and uses that as the basis for planning.

___   8.   A compilation of data on the skills and characteristics of employees.

___   9.   Uses information on the past and present to identify expected future conditions.

___   10.   Reducing the size of an organizational workforce.

___   11.   Addresses the strengths and weaknesses of the current workforce.

True/False Questions

___   1.   A key element of total organizational planning is the development of an effective human resources strategy.

___   2.   HR planning should be conducted as a process totally separate from the overall strategic planning process in an organization.

___   3.   The HR unit is responsible for overall strategic planning.

___   4.   The mission statement clarifies how this organization is different from other competing entities.

___   5.   Contingent workers represent about 20% of today's work force.

___   6.   Environmental scanning is concerned primarily with the demand for labor.

___   7.   When the unemployment rate is high, it is more difficult to find qualified workers.

___   8.   The time frame for intermediate planning is 1 - 5 years.

___   9.   Government's influence on HR planning has stayed relatively stable over time.

___   10.   Succession analysis is a widely used internal method to forecast the supply of people for certain positions.

___   11.   Early retirement buyouts do not tend to save organizations money in the long run.

___   12.   HR planning is not effective unless the plans are continuously monitored and reviewed.

Idea Completion Questions

1.   The four steps in the strategic human resources planning process are:
_____, _____, _____, and
_____.

2.   The external environmental factors affecting labor supply are:
_____, _____, _____, and
_____.

3.   The judgmental/subjective methods of forecasting include:
_____, _____, _____, and
_____.

4.   Mathematical approaches to forecasting demand include:
_____, _____, _____, and
_____.

5.   Frequently used methods of downsizing are:
_____, _____, and _____.

Multiple Choice Questions

___   1.   The process of identifying organizational objectives and actions needed to achieve those objectives is
a.   H R planning.
b.   forecasting.
c.   managing human resources.
d.   strategic planning.

___   2.   Strategic planning must _____ managing human resources in order for overall organizational planning efforts to be comprehensive.
a.   include
b.   supersede
c.   ignore
d.   specialize in

___   3.   The _____ clarifies how this organization is different from other competing entities.
a.   organizational culture
b.   strategic plan
c.   mission statement
d.   life cycle

___   4.   The characteristics of Human Resource strategy for an organization following a prospector strategy include which of the following?
a.   build skills in existing employees
b.   production and control skills needed
c.   shorter Human Resource Planning horizon
d.   all of the above.
e.   Only a and b above.

___   5.   A typical skills inventory would include
a.   education and training.
b.   mobility and geographic preferences.
c.   promotability ratings.
d.   specific aptitudes, abilities, and interests.
e.   all of the above.

___   6.   Training is less important in which stage of the organizational life cycle?
        a.   introduction
        b.   growth
        c.   maturity
        d.   decline

___   7.   Factors that affect the supply of potential employees available to an organization include
        a.   government regulations and pressures.
        b.   changing workforce composition and patterns.
        c.   economic conditions.
        d.   all of the above.
        e.   a and b only.

___   8.   Which of the following are characteristics of the HR strategy for organizations following a defender strategy?
        a.   long HR planning horizon
        b.   builds skills in existing employees
        c.   marketing and Research and Development skills needed
        d.   all of the above
        e.   and b above only

___   9.   Which of the following factors determine HR Plans?
        a.   competitive/financial environment
        b.   current organizational situation
        c.   strategy of the organization
        d.   culture of the organization
        e.   all of the above

___   10.   Which of the following are reasons why organizations should use outplacement services?
        a.   cost control
        b.   company image
        c.   social responsibility
        d.   all of the above
        e.   only b and c above

___   11.   The starting point for evaluating internal strengths and weaknesses is a(n)
        a.   audit of jobs and skills.
        b.   human resource plan.
        c.   system of performance evaluation.
        d.   trend projection.

___   12.   A widely used forecast method that relies on replacement charts is
        a.   the Delphi technique.
        b.   regression analysis.
        c.   succession analysis.
        d.   a simulation.

___   13.   Forecasting methods that rely on statistical comparison of past relationships among various factors are
        a.   simulations.
        b.   regression analyses.
        c.   rule-of-thumb forecasts.
        d.   trend projections.

___   14.   _____ rely upon general guidelines being applied to a specific situation within the organization.
        a.   Succession analyses
        b.   Simulations
        c.   Regression analyses
        d.   Rule-of-thumb forecasts

___   15.   A human resources surplus can be managed by downsizing the organization through
        a.   attrition.
        b.   early retirement buy-outs.
        c.   outplacement.
        d.   all of the above.
        e.   a and b only.

___ 16. If forecasts identify a shortage of workers with particular skills, the HR plan should include plans for
   a.   identifying possible sources of labor.
   b.   outplacement.
   c.   training and development of current employees.
   d.   all of the above.
   e.   a and c only.

Essay Questions

1. Describe the possible consequences for a large organization that does not conduct HR planning.

2. Discuss the differences in HR strategy in defender and prospector organizations.

3. Identify the various factors that affect the supply of labor to a large manufacturing firm. How can the firm minimize the impact of these factors?

4. Explain the relationship of HR Planning to organizational strategic planning.

5. Assume that you are the Director of Human Resources at a large national bank, and that your bank has just acquired a large regional bank. What plans would you implement to manage the excess and overlapping employees?

ANSWER KEY

Matching

1.	c	2.	i	3.	h	4.	k	5.	j
6.	d	7.	a	8.	g	9.	f	10.	b
11.	e								

True/False

1.	T	2.	F	3.	F	4.	T	5.	T
6.	F	7.	F	8.	T	9.	F	10.	T
11.	F	12.	T						

Idea Completion

1. Scanning the external environment
   internal analysis of jobs and people
   forecasting
   managing a human resource plan

2. Workforce composition and work patterns
   government influences
   geographic and competitive conditions
   economic conditions

3. Delphi technique
   rule-of-thumb
   estimates
   nominal-group technique

4. statistical regression analysis
   simulation models
   productivity ratios
   staffing ratios

5. attrition
early retirement buyouts
layoffs

Multiple Choice

1.	d	2.	a	3.	c	4.	c	5.	e
6.	d	7.	d	8.	e	9.	e	10.	d
11.	a	12.	c	13.	b	14.	d	15.	d
16.	e								

SAINT HELLEN'S UNIVERSITY

Located in Massachusetts, Saint Hellen's College for Women was founded in 1888 as a private liberal arts college for women. In the late 1960s, responding to the professional aspirations of its students, the faculty expanded the undergraduate curriculum to include a major in business administration. Thus, in addition to the traditional Bachelor of Arts and Bachelor of Science degrees in the College of Arts and Sciences, Saint Hellen's offered a Bachelor of Business Administration degree in a fully accredited School of Management. By the late 1970s, Saint Hellen's College for Women enrolled almost 1,500 undergraduate students, approximately 25 percent of whom majored in business administration. The college was proud of its unique national reputation as a selective liberal arts college with an accredited business school.

As the college entered the 1990s, its future looked daunting. The faculty had observed that the number of high school students seeking admission to Saint Hellen's was falling, and complained that student test scores were declining. In 1992, following an extensive self study, the faculty concluded that a single-sex college was becoming less and less attractive to female high school graduates. Responding to the faculty's recommendation, Saint Hellen's Board of Governors voted to "admit all qualified students without regard to gender." In addition, the Board decided to change the name of the college to "Saint Hellen's University."

It was anticipated that in ten years the composition of the student body would be approximately two-thirds female and one-third male. The decision to admit male students, together with extensive media coverage, resulted in an increase of nearly 50 percent in the number of high school seniors applying for admission to the first coed class which entered as freshmen in the fall of 1993. The students applying to Saint Hellen's University were, on average, better qualified in terms of SAT scores, secondary school grades, and achievements tests than the applicants in recent years.

This trend continued, and in May 1996 the admissions office reported that less than forty-five percent of applicants were being admitted to Saint Hellen's University. In addition, approximately fifty percent of the applicants were men.

The faculty were overwhelmed. Rather than deny admission to so many obviously qualified students, the faculty voted to gradually increase the size of the student body to 2,000 undergraduates, and to be truly gender-blind in admissions procedures. This plan required that freshmen enrollment be increased by 100 students per year for five years. University president, Dr. Janice McGill, appointed several task forces to study the potential impact of increasing the size and composition of the student body on the various programs of the university.

One task force was charged with studying the composition, development, and effectiveness of the faculty. In January 1997, this task force presented its report to President McGill. Their report included the following observations:

Student/Faculty Ratio - In the fall of 1996 there were 166 full-time faculty members. This translated into a 9 to 1 student/faculty ratio. To maintain this ratio, the university will need an additional 56 faculty positions before 2002. However the present faculty were not proportionally distributed between the College of Arts and Sciences and the School of Management. In the College, the average class size was 10 students, while classes averaged 25 in the School of Management.

The task force recommended a university-wide class size of 15, which was in keeping with the figures quoted in the student recruitment literature.

In a survey of the 1996 freshman class, it was learned that 50 percent of the men and 25 percent of the women planned to major in business administration, with the remainder planning majors in the various departments of the College of Arts and Sciences. (Students earning degrees in the School of Management are required to complete a general education distribution within the College of Arts and Sciences.) In light of this, the task force recommended that of the 56 new faculty positions, 40 should be in the School of Management.

Faculty Recruitment - The College of Arts and Sciences reported that they were having little difficulty in hiring new faculty. But this was not the case for the School of Management. Whereas there was a limited market for a scholar with a Ph.D. in classical literature, history, or philosophy, business schools were in direct competition with industry for top Ph.D. graduates. In addition, it was not unusual for a graduating senior with a BBA degree and a good GPA to receive initial job offers paying over $35,000. This, of course, meant that fewer and fewer students were eager to pursue doctoral studies in business disciplines.

Faculty Salaries - It was here that the task force uncovered considerable feelings of inequity. A newly graduated Ph.D. in business administration can expect an initial salary exceeding $60,000 as an assistant professor at Saint Hellen's University. The dean of the School of Management complained that this salary level, while competitive with other small colleges, is considerably less than that offered by either consulting firms or industry. This competition with industry has resulted in acute shortages of business faculty nationwide. The dean argued that, to attract and retain superior faculty, the university must implement an across-the-board salary increase of at least 20 percent for all professors in the School of Management.

Faculty in the College of Arts and Sciences also expressed feelings of inequity. When compared to the School of Management their salaries are considerably lower. A newly graduated Ph.D. can expect a starting salary of less than $30,000. The average salary for senior faculty with at least 15 years service is $50,000.

Benefits - In addition to the usual retirement, medical, disability, and life insurance, and faculty leave packages, Saint Hellen's offers a generous educational grant for children of faculty members. This grant provides for tuition to be waived for faculty children attending Saint Hellen's University. Children attending other universities will be awarded educational grants up to 90 percent of Saint Hellen's tuition.

Faculty Demographics - In the past, Saint Hellen's College for Women attracted a faculty, approximately fifty/fifty male and female, that was dedicated to teaching. Turnover has been very low. The professors, staff, and students speak of "community" when they describe university life.

In the School of Management, the average age of the faculty is 37, with 80 percent of the professors less than 45 years old. In the College of Arts and Sciences, 50 percent of the professors are over 55, and 35 percent are under 30 years old.

Even prior to admitting male students, most of the professors in the School of Management were male. Since 1993, only one of the new professors hired by the School of Management was female. With regard to race, all the faculty in the School of Management are white. In the College of Arts and Sciences, there is one tenured and two untenured African-American professors. The only other non-white professor is an Asian teaching in the language department.

Student Concerns - A recent survey conducted by the Student Senate reported that female business students complained that they lacked suitable role models at the university. Many women responded that the admission of male students was having a negative effect on the status of women at Saint Hellen's.

A significant number of students, both male and female, commented that the younger professors seemed less committed to the traditions of Saint Hellen's University. Students and alumnae observed that they appeared more interested in their own academic careers, especially with regard to research and consulting, than in teaching or student advising.

Questions

1. Is strategic HR planning appropriate for Saint Hellen's University?

2. What HR issues do you expect to become critical in the next ten years? What short-term, intermediate, and long-range plans should Saint Hellen's University develop to address these issues?

3. What factors must President McGill consider as she forecasts the supply and demand for faculty at the university?

4. Describe the organizational culture at Saint Hellen's University. How is it likely to change in the next few years?

5. How can the Board of Governors evaluate the success of HR planning at the university?

AUDITING JOBS

Obtaining a profile of the existing workforce is an important part of the assessment of an organization's internal strengths and weaknesses. This exercise provides an opportunity for you to develop a workforce profile of a small company or a department in a larger firm.

Assignment

1.   Contact a local firm and explain that you wish to do a workforce profile of approximately 25 employees, all in the same department or small firm.

2.   Complete the workforce profile and HR forecast on the next pages and share the results with the appropriate management of the firm.

3.   With the profile and forecast completed, write a report that addresses the following:

   a)   How could the limited information you obtained about the current workforce be useful in HR planning?

   b)   Are there any potential human resource problems in the organization? (For example, is there an aging workforce, a potential labor surplus or shortage?)

   c)   What difficulties did you experience in getting the managers to forecast anticipated demand? What are the implications of those difficulties?

   d)   Identify at least three other factors that would be beneficial to obtain on the current workforce. How would they be useful?

Workforce Profile

Current Workforce	Category*			
	1	2	3	4
Age of Workers				
Under 25 years				
25-39 years				
40-55 years				
Over 55 years				
More than 10 years				
Sex				
Female				
Male				
Racial and Ethnic Group				
African American				
Asian				
Hispanic				
Native American				
White				
Other				

* Category 1 - Managerial employees
  Category 2 - Professional employees
  Category 3 - Office and clerical employees
  Category 4 - Operations and other employees

Workforce Profile
page 2

Current Workforce	Category*			
	1	2	3	4
Educational Levels				
Less than high school				
High school diploma				
Some post high school				
Bachelors degree				
Advanced degree				
Years with Firm				
Less than 2 years				
2-5 years				
5-10 years				
More than 10 years				

```
  * Category 1  -  Managerial employees
    Category 2  -  Professional employees
    Category 3  -  Office and clerical employees
    Category 4  -  Operations and other employees
```

HR Forecast

Anticipated Workforce	Category*			
	1	2	3	4
Short-term Forecast Immediate HR needs				
Intermediate Forecast Five years from now				
Long-range Forecast Ten years from now				

* Category 1 - Managerial employees
  Category 2 - Professional employees
  Category 3 - Office and clerical employees
  Category 4 - Operations and other employees

Chapter 3

Human Resources and Organizational Competitiveness

CHAPTER OBJECTIVES

1. Discuss why and how the psychological contract between employees and employers is being transformed.

2. Explain the expectancy theory of motivation.

3. Define *job design* and identify the five components of the job-characteristics model.

4. Describe three types of teams used for jobs.

5. Define *job satisfaction* and *organizational commitment* and discuss how they relate to absenteeism and turnover.

6. Identify several ways to control absenteeism and turnover.

7. Describe the importance of national, organizational, and individual productivity.

8. Define *Total Quality Management (TQM)* and explain HR's role in it.

9. Identify the five dimensions of service.

SUMMARY OF THE CHAPTER

As organizational mergers, restructuring and "rightsizing" have become widespread, employees believe that their loyalty and effort are not being returned by their employers. Thus, there is a need to transform the relationships between organizations and individuals. The old *psychological contract*, the unwritten expectation that employees would exchange their efforts and capabilities for a secure job, rising wages, and comprehensive benefits, is no longer realistic. The pressure of globalization, maintaining international competitiveness, and rapid changes in technology call for a new focus in the employee/ employer relationship. The new expectation is that employees will contribute jointly with other employees to accomplish organizational success in a competitive marketplace for goods and services. Organizations can foster individual and team productivity, innovation, and commitment by providing employees with jobs that motivate them, offer them job satisfaction, and encourage their involvement.

Motivation is an emotion or desire causing a person to act. All the theories about motivation are based essentially upon assumptions about why people behave as they do. The content theories of motivation are concerned with the needs that people are attempting to satisfy. Two of the major content theories are Maslow's Hierarchy of Needs and Herzberg's Motivation/Hygiene Theory. The process theories of motivation focus on how organizations and managers can tap employee motivation through the satisfaction of needs to enhance individual performance. The most prominent process theory is expectancy theory. *Expectancy theory* is based on the assumption that people act in order to reach a goal, but whether they will act depends on whether they believe their behavior will help them achieve their goals.

Whether or not people are motivated to perform also depends on the job itself and how that job is designed. *Job design* refers to organizing tasks, duties, and responsibilities into a productive unit of work. It considers the content of jobs and the effect of jobs on employees. Today much attention is paid to the design of jobs, since job design can impact performance, affect job satisfaction, and affect both physical and mental health.

Job enlargement and *job enrichment* have attempted to alleviate some of the problems encountered with excessive job simplification. Job enlargement broadens the scope of the job by expanding the number of different tasks to be performed. Job enrichment affects the depth of the job by adding responsibility for planning, organizing, controlling, and evaluating the job.

The *job-characteristics model* suggests that three critical psychological states can be influenced by five different design characteristics of jobs. The model illustrates the effect of these psychological states on job satisfaction and work outcomes, while recognizing the operation of individual differences.

A movement which has affected the design and characteristics of jobs and work is *reengineering*, which is rethinking and redesigning work to improve cost, service, and speed. Another aspect of job design is the use of alternative work schedules and arrangements. These alternatives include the use of compressed work weeks, flextime, working at home, and telecommuting.

Another aspect of the changing job design is the increased use of teams. Several types of teams are used in organizations today. A *special-purpose team* is one which is formed to address specific problems. Another kind of team is the *quality circle*, a small group of employees who monitor productivity and quality and suggest solutions to problems. Yet another way work is restructured is through the use of *production cells* which are groupings of workers who produce entire products or components of products. *Self-directed work teams* are organizational teams composed of individuals who are assigned a cluster of tasks, duties and responsibilities to be accomplished. Successful self-directed teams have three characteristics: they value and endorse dissent, they use *shamrock* structures and have some variation in membership, and they have authority to make decisions.

The characteristics of individuals and the design of jobs interact to affect the job satisfaction and commitment of employees. *Job satisfaction* is a positive emotional state resulting from evaluating one's job experiences. It has many dimensions including satisfaction with the work itself, wages, recognition, supervisor, co-workers, and the organization. Although the relationship between productivity and job satisfaction is not entirely clear, there is good evidence that job satisfaction leads to organizational commitment, which influences absenteeism and turnover. *Organizational commitment* is the degree to which employees believe in and accept organization goals and desire to remain with the organization. Three types of organizational commitment have been identified: affective commitment, continuance commitment, and normative commitment. The continuance commitment factor relates commitment to individual withdrawal from organizations, either occasionally through absenteeism or permanently through turnover.

Employees are absent for numerous reasons. Some absenteeism such as that due to personal or family illness is unavoidable and is called involuntary absenteeism. Voluntary absenteeism is, however, avoidable and it is this type of absenteeism that organizations must control. Absenteeism control falls into three categories: discipline, positive reinforcement, and a combination of both.

Turnover occurs when employees leave an organization and have to be replaced. Turnover also can be classified as voluntary and involuntary. Involuntary turnover occurs when an employee is fired. Voluntary turnover occurs when an employee leaves by his or her own choice. Ways of reducing voluntary turnover include realistic job previews, improving the selection process, providing good employee orientation, insuring a fair and equitable pay system, and providing career planning and internal promotions.

The means of determining organizational competitiveness is through productivity. *Productivity*, a measure of the quantity and quality of work done considering the cost of resources it took to do the work, is the concern of individuals, companies, and nations. A useful way to measure organizational productivity is by unit labor cost, which is computed by dividing the average wage of workers by their level of productivity. In order to succeed in a competitive environment, organizations need individual productivity from their human resources. Individual productivity depends on three factors: a person's innate ability to do the job, the level of effort he or she is willing to exert, and the support given the person.

In addition to productivity, quality is becoming increasingly important throughout the world. A set of quality standards called the ISO 9000 Standard have been derived by the International Standards Organization in Geneva, Switzerland. The U. S. Department of Commerce has established the Malcolm Baldridge awards given annually to companies that improve their quality. To gain quality improvements, many organizations have adopted the concept of *Total Quality Management (TQM)* which is a comprehensive management process focusing on the continuous improvement of organizational activities to enhance the quality of the goods and services supplied. Important characteristics of TQM are a customer focus, employee involvement, and benchmarking. HR plays a major role in successful TQM endeavors. Training, job redesign, team formation, and modification of compensation systems are major HR functions impacted by TQM.

Delivery of high quality service is another important outcome that affects organizational competitiveness. Important dimensions of service include reliability, responsiveness, assurance, empathy and tangibles. In order to have high quality service, HR must insure that appropriate employees are selected and properly trained and that recognition and reward programs focus on rewarding employees for exceptional customer service.

STUDY QUESTIONS

Matching Questions

Match the key term from the list below with its most appropriate definition.

a.	Motivation	k.	Autonomy
b.	Flextime	l.	Unit labor cost
c.	Compressed Work Week	m.	Job rotation
d.	Valence	n.	Psychological Contract
e.	Instrumentality	o.	Turnover
f.	Production cells	p.	Job enlargement
g.	Task significance	q.	Job enrichment
h.	Productivity	r.	Telecommuting
i.	Job satisfaction	s.	Reengineering
j.	Job Design	t.	Expectancy

____ 1.   The process of shifting a person from job to job.

____ 2.   The concept of broadening the scope of a job by expanding the number of different tasks to be performed.

____ 3.   A work schedule in which the full week's work is accomplished in less than five days.

____ 4.   The unwritten expectations that employees and employers have about the nature of their work relationships.

____ 5.   Increasing the depth of a job by adding employee responsibilities.

____ 6.   Occurs when employees leave an organization and have to be replaced.

___   7.   Rethinking and redesigning work to improve cost, service and speed.

___   8.   The strength of the individual's valuation of the reward.

___   9.   Organizing tasks, duties, and responsibilities into a productive unit of work.

___   10.   An emotion or desire causing a person to act.

___   11.   Groupings of workers who produce entire products or components of products.

___   12.   The average wage of workers divided by their level of productivity.

___   13.   The process of "going to work" via electronic computing equipment.

___   14.   A pleasurable or positive emotional state resulting from the appraisal of one's job or experiences.

___   15.   Occurs when employees work a set number of hours but vary starting and ending times.

___   16.   The probability that performance will lead to the desired rewards.

___   17.   The amount of impact the job has on other people.

___   18.   The extent of individual freedom and discretion in the work and its scheduling.

___   19.   A measure of the quantity and quality of work done considering the cost of the resources it took to do the work.

___   20.   The probability that if the employee puts forth more effort, it will lead to performance.

True/False Questions

____   1.   By observing a person's behavior one can directly infer what motivated that behavior.

____   2.   The widespread organizational restructuring that has occurred in recent years has had little impact on the traditional psychological contract which exists between employers and employees.

____   3.   The content theories of motivation are concerned with the needs that people are attempting to satisfy.

____   4.   Reengineering is just another name for job design.

____   5.   According to Maslow, esteem is more important (higher order need) than belonging and love needs.

____   6.   Job enrichment is the process of shifting a person from job to job.

____   7.   Increasing job depth refers to increasing the influence and self-control employees have over their jobs.

____   8.   Employees are alike in one aspect. They all want their job enlarged in scope and depth.

____   9.   Skill variety refers to the extent that the job includes a complete "whole" identifiable unit of work.

____   10.   Stimulating and maintaining productivity is an important goal for companies in a changing competitive environment.

____   11.   A fair and equitable pay system can help prevent turnover.

____   12.   Self-directed work teams have no team leaders.

____   13.   Job design considers the content of jobs, but ignores their impact on employees.

____   14.   Productivity is the quantity and quality of work done divided by the cost of resources to do the work.

____   15.   Job design can affect both the physical and mental health of the employees.

____   16.   TQM programs have become quite popular as companies try to improve the quality of their HR departments.

___   17.   The Malcolm Baldridge Awards are given annually for quality improvement in American companies.

___   18.   Organizational productivity can be measured by unit labor costs.

___   19.   There is good evidence that job satisfaction leads to organizational commitment.

___   20.   Absenteeism can best be controlled by a combination of positive reinforcement and disciplinary actions.

Idea Completion Questions

1.   Three common forms of alternative work schedules include: _____, _____, and _____.

2.   Three characteristics of successful self-directed teams are: _____, _____, and _____.

3.   To succeed in a competitive environment organizations need: _____, _____, and _____ from their human resources.

4.   The five job characteristics in the job-characteristics model are: _____, _____, _____, _____, and _____.

5.   The three components of individual productivity are: _____, _____, and _____.

Multiple Choice Questions

___   1.   Broadening the scope of a job by expanding the number of different tasks to be performed
is called
   a.   job design.
   b.   job enlargement.
   c.   job enrichment.
   d.   job rotation.

___   2.   The HR components necessary for organizational success include which of the following?
   a.   individual productivity
   b.   innovation
   c.   loyalty
   d.   all of the above
   e.   only a and b above

___   3.   The job characteristic that influences "responsibility for the results" of the work is
   a.   autonomy.
   b.   task identity.
   c.   task significance.
   d.   feedback from the job.

___   4.   Skill variety, task identity, and task significance together stimulate
   a.   knowledge of results.
   b.   autonomy.
   c.   responsibility for the results.
   d.   meaningfulness of the work.

___   5.   The extent to which the job includes a "whole" identifiable unit of work is the _____
job characteristic.
   a.   skill variety
   b.   task identity
   c.   task significance
   d.   autonomy
   e.   feedback from the job

___   6.   Which of the following is not considered a compressed work week?
    a.   five days - eight hours per day
    b.   four days - ten hours per day
    c.   three days - twelve hours per day
    d.   two twelve hour days on the weekend

___   7.   A shamrock team is composed of all the following members except:
    a.   core members.
    b.   resource experts.
    c.   part-time/temporary members.
    d.   supervisors.

___   8.   _____ refers to conscious efforts to organize tasks, duties, and responsibilities into a unit of work to achieve a certain objective.
    a.   Job design
    b.   Job analysis
    c.   Organizational development
    d.   Work ethic

___   9.   Individual productivity depends on
    a.   a person's innate ability to do the job.
    b.   a person's willingness to exert effort.
    c.   the support given the person.
    d.   all of the above.
    e.   only a and b above.

___   10.   Increasing the depth of a job by adding employee responsibility for planning, organizing, controlling, and evaluating the job is
    a.   job enlargement.
    b.   job scope.
    c.   job enrichment.
    d.   job rotation.

___ 11. Which of the following is not included in Maslow's hierarchy of needs?
      a. power needs
      b. self-esteem needs
      c. physiological needs
      d. safety needs
      e. all of the above are included

___ 12. In Herzberg's Motivation/Hygiene Theory, all but which of the following are considered motivators?
      a. achievement
      b. recognition
      c. salary
      d. advancement
      e. responsibility

___ 13. In the Expectancy Theory of motivation the probability that performance will lead to the desired rewards is known as
      a. valence.
      b. expectancy.
      c. instrumentality.
      d. equity.

___ 14. Herzberg's hygiene factors would include all but
      a. achievement.
      b. interpersonal relations.
      c. working conditions.
      d. supervision.
      e. both b and d above.

___ 15. All of the following are types of organizational commitment except _____.
      a. affective commitment
      b. cognitive commitment
      c. continuance commitment
      d. normative commitment

Essay Questions

1.   Compare and contrast the content and process theories of motivation.

2.   Discuss the advantages and problems associated with trying to match individual characteristics with the requirements and characteristics of jobs.

3.   Discuss the components necessary for organizational success in today's competitive environment.

4.   Illustrate how an organization can utilize Hackman and Oldham's job-characteristics model in redesigning an assembly line job.

5.   Discuss the relationship between job satisfaction and absenteeism, turnover, and individual productivity.

ANSWER KEY

Matching

1. m	2. p	3. c	4. n	5. q
6. o	7. s	8. d	9. j	10. a
11. f	12. l	13. r	14. i	15. b
16. e	17. g	18. k	19. h	20. t

True/False

1. F	2. F	3. T	4. F	5. T
6. F	7. T	8. F	9. F	10. T
11. T	12. F	13. F	14. T	15. T
16. F	17. T	18. T	19. T	20. T

Idea Completion

1. flextime
   compressed work week
   telecommuting

2. they value and endorse dissent
   they use shamrock structures
   they have authority to make decisions

3. individual productivity
   quality
   service

4.   skill variety
        task identity
        task significance
        autonomy
        feedback

5.   ability
        effort
        organizational support

Multiple Choice

1.	b	2.	d	3.	a	4.	d	5.	b
6.	a	7.	d	8.	a	9.	d	10.	c
11.	a	12.	c	13.	c	14.	a	15.	b

TEXAS FISH FRY

It is a Friday afternoon. Sally Anne Templeton arrives home from school, but instead of resting up after a busy week of school activities, Sally Anne changes into her brown and gold uniform and drives to work.

Like many high school students, Sally Anne has an after school job. But unlike most seventeen year-old students, she is the night manager at a fast-food restaurant. This position at Texas Fish Fry gives Sally Anne many responsibilities not held by her peers. Last night, for example, there was a one hundred dollar shortage in the cash register. She has been worrying about this loss all day, and is concerned about the likely consequences.

Sally Anne's Career

Sally Anne has been working at Texas Fish Fry for just under two years. She started out working Saturday mornings cleaning the store, and was soon promoted to counter sales. Since this was her first job, she strove for perfection - always punctual, never complaining about her work schedule, and could always be depended upon in a pinch. Being intelligent was another point in her favor. Texas Fish Fry, like other fast-food businesses, had a reputation for hiring just about anyone who could count to ten. This factor limited the selection of people for advancement.

William Andrews, the store manager, noticed Sally Anne's potential and promoted her to night manager nine months ago. William was wary at first because of Sally Anne's age and her limited experience. However, Sally Anne proved to be an efficient and fair manager.

Sally Anne's duties included responsibility for all moneys after 4 p.m., taking hourly cash register readings, signing voids, and estimating how much fish, french fries, and hush puppies should be fried for the night's business. When the store closed at 11:30, she had to take inventory, balance the night's receipts, and lock up the store. Most nights, she would leave for home at midnight. There were usually eight people working every night and Sally Anne had to write daily reports on each. These reports were submitted to the district supervisor. Sometimes, Sally Anne found her job difficult when she had to reprimand people her own age. Often they didn't take too kindly to her criticism.

Texas Fish Fry

Texas Fish Fry is a privately-owned operation with twenty-eight stores in Texas, Louisiana, and Arkansas. Revenues are expected to exceed $25 million this year. Jonathan J. Klein, the sole owner, is a shrewd businessman. Twenty years ago, he started out with a booth at the Texas State Fair. Today he is a multi-millionaire in charge of his own hierarchy of employees.

Mr. Klein has deep moral convictions, and is on a personal anti-drug crusade. Every month he visits each of his stores, and meets with all the employees. He will always emphasize to his employees the danger of drugs, charging that they are the primary cause of the decline in morality, the increasing number of teenage pregnancies, and the increase of crime in society. Mr. Klein has very little contact with his employees outside of these monthly meetings.

Mr. Klein employs three district supervisors, among whom the stores are divided. These supervisors visit each store in their district at least twice a week. They are responsible for the cleanliness of the store and its employees, and they handle all complaints and any major problems related to their stores. Sally Anne's district supervisor was T.J. Chase. T.J. is 43 years old and has worked for Texas Fish Fry for the past twelve years. He is a very nervous man who has a tendency to lose his temper. While inspecting a store, if he found something especially dirty or out of place, it was not uncommon to see him throwing cooking utensils across the kitchen accompanied by a volley of insulting remarks. He seemed to take pride in reducing his employees to tears. To say the least, T.J. Chase was a man who kept his employees on their toes.

Each store has its own manager. The Garland store, where Sally Anne worked, was managed by William Andrews. William was a hard working man who took great pride in his store. He was very strict with his employees but very fair. If they were unhappy for some reason, William was always ready to listen. Basically, William's job entailed the day-to-day management of the store, including responsibility for the hiring and firing of employees and preparing the work schedules. William had very little to do with long range planning for the organization. His right-hand man (person) was always the night manager. Having a responsible night manager enabled him to relax at home at night with his young family, without worrying about the store.

The typical fry cook and counter-sales person at Texas Fish Fry was sixteen or seventeen years old. In the past, Texas Fish Fry had hired unambitious sixteen year-olds who have no plans for long term employment. They work for a few months and quickly get tired of the job. They quit, relax for a while, and then they find another job at a fast-food restaurant. The pay is minimum wage and the work is hard and sometimes dangerous. It is up to the store manager and night manager to keep morale up, but morale is never very high.

Friday Evening

That afternoon, just like every other afternoon, Sally Anne reported for work at 4 p.m. She punched the time clock and went directly to the little cubbyhole designed as her office. Before she had a chance to sit down, one of the cooks informed her that two of his fellow workers called off work for that evening. Sally Anne sighed and told him to do the best he could until she could find replacements. As Sally Anne dialed her list of "on-call" workers, she thought, *"this is the fourth time this month that those girls have called off. I think the store manager should hear about this."* Seeing that the lone cook needed help, Sally Anne fried fish until the replacements arrived.

After the replacements arrived Sally Anne was finally able to sit down. As she shuffled through the day's mail, one letter caught her attention. It was a memo addressed to her. She had an idea as to what the memo was about and she became very angry. She opened it and read:

Dear Miss Templeton:

   Please report to the company physician, Dr. Frank, at 3:00 p.m. Monday for urinalysis testing. A shortage has been detected in yesterday's receipts and we are very concerned that the theft may be drug related. It is a pity that we have to resort to such measures. We know you will oblige since we are sure that you also are very concerned. Your cooperation is greatly appreciated.

   Sincerely,
   T.J. Chase
   District Supervisor, Texas Fish Fry, Inc.

The letter was no surprise to Sally Anne because in the past year and a half she had seen seven others just like it. Also, in the past year and a half she had been the first to be tested since she worked closer to the money than anyone else. All seven times she was clean. After her, the other employees were tested. If not for anything else, she was going to quit for her own personal integrity. If the company didn't trust her by now, they never would.

Actually, this had been building up for a while. Sally Anne was not happy with most of the store's policies and this was no exception. She dialed the store manager's home phone number and then hung up. *"Why should I quit to Mr. Andrews,"* she thought. *"He didn't write the memo, and he isn't responsible for all of the store's policies anyway. If changes are to be made, complaints should be directed to the person who makes the policies."* Sally Anne was determined and proceeded to call the district supervisor:

CHASE: *Hello, T.J. Chase here.*

SALLY ANNE: *Hello, Sir. This is Sally Anne Templeton of the Garland store.*

CHASE: *Yes Sally Anne, what can I do for you?*

SALLY ANNE: *Mr. Chase, I'm sorry but this will be my last night working for you. I've had it with Texas Fish Fry. The latest urinalysis memo was the last straw. If you people don't trust me by now you never will. Mr. Chase, I could go on and on about why I am unhappy here but I don't think it would do any good.*

CHASE:	*I see. Well Sally Anne, let's not be too hasty here. I can see your point. I'm interested in what you have to say about our firm. Please come to work as usual on Monday and I'll be there so we can talk. Is that all right with you?*
SALLY ANNE:	*I guess so. I don't think I will change my mind though, but it can't hurt.*
CHASE:	*Fine. I'll see you on Monday. Goodbye!*

Monday Evening

When Sally Anne arrived at work on Monday evening she was nervous because she knew that T.J. Chase would be there soon and she was losing her nerve. She still wanted to quit, but was less determined than on Friday. Within a few minutes T.J. came striding through the front door. After his usual inspection and round of insults he turned his attention to Sally Anne. They went into the office and sat down.

At first, T.J. just listened and Sally Anne did all the talking. Yes, she was upset about the urinalysis memo, but that wasn't the real problem. The real problem, she felt, was the lack of concern between management and workers. Management expected the night workers to work an eight-hour shift in a hot kitchen without a break. Legally, the employees were required to take a break, but there was so much work to be done that if they took a break they would get behind. If they punched out late, the workers would be severely reprimanded. The work itself didn't bother them too much, but the dangers associated with it worried the employees. Every night the fry cooks had to handle hot, burning grease. In the past year, there had been five serious injuries due to the hot grease. Most of the employees felt that minimum wages were not enough considering the danger associated with the work. Also, the store had been robbed twice this year. It is a pretty scary situation for a sixteen year-old to face a gunman. Besides the robberies, numerous obscene phone calls and a bomb threat have unsettled the employees. Added security would at least curb some of these antics. Also the constant insulting by top management and the "guilty until proved innocent" attitude make work miserable.

On a personal level, Sally Anne was upset about the lack of trust management had for her. If she had passed the urinalysis seven times, why make it an eighth? Another thing that bothered Sally Anne was her pay. For all her responsibilities, she only received fifty cents an hour more than the other workers. Obviously, the company was receiving quality labor for a cheap price. As an added insult, the employees were required to purchase their own uniforms at $40 each. Problems like these lower the morale of the employees and lessen their sense of loyalty to the business.

The other side of the coin is no better. The employees learn very early to take a careless attitude towards their job. Sally Anne was very aware of the shortages in the inventory record. She knew that employees were constantly stealing food, and also serving meals to their friends without charging for them.

Maybe the reason the employees were only paid minimum wage was because management knows they steal and tries to compensate. The employees also show a lack of commitment by calling off work, coming in late, and quitting without notice.

Now it was T.J. Chase's turn to speak. He understood all that Sally Anne had to say. But, of course, none of it was new to him. T.J. tried to explain to Sally Anne that in the fast-food business, all was not perfect, and that management was trying its best to remedy the problems it faced. But like everything else, solutions take time and cost money. *"Unfortunately, our people don't stay around long enough to get what they want done. I'm sure that if we could cut our budget in certain places we could relieve some of the problems that seem to upset you. Sally Anne, we'd hate to see you go. Will a fifty cent raise be sufficient to keep you here?"*

Sally Anne just looked at him with a blank stare on her face. As she was about to answer him, the door opened and Charles, the fry cook, stood there with a broken pot in his hand.

Questions

1.   Do you approve of the company's policy of hiring mostly teenagers at minimum wage? Is it ethical?

2.   Do teenagers make for a good job fit? Can you suggest any alternatives?

3.   How should the business address the problems of turnover, absenteeism, and tardiness? Is it endemic to the fast-food industry?

4.   How is Texas Fish Fry attempting to address some serious social issues? Is drug testing an appropriate organizational response to the problem of substance abuse? Is it legal? Is it ethical? Can you suggest any alternatives?

5.   Is it appropriate for Sally Anne Templeton to be occupying such a responsible position? Why do you think she has remained committed to the firm for so long?

6.   Do you think Sally Anne will follow through with her threat to resign? Should she change her mind? Why? Do you think she has a career at Texas Fish Fry?

7.   What advice would you give to Sally Anne?

THE IDEAL JOB

Assumption

Graduation is approaching and you are beginning your job search in earnest. Before scanning the employment pages of the newspapers or visiting your college career development office, you spend some time reflecting on the type of job you would really like. Be realistic! First, review your academic qualifications, grades, and work experience. Remember, very few college graduates begin their careers as a corporate comptroller, a vice president for human resources, or CEO (unless their parents or in-laws own the company).

Assignment

Complete the *Ideal Job Questionnaire* on the following page. Be honest. What will determine whether or not you accept a job offer? What would you consider if trying to decide between two or more job offers.

Questions

1. In view of your priorities highlighted in the questionnaire, what need(s) are potent according to Maslow's hierarchy?

2. Which of the characteristics would Herzberg classify as hygiene factors? Motivators? Do you agree with Herzberg's classification of your job characteristics?

3. With reference to the expectancy theory of motivation, what outcomes have the highest valence? How will your qualifications, academic and personal, enable you to capture an "ideal" job offer (effort-performance expectancy)? What makes you think that job will result in the outcomes highlighted in your questionnaire (performance-reward instrumentality)?

4. Review Hackman and Oldham's job-characteristics model. Do you expect this "ideal" job will result in your being motivated, productive, and satisfied? How?

5. Under what circumstances can you see yourself leaving the job? After you started work and experienced the "real" job, which of these job characteristics would need to be lacking for you to quit?

6. When will you consider yourself to be a committed employee? What needs to happen first?

Ideal Job Questionnaire

Below is a list of 20 job characteristics. Rank them in terms of their importance to you when looking for a job. Write **"1"** beside the most important; **"2"** beside the second most important, etc.

____ Starting pay

____ Signing bonus

____ Potential future earnings

____ Benefits package

____ Training program

____ Opportunity to develop specialized skills

____ Receive recognition for contributions

____ Opportunity to use education and skills

____ Assistance with graduate education

____ Career opportunities within the firm

____ Prestige of the firm

____ Opportunity to use this position as a stepping stone to obtain a desired position in another firm in the future

____ The personalities of the people currently working in the firm

____ Geographic location

____ Work assignments

____ HR policies

____ Opportunity for advancement

____ Likelihood of fair treatment

____ Hours of work

____ Job security

Chapter 4

Global Human Resource Management

CHAPTER OBJECTIVES

1. Discuss the major factors influencing global HR management.

2. Define *culture* and explain how national cultures can be classified.

3. Differentiate among importing and exporting companies, multinational enterprises, and global organizations.

4. List and define several types of international employees.

5. Explain why staffing activities are more complex for international jobs than for domestic ones.

6. Discuss three areas of international training and development.

7. Identify several international compensation practices.

8. Describe several international health, safety, and security concerns.

SUMMARY OF THE CHAPTER

With growing numbers of U.S. firms establishing operations abroad and foreign firms establishing plants in the U.S., international HR management is becoming increasingly important. The signing of the North American Free Trade Agreement (NAFTA) in 1992 expanded trade opportunities among Canada, United States and Mexico. The General Agreement on Tariffs and Trade (GATT) signed in 1994 by many nations provided general guidelines on trade practices among nations and has an impact on HR practices in various countries including the U.S. Growing economies in Latin America, and Asia have provided many opportunities for organizations to successfully establish operations in those areas.

There are four basic sets of factors--legal, political, economic, and cultural--which must be considered by HR managers with global responsibilities. The legal and political systems of many countries are not as stable as those we are accustomed to in the U.S.. Economic conditions vary from country to country. Although labor costs often are significantly less than in the U.S., whether or not actual profits can be realized by operating in these countries depends upon currency fluctuations, restrictions on transfer of earnings, and other unusual costs such as upgrading the infrastructure which may be incurred just to do business in these countries. Culture, the societal forces affecting the values, beliefs, and actions of a distinct group of people, is another important concern affecting international HR management. Hofstede's five dimensions of culture - power distance, individualism, masculinity/femininity, uncertainty avoidance, and long-term orientation - provide a useful way of identifying and comparing cultures. An understanding of each of these dimensions provides managers with useful insights into international HR management.

In light of the growing globalization of business, many organizations that operate only in one country are realizing they must develop an international perspective. Globalization typically evolves through three stages. The first stage of international interaction is *importing and exporting* in which an organization begins selling and buying goods and services with organizations in other countries. In the second stage the firm becomes a *multinational enterprise (MNE)* by locating units in foreign countries. Finally, a firm may become a *global organization* with corporate units in a number of countries that are integrated to operate as one organization worldwide. There are differing HR implications as firms move through these three stages.

Large MNEs and global organizations must establish a staffing philosophy. Four distinct attitudinal sets - ethnocentric, polycentric, regiocentric, and geocentric - have been identified. International employees can be placed in three different classifications. An *expatriate* is an employee working in a unit or plant who is not a citizen of the country in which the unit or plant is located, but is a citizen of the country in which the organization is headquartered. A *host-country national* is an employee working in a unit or plant who is a citizen of the country in which the unit or plant is located, where the unit or plant is operated by an organization headquartered in another country. A *third-country national* is an employee who is a citizen of one country, working in a second country, and employed by an organization headquartered in a third country. Many MNEs use expatriates to ensure that foreign operations are linked effectively with the parent corporation. However, other companies choose to use host-country nationals because they understand the politics and laws of the country better and/or because lower pay rates for these people provides a cost advantage. The use of third-country nationals is a way to emphasize that a global approach really is being taken.

When expatriates are used, the selection process should provide a realistic picture of the life, work, and culture to which the employee may be sent. Cultural adaptability is likely to be the most important factor to consider during the staffing and selection process. Also an expatriate must be able to communicate orally and in writing in the host-country language. Family factors such as the availability of good schooling for children and work opportunities for spouses, also are key factors to consider in the selection of expatriates.

Employees working internationally face special situations and pressures, and training and development activities must be tailored to address them. Training and development for international assignments falls into three categories--pre-departure orientation and training, continuing employee development, and readjustment training and development. The major focus of pre-departure orientation and training is training in the foreign language and culture familiarization for not only the expatriate, but also for his or her family. Once the global employee and his or her family arrive in the host country, they will need assistance in many areas such as obtaining housing, establishing bank accounts, obtaining medical services, and arranging for school admissions for dependent children. Provision for continuing employee development for expatriates must be made so that the employee does not experience anxiety about their continued career progression. When it is time for the expatriate to return home, readjustment training and development must be available. The repatriated employee must learn to deal with a net decrease in compensation, adjust to closer working and reporting relationships, and become reacclimatized to home country customs in general.

Organizations with employees in many different countries face some special compensation pressures. In addition to their normal salary, an expatriate typically receives allowances for relocation and moving, housing and utilities, dependent education, and home leaves and travel. In addition there is usually cost of living adjustments, foreign service and hardship premiums and tax equalization payments. Compensation for international assignments typically is based on one of two approaches, either the *balance-sheet approach* or the *global market approach*. The balance-sheet approach provides the employee with a compensation package that equalizes the cost differences between the international assignment and the same assignment in the home country of the individual or the corporation. The global market approach recognizes that the assignment is continual, not temporary and may take employees to different countries for differing lengths of time. Using this approach allows the core components of compensation to be present regardless of the country to which the employee is assigned, but varies other components based upon the country to which the individual is assigned and the individual's performance in the assignment.

Employee relations is an important topic for global employees. Although the nature of the various facets may vary from country to country, the basic components of concern remain constant. Of particular importance are the areas of health, safety, and security. Labor-management relations also are likely to vary from country to country as well. In some countries unions do not exist or are relatively weak, however in other countries unions are extremely strong and are tied closely to political parties. These differences cause noticeable differences in how collective bargaining occurs.

STUDY QUESTIONS

Matching Questions

Match the key term from the list below with its most appropriate definition.

a.	Culture	f.	Expatriate
b.	Importing and exporting	g.	Host-country national
c.	Multinational Enterprise	h.	Third-country national
d.	Global Organization	i.	Repatriation
e.	Balance-sheet approach	j.	Tax equalization plan

___   1.   An approach to international compensation that provides international employees with a compensation package that equalizes cost differences between the international assignment and the same assignment in the home country of the individual or the corporation.

___   2.   Plan used to protect expatriates from negative tax consequences.

___   3.   An organization with units located in foreign countries.

___   4.   The societal forces affecting the values, beliefs, and actions of a distinct group of people.

___   5.   The phase of international interaction in which an organization begins selling and buying goods and services with organizations in other countries.

___   6.   An employee working in a unit or plant who is a citizen of the country in which the unit or plant is located, where the unit or plant is operated by an organization headquartered in another country.

___   7.   The process of bringing expatriates home.

___   8.   An employee working in a unit or plant who is not a citizen of the country in which the unit or plant is located but is a citizen of the country in which the organization is headquartered.

___   9.   An organization that has corporate units in a number of countries that are integrated to operate as one organization worldwide.

___   10.   An employee who is a citizen of one country, working in a second country, and employed by an organization headquartered in a third country.

True/False Questions

____ 1. Inability of spouse and other family members to adapt to life in another country is the most significant reason for expatriates not finishing out their assignments overseas.

____ 2. Increased global competition is projected to have little impact on the management of human resources.

____ 3. Women have typically had equal opportunity to overseas assignments.

____ 4. "Balance-sheet compensation" is a system of compensation for expatriates used to insure tax equalization for these employees.

____ 5. Inability to communicate adequately in the host-country language typically is not a significant inhibition to the success of an expatriate.

____ 6. Only a small percentage of expatriates fail to complete their foreign assignments.

____ 7. GATT specifically expanded trade opportunities among Canada, the U.S. and Mexico.

____ 8. The lower labor cost in less developed countries does not always translate into increased profits for the global organization because other costs of doing business in these countries are higher.

____ 9. The last stage of international interaction is known as importing and exporting.

____ 10. A polycentric staffing philosophy would call for the assignment of host-country nationals to professional and managerial jobs.

____ 11. The actual costs of placing a key manager outside the U.S. may be twice the manager's actual salary.

____ 12. A major reason that MNEs use expatriates is to insure that the foreign operations are linked effectively with the parent company.

____ 13. Reverse culture shock is one component of pre-departure orientation and training.

____ 14. Generally repatriated employees retain their expatriate compensation package as a bonus for having accepted the overseas assignment.

____ 15. Co-determination is a practice whereby union or worker representatives are given positions on a company's board of directors.

Idea Completion Questions

1.   The major factors affecting global HR management are:

   _____, _____, _____, and
   _____.

2.   Hofstede's five dimensions for identifying and comparing culture are:

   _____, _____, _____,
   _____, and_____.

3.   The four attitudinal sets that affect the assignment of managers and professionals to international operations are:

   _____, _____, _____, and
   _____.

4.   Three types of international employees are:

   _____, _____, and _____.

5.   Four types of expatriates are:

   _____, _____, _____, and
   _____.

6.   The three categories of international training and development are:

   _____, _____, and _____.

Multiple Choice Questions

_____   1.   The components of pre-departure orientation and training should include all of the following except
a.   language.
b.   culture.
c.   history.
d.   career planning.
e.   living conditions.

_____   2.   The main reason to have continuing employee development type of training for the expatriate is
a.   to allay the expatriate's anxiety over career progression.
b.   to insure that the person will be repatriated correctly.
c.   to be sure the person understands his or her compensation package.
d.   to insure the person learns the language and customs of the host country.

_____   3.   Components of expatriate compensation include which of the following?
a.   tax equalization payments
b.   relocation and moving allowance
c.   home leaves and travel allowances
d.   all of the above
e.   only a and b above

_____   4.   When firms have union representatives on their boards of directors the practice is called
a.   expatriation.
b.   co-determination.
c.   arbitration.
d.   repatriation.

_____   5.   The purpose of a tax equalization plan is
a.   to exempt expatriates from paying U.S. income tax.
b.   to exempt expatriates from paying income tax in their host country.
c.   to adjust an employee's base income down by the amount of estimated U.S. tax to be paid for the year.
d.   to provide employment for the employee's spouse overseas.

6.   When expatriates return home, they typically must readjust to which of the following?
   a.   a net decrease in total income
   b.   less flexibility, autonomy, and independence than they had overseas
   c.   U.S. lifestyles and culture
   d.   all of the above
   e.   only b and c above

7.   Poor staffing for international assignments occurs for which of the following reasons?
   a.   inability of spouse to adapt
   b.   inappropriate personality of selected individual
   c.   inability of manager to handle expanded overseas responsibility
   d.   all of the above
   e.   only a and b above

8.   All of the following factors except _____ affect global HR Management?
   a.   technology
   b.   legal
   c.   political
   d.   economic
   e.   cultural

9.   _____ is the dimension of culture referring to the inequality among the people of a nation.
   a.   Individualism
   b.   Power distance
   c.   Masculinity/Femininity
   d.   Long-term orientation

10.   The phase of international interaction in which an organization begins selling and buying goods and services with organizations in other countries is referred to as
   a.   importing and exporting.
   b.   multinational enterprise.
   c.   global organization.
   d.   none of the above.
   e.   both b and c above are correct.

___ 11. If an organization assigns managers and professionals from the home-country office to overseas assignments, it is following which international staffing philosophy?
a. ethnocentric
b. polycentric
c. regiocentric
d. geocentric

___ 12. _____ is the dimension of culture referring to the preference of people in a country for structured situations instead of unstructured situations.
a. Long-term orientation
b. Power distance
c. Uncertainty avoidance
d. Individualism

___ 13. MNEs use host-country nationals for all the following reasons except:
a. they know the culture, politics, and laws better.
b. they know how to get business done better than an outsider.
c. they can tap into the informal power network.
d. they can more effectively link the foreign operation to the parent corporation.

___ 14. Professionals and managers assigned to work in foreign operations for one to three years after which time they rotate back to the parent corporation in the home country are referred to as
a. volunteer expatriates.
b. traditional expatriates.
c. career development expatriates.
d. global expatriates.

___ 15. Which of the following statements is true regarding women and international assignments?
a. Women often do not want overseas assignments.
b. Women are likely to be less qualified than men for overseas assignments.
c. From 1995 to 2000 the number of women receiving overseas assignments i projected to increase by 13%.
d. all of the above are true.

Essay Questions

1.   Discuss the three phases of international training and development.

2.   Describe the components of an international compensation package.

3.   Explain how an understanding of Hofstede's dimensions of culture can help in effective international HR management.

4.   Compare and contrast the various types of international involvement in which a firm might engage.

5.   Discuss the various types of international employees and explain the reasons why organizations might choose to use each type.

ANSWER KEY

Matching Questions

1. e	2. j	3. c	4. a	5. b
6. g	7. i	8. f	9. d	10. h

True/False

1. T	2. F	3. F	4. F	5. F
6. F	7. F	8. T	9. F	10. T
11. T	12. T	13. F	14. F	15. T

Idea Completion

1. legal
    political
    economic
    cultural

2. power distance
    individualism
    masculinity/femininity
    long-term orientation
    uncertainty avoidance

3. ethnocentric
    polycentric
    regiocentric
    geocentric

4. expatriates
    host-country nationals
    third-country nationals

5.   volunteer
       traditional
       career development
       global

6.   pre-departure orientation and training
       continuing employee development
       readjustment training and development

Multiple Choice Questions

1. d	2. a	3. d	4. b	5. c
6. d	7. d	8. a	9. b	10. a
11. a	12. c	13. d	14. b	15. c

DEWITT WOOLEN MILLS

1829 - In the Beginning

Theodore DeWitt immigrated to the United States in 1829. He settled in western Pennsylvania and began raising sheep. In 1934, DeWitt built his first woolen mill. The first wool products manufactured by DeWitt Woolen Mills were simple yet integral to the building of a nation. Originally, Theodore DeWitt travelled from logging camp to logging camp selling fabric, socks, and yarn to lumbermen from the back of a mule cart. The loggers' wives made clothes from the fabric.

From this humble beginning, DeWitt grew and developed more sophisticated products with new production methods. By 1900, the mill was manufacturing a full range of products, from fabrics to finished garments. It was a fully integrated business, from sheep to clothing. Salesmen traveled to clothing stores in the midwestern and northeastern states, and the firm mailed catalogs to customers throughout the United States.

Many of DeWitt's employees, like Theodore DeWitt, were immigrants who came to the United States willing to work hard and build a new life. Over the years, DeWitt built cottages for the employees and their families, a hospital, a school, and a Church which also served as the community center. Most of the employees lived in DeWitt Township and were proud when their children began working at the mill. The employees shared in the firm's success.

1992 - Reorganization

By 1992, the company's fortunes had taken a nosedive. The firm had stopped raising sheep years ago, and was purchasing raw wool from both domestic and foreign suppliers. The catalog business was losing money. The manufacturing process, from spinning to dyeing to weaving to sewing, was very labor intensive. The labor union had demanded, and received, significant increases in wages and benefits over the years.

The Board brought in a new management team, instructing them to turn the company around. The production manager totally automated the spinning, dyeing, and weaving processes. The garments still had to be sewn by semiskilled workers. This was one process that remained labor intensive.

The marketing manager eliminated the catalog-sales department and signed contracts with national catalog companies such as Lands End and L.L. Bean. A newly-focused sales team targeted department stores and upscale sporting-good stores in the U.S. and Canada. Because of the high cost of production, the products too expensive for the high-volume discount stores. Nevertheless, sales volume increased. However, margins were still too small for the long-term financial health of the company.

The human resource manager inherited a workforce that was well compensated and loyal to DeWitt. So he didn't relish the task of reducing the size of the workforce as the production processes were automated. During the next five years DeWitt would lay-off, fire, or offer early retirement to more than half of the employees.

1997 - An International Challenge

The management team was not satisfied with their accomplishments. While sale volume was up and production costs were down, the company was only marginally profitable. The managers agreed that they needed to reduce production costs so that they could compete in the discount-store market and improve their profit margins in the catalog and department store markets.

They acknowledged that the only place where they could cut costs was in the sewing department. The sewers were all women earning between $5.50 and $8.50 an hour. The workers were unionized and wages were based on job classification and length of service.

Many of DeWitt's competitors either manufactured their garments overseas or simply imported ready-made garments. The management team discussed the possibility of manufacturing the garments off-shore:

Production Manager   *We can contract-out the sewing to a sweat shop, or we could build our own factory on foreign soil where we can capitalize on the lower wage costs. My concern is, can we produce quality items with foreign labor? Will the finished clothing meet our high standards?*

To ensure that the DeWitt label still means quality, we must build our own factories overseas. Either we use American managers and supervisors or else we train host-country nationals in our U.S.-based factories.

Marketing Manager   *I, too, am concerned about quality. We could consider marketing reduced-quality, imported clothing under another brand name, but this would mean using a differentiated sales force and setting up separate distribution systems. I could not tolerate selling second-rate goods under the DeWitt label. No, I am convinced that, if we manufacture off-shore, we must take every step to ensure the integrity of our label.*

HR Manager   *Do you realize what this proposal would mean for my department? I will have to pension-off all our sewers, hire new ones in another country, not to mention the problems of the management and supervision of the international operations. Please consider my situation.*

Questions

1. Are the managers being realistic in seeking to establish a production facility in another country? What problems will DeWitt face in moving part of its manufacturing process overseas?

2. What would a decision to manufacture off-shore mean for the HR unit? Is the HR manager simply raising barriers to a rational business decision?

3. Illustrate how the passage of NAFTA and GATT has make it possible to shift manufacturing processes overseas. What could be the long-term effects of these agreements on American manufacturing?

4. Assume that the DeWitt management decides to build a production facility off-shore to sew the garments, package them, and ship the completed orders direct to the major customers. Develop at least two alternate plans for the HR unit that involves expatriate and host-country managers and supervisors.

5. Do you anticipate any host-country problems in establishing a factory in another country?

6. Discuss any ethical concerns you have about DeWitt's options.

AN INTERNATIONAL ASSIGNMENT

Assume that you are working for a global organization and that you can expect one or more overseas assignments during your career. Select a country where you would like to work as a regional manager. Assume that you are unmarried, and that your assignment will be for three to four years.

Assignment

1. Research and list the differences in customs and culture between where you are living now and that country.

2. Based on your research, would you accept or reject the assignment regardless of the salary involved? Explain your reasons.

3. Assuming you decide to accept the assignment, what are the minimum increments in salary, benefits and perks that you would require?

4. How would you prepare for the international assignment? What assistance and orientation would you want to receive from your employer before you leave home? What assistance would you expect upon arrival?

5. At the conclusion of your assignment, do you expect your transition back to the domestic office to be easy? Why or why not? What preparations should you make before returning?

6. Now, assume that you are married and have two children, one in elementary school and the other in high school. Would your responses to the above questions be any different? Explain your answer.

Chapter 5

Diversity and Equal Employment Opportunity

CHAPTER OBJECTIVES

1. Define *diversity management,* and discuss what it encompasses.

2. Differentiate among diversity management, equal employment opportunity (EEO), and affirmative action.

3. Discuss several reasons for supporting and opposing affirmative action.

4. Explain how to identify when illegal discrimination occurs, and define five basic EEO concepts.

5. Discuss the key provisions of the Civil Rights Act of 1964, Title VII, and the Civil Rights Act of 1991.

6. Discuss the two general approaches that can be used to comply with the 1978 Uniform Guidelines on Employment Selection Procedures.

7. Define *validity* and *reliability* and explain three approaches to validating employment requirements.

SUMMARY OF THE CHAPTER

The workforce today is composed of individuals of differing races, ages, cultural and geographic origins, abilities and disabilities, and genders. In addition, varied lifestyles, personalities, family arrangements, and other factors affect individual performance.

Diversity provides organizations opportunities to tap a broader, more diverse set of ideas and experiences of people, and can be valuable because it often reflects the diversity of customers and the marketplace. On the other hand, diversity may initially lead to increased tensions and conflicts in the workplace.

A major component of diversity has been the influx of women into the workforce, including the fact that half of all working women are single, separated, divorced, widowed, or otherwise single heads of households. Balancing work and family will continue to grow in importance. The *Family and Medical Leave Act* (FMLA) has been one attempt to address this issue.

The fastest-growing segments of the U.S. population are in minority racial and ethnic groups, primarily Hispanics, African Americans, and Asian Americans. Much of the growth is due to immigration.

Another component of diversity is the aging of the workforce. With fewer young people to fill entry-level jobs, organizations, particularly in the service sector, are facing significant staffing difficulties. Employers are attracting older persons to return to the workforce through the use of part-time and other scheduling options.

Individuals with disabilities are another group adding diversity to the workforce. With the passage of the *Americans with Disabilities Act*, greater numbers of individuals with disabilities will be employed, requiring employers to more precisely define essential tasks in jobs and to make reasonable accommodation for disabled workers through more flexible work schedules, altering facilities, and purchasing special equipment.

Individuals with differing sexual orientations and lifestyles create yet another dimension to workforce diversity. Although few laws exist to protect such individuals from employment discrimination, there are growing concerns about balancing employee privacy rights with legitimate employer requirements.

Diversity management is concerned with developing organizational initiatives that value all people equally, regardless of their differences. By addressing diversity issues and managing them effectively, organizations benefit in various ways: conflicts within the organization can be ameliorated, better productivity can result, and the organization can be more attractive to potential applicants and current employees.

Equal employment opportunity (EEO) is a broad concept that states that individuals should have equal treatment in all employment-related actions. Various laws have been passed to protect individuals who share certain characteristics, such as race, age , or gender. A *protected class* is composed of individuals who fall within a group identified for protection under equal employment laws and regulations. Federal laws provide protection against discrimination based on race, ethnic origin, color, gender, age, disability, military experience, and religion.

Affirmative action occurs when employers identify problem areas, set goals, and take positive steps to guarantee equal employment opportunities for people within a protected class. Affirmative action focuses on hiring, training, and promoting of protected-class members where they are underrepresented in an organization. Those not members of a protected class have claimed that affirmative action leads to quotas, preferential selection, and reverse discrimination.

Numerous federal, state, and local laws address equal employment opportunity concerns. The keystone of antidiscrimination legislation was the *Civil Rights Act of 1964, Title VII* which was passed in part to bring about equality in all employment-related decisions. The act made it an unlawful employment practice to discriminate against any individual on the basis of that individual's race, color, religion, sex, or national origin.

The major purpose for the passage of the *Civil Rights Act of 1991* was to overturn or modify seven U.S. Supreme Court decisions handed down during the 1988-1990 period. The major decision that was overturned had been issued in the *Ward's Cove Packing v. Atonio (1989)* case. The act requires that employers show that an employment practice is job-related for the position and is consistent with business necessity if disparate impact occurs.

The 1991 act overturned several court decisions that had made it more difficult for plaintiffs to bring suits based on intentional discrimination. The act makes an employer liable if the protected-class status of an individual was a motivating factor that caused a discriminatory action to occur.

The 1991 act also allows victims of discrimination on the basis of sex, religion, and disabilities to receive both compensatory and punitive damages in the cases of intentional discrimination. Jury trials are allowed to determine the liability for, and the amount of, compensatory and punitive damages, subject to caps.

The *Equal Employment Opportunity Commission* (EEOC), established by the Civil Rights Act of 1964, is responsible for enforcing the employment-related provisions of the act. The agency initiates investigations, responds to complaints, and develops guidelines to enforce various laws.

The *Office of Federal Contract Compliance Programs* (OFCCP), a part of the Department of Labor, was established by executive order to ensure that federal contractors and subcontractors have nondiscriminatory practices and take affirmative action to overcome the effects of prior discriminatory practices.

The *Uniform Guidelines on Employee Selection Procedures* were developed to provide a framework used to determine if federal laws on discrimination are being adhered to by employers. There are two major means of compliance identified in the guidelines. The first strategy is to insure that there is no disparate impact on protected classes. The 4/5ths rule is a yardstick that employers can use to determine if there is disparate impact on protected-class members.

The second strategy is to insure job-related validity of all instruments used in the employment process. Employment practices that must be valid include such practices and tests as job descriptions, educational requirements, experience requirements, work skills, application forms, interviews, paper-and-pencil tests, and performance appraisals. The three basic approaches to job-related validation which current EEOC guidelines recognize are: content validity, criterion-related validity (concurrent and predictive), and construct validity.

STUDY QUESTIONS

Matching Questions

Match the key term from the list below with its most appropriate definition.

a.	Title VII Civil Rights Act		j.	Disparate impact
b.	EEOC		k.	4/5th rule
c.	OFCCP		l.	Predictive validity
d.	Validity		m.	Concurrent validity
e.	Reliability		n.	Content validity
f.	Criterion-related validity		o.	Construct validity
g.	Disparate treatment		p.	Retaliation
h.	Affirmative action		q.	Reverse discrimination
i.	Diversity management		r.	Validity generalization

____ 1. A "test" actually measures what it says it measures.

____ 2. Discrimination generally occurs if the selection rate for a protected group is less than 80 percent of their representation in the relevant labor market or 80 percent less than the majority group.

____ 3. Was established to ensure that federal contractors and subcontractors have nondiscriminatory practices.

____ 4. The keystone of anti-discrimination legislation which prohibits discrimination in employment on basis of race, religion, color, sex, or national origin.

____ 5. Validity measured by means of a procedure that uses a test as the predictor of how well an individual will perform on the job.

___   6.   Efforts concerned with developing organizational initiatives that value all people equally, regardless of their differences.

___   7.   The consistency with which a test measures an item.

___   8.   Giving a test to current employees and the scores are correlated with their performance ratings.

___   9.   The agency responsible for enforcing employment-related provisions of the 1964 Civil Rights Act.

___   10.   A process in which employers identify problem areas, set goals, and take positive steps to guarantee equal employment opportunities for people in a protected class.

___   11.   Occurs when there is a substantial underrepresentation of protected-class members as a result of employment decisions that work to their disadvantage.

___   12.   A logical, nonstatistical method used to identify the KSAs and other characteristics necessary to perform a job.

___   13.   Occurs when protected-class members are treated differently from others.

___   14.   Test results of applicants are compared with their subsequent job performance.

___   15.   Shows a relationship between an abstract characteristic inferred from research and job performance.

___   16.   Occurs when an employer takes punitive action against individuals who exercise their legal rights.

___   17.   A condition that may exist when a person is denied an opportunity because of preferences given to protected-class individuals who may be less qualified.

___   18.   The extension of the validity of a test to different groups, similar jobs, or other organizations.

True/False Questions

____ 1. Federal civil rights laws prohibit discrimination based on sexual orientation, except where lifestyle is a *bona fide* occupational qualification.

____ 2. The Age Discrimination in Employment Act makes it illegal to discriminate against persons over 40 years of age.

____ 3. The Civil Rights Act of 1991 specifically permits the use of quotas in affirmative action plans.

____ 4. Affirmative action occurs when an employer sets specific numbers of protected-class members that must be hired.

____ 5. About one half of all women in the workforce are single heads of households.

____ 6. Younger workers will make up a smaller proportion of the workforce in the 1990s.

____ 7. Disparate treatment occurs when there is a substantial underrepresentation of protected-class members as a result of employment decisions that work to their disadvantage.

____ 8. EEO laws permit employers to discharge individuals who file discrimination charges with government agencies rather than with the employer's HR department.

____ 9. A test is useful only if it is either valid or reliable.

____ 10. The philosophy of enforcement of laws by the EEOC and the OFCCP are unaffected by the political party in office.

____ 11. A problem with concurrent validity is that a relatively large number of people have to be hired initially.

____ 12. The Uniform Guidelines apply to most employment-related decisions, not just to the initial hiring process.

____ 13. Validity refers to the consistency with which a test measures an item.

____ 14. The affirmative action requirements of Executive Orders 11246 and 11375 apply only to federal contractors and subcontractors.

___ 15.   Since EEO laws are enforced by agencies staffed by presidential appointees, differing degrees of activism and emphasis result, depending on the philosophical beliefs held by a particular administration.

___ 16.   Back pay in discrimination cases has generally not been significant enough to pressure management to be fair in their staffing policies and practices.

___ 17.   Intent is a major consideration courts have used when determining whether an organization is guilty of discrimination.

___ 18.   If a charge of discrimination is brought against an employer on the basis of disparate impact, the employer must be able to demonstrate that its employment procedures are valid.

___ 19.   Criterion-related validity is a logical, nonstatistical method used to identify the KSAs necessary to perform a job.

___ 20.   The *Griggs v. Duke Power* decision prohibits the use of tests in selection.

___ 21.   The 1964 Civil Rights Act specifically states that employers may discriminate on the basis of sex, religion, or national origin if the characteristic can be justified as a *bona fide* occupational qualification.

___ 22.   The Civil Rights Act of 1991 reversed the *Griggs v. Duke Power* decision.

___ 23.   In *Hopwood v. State of Texas*, it was ruled that the use of race in educational admissions contradicts, rather than furthers, the aims of equal protection.

___ 24.   The Civil Rights Act of 1991 permits the practice of race norming whereby test scores are adjusted on the basis of the race or gender of the test taker.

___ 25.   Diversity management is based on the premise that individuals should have equal access to all employment-related activities.

Idea Completion Questions

1.　Title VII of the Civil Rights Act of 1964 prohibits discrimination in employment on the basis of:
_____, _____, _____,
_____, and_____.

2.　The enforcement agency created by the Civil Rights Act of 1964 is the
_____, which is responsible for: _____.

3.　The major thrust of OFCCP efforts is to require that: _____
_____.

4.　Validity means that _____
_____,
while reliability refers to _____
_____.

5.　The three validation strategies recognized by the 1978 uniform selection guidelines are:
_____, _____, and _____.

6.　The 4/5ths rule states that discrimination generally is considered to occur if the selection rate for a protected group is: _____,
or _____.

Multiple Choice Questions

___   1.   Increasing numbers of women in the workforce will cause increased pressure for which of the following?
    a.   more variety in benefit programs
    b.   more flexible work schedules
    c.   different relocation programs
    d.   all of the above
    e.   only a and b above

___   2.   Projections suggest that the African American labor force will grow about _____ as fast as the white labor force from 1990-2000.
    a.   twice
    b.   three times
    c.   four times
    d.   one-half
    e.   one-third

___   3.   It is projected that _____ will be the largest minority group in the U.S. by 2010.
    a.   African Americans
    b.   Asian Americans
    c.   Hispanics
    d.   Caucasians

___   4.   The concept of reliability refers to
    a.   how difficult it is for applicants to "fake" out the test.
    b.   the consistency with which a test measures an item.
    c.   how well the test measures what it is supposed to measure.
    d.   the environmental conditions present when the test is given (for example: heat, lighting, etc.)

___   5.   The Equal Pay Act of 1963
    a.   prohibits wage discrimination based on sex.
    b.   requires equal pay for jobs of comparable worth.
    c.   prohibits pay differentials based on race, religion, color, sex, or national origin.
    d.   all of the above are provisions of the Act.
    e.   only a and b above.

___ 6. The Pregnancy Discrimination Act (1978) requires that
    a. the costs of childbirth must be covered by the firms' medical insurance plans.
    b. pregnant employees shall be provided with a four weeks paid leave of absence.
    c. pregnancy must be treated just as any other medical condition.
    d. it requires all of the above.

___ 7. The Age Discrimination in Employment Act, as amended, prohibits discrimination against
    a. teenagers.
    b. any person of any age.
    c. employees over 70 years of age.
    d. employees over 40 years of age.

___ 8. Disparate impact occurs when
    a. reverse discrimination is practiced.
    b. protected-class members are treated differently from others.
    c. there is substantial underrepresentation of protected-class members.
    d. all of the above represent disparate impact.
    e. only b and c above.

___ 9. In the *Ward's Cove Packing v. Atonio (1989)* case, the Supreme Court ruled
    a. that the statistical imbalance between job groups was not a sufficient basis for establishing a *prima facie* case of illegal discrimination.
    b. that an employer show that an employment practice is job related for the position.
    c. that the appropriate statistical comparisons should be made between the racial percentage of jobs in question and the racial composition for the local labor market.
    d. all of the above.
    e. only a and c above.

___ 10. The Immigration Reform and Control Act of 1986
    a. prohibits employment discrimination on the basis of national origin or citizenship.
    b. only pertains to Latin-Americans.
    c. prohibits employers from knowingly hiring illegal aliens.
    d. all of the above are true according to the act.
    e. only a and c above.

___   11.   A test is considered valid if
      a.   it actually measures what it says it measures.
      b.   it is developed by a professionally-qualified testing service.
      c.   it consistently measures an item the same way.
      d.   it has a reliability coefficient of .60 or above.
      e.   only c and d above.

___   12.   Which type of validity requires a fairly large number of people and a time gap between the test and the performance.
      a.   predictive
      b.   concurrent
      c.   content
      d.   construct
      e.   criterion-related

___   13.   In _____ validity, a prospective employee would perform a test which is an actual sample of work done on the job.
      a.   predictive
      b.   concurrent
      c.   content
      d.   construct
      e.   criterion-related

___   14.   The 4/5ths rule for determining disparate impact suggests that
      a.   4/5ths of all minorities interviewed must be hired.
      b.   discrimination exists if the selection rate for any protected group is less than 80% of the selection rate of the majority groups.
      c.   4/5ths of all minorities hired must be African Americans.
      d.   discrimination occurs if there is a proportional underrepresentation in relation to the relevant labor market.
      e.   both b and d above.

___   15.   The agency(ies) responsible for enforcing employment-related provisions of the 1964 Civil Rights Act is
      a.   the EEOC.
      b.   the Department of Labor.
      c.   the Justice Department.
      d.   the OFCCP.
      e.   both a and d above.

___ 16. In overturning the *Price Waterhouse v. Hopkins (1989)* decision, the Civil Rights Act of 1991 says that
   a.   when an employment decision is based on both legitimate and impermissible factors, the employer can avoid liability if the same decision would have been reached without the impermissible factor.
   b.   an employer is liable if the protected-class status of an individual was a motivating factor that caused discriminatory action to occur.
   c.   victims of discrimination cannot receive both compensatory and punitive damages.
   d.   race norming is permissible if the intent is to hire previously underrepresented protected-class members.
   e.   both b and c above.

___ 17. With regard to U.S. firms operating internationally, the Civil Right Act of 1991 states
   a.   that if customs or cultural conditions of a foreign country conflict with U.S. EEO laws, the U.S. laws do not apply.
   b.   specifically that Title VII did not cover U.S. employees working for U.S. firms internationally.
   c.   that if laws in a foreign country require actions in conflict with U.S. EEO laws, the foreign laws will apply.
   d.   all of the above.
   e.   only a and c above

___ 18. _____ is the extension of a test to different groups, similar jobs, or other organizations.
   a.   Validity generalization
   b.   Judgment validity
   c.   Concurrent validity
   d.   Construct validity
   e.   Validity rationalization

___ 19. Provisions of the Americans with Disabilities Act include:
   a.   a covered employer must make reasonable accommodation for persons with disabilities.
   b.   discrimination is prohibited against individuals if they can perform the essential functions of the job.
   c.   pre-employment medical examination are prohibited.
   d.   all of the above.
   e.   only a and b above.

___ 20.   The Immigration Reform and Control Act
          a.   requires that U.S. employers pay at least the minimum wage to undocumented aliens.
          b.   makes it illegal for an employer to hire a non-U.S. citizen.
          c.   prohibits employers from requiring more documentation for some prospective employees than for others.
          d.   all of the above.
          e.   both b and c above.

Essay

1.   How will the workforce of 2005 differ from that of today? What actions can an employer take to manage a more diverse workforce?

2.   Define the following concepts, and illustrate their impact on HR management:
          a.   diversity management,
          b.   equal employment opportunity,
          c.   affirmative action.

3.   Has the Civil Rights Act of 1964 been successful in bringing about equality in all employment-related decisions?

4.   Illustrate how the Civil Rights Act of 1991 has affected staffing practices.

5.   Define reliability and validity. How are both essential to complying with the 1978 Uniform Guidelines on Employee Selection Procedures.

6.   Describe the three validation strategies recognized by the 1978 Uniform Guidelines on Employee Selection Procedures, clearly indicating the usefulness and limitations of each.

ANSWER KEY

Matching

1. d	2. k	3. c	4. a	5. f
6. i	7. e	8. m	9. b	10. h
11. j	12. n	13. g	14. l	15. o
16. p	17. q	18. r		

True/False

1. F	2. T	3. F	4. F	5. T
6. T	7. F	8. F	9. F	10. F
11. F	12. T	13. F	14. T	15. T
16. F	17. F	18. T	19. F	20. F
21. T	22. F	23. T	24. F	25. F

Idea Completion

1. race
   religion
   color
   sex
   national origin

2. Equal Employment Opportunity Commission (EEOC)
   enforcing the employment-related provisions of the act

3. federal contractors and subcontractors take affirmative action to overcome the effects of prior discriminatory practices

4. a "test" actually measures what is says it measures
   the consistency with which a test measures an item

5.   content validity
        criterion-related validity
        construct validity

6.   less than 80 percent of the group's representation in the relevant labor market
        80 percent of the selection rate for the majority group

Multiple Choice

1.	d	2.	a	3.	c	4.	b	5.	a
6.	c	7.	d	8.	c	9.	e	10.	e
11.	a	12.	a	13.	c	14.	e	15.	a
16.	b	17.	e	18.	a	19.	d	20.	c

PRESIDENT SHIPLEY'S DILEMMA

Maurice Shipley is President of Ocean View College, a small private liberal arts college in south Florida. With the exception of the Vice President for Administration who is hispanic, all the senior administrators at Ocean View are white.

The college's Vice President for Student Affairs and Dean of Students is due to retire at the end of the semester. President Shipley established a search committee and charged them to make every attempt to recruit African-American candidates for this position. In addition to advertising the position in the *Chronicle of Higher Education*, the search committee placed advertisements in the newsletter of the Association of Minority Deans, and in the Minority Faculty Data Bank.

After sifting through dozens of resumes, reading many letters of recommendation and conducting countless telephone interviews, the search committee has invited the first of five finalists to campus for a series of interviews. This candidate, Dr. Josiah Washington, was the only African-American applicant to meet all the experience and educational qualifications specified by the search committee. Dr. Washington has an impressive resume and has held a similar position at a prestigious college in the northeast for the past eight years. On paper, he was by far the most suitable applicant for the position. When contacted by phone, he indicated that he was tired of the long cold winters, and wished to move south.

January 26

Dr. Washington has just spent two days at Ocean View meeting with a variety of faculty, administrators, and students. After he had left campus, President Shipley began receiving reviews from the various people who had interviewed Dr. Washington. The written reports were unanimous in their assessment that Dr. Josiah Washington was an outstanding candidate with impeccable credentials. But President Shipley sensed that there were some reservations. When questioned privately, several of the administrators and faculty, and all of the students who had met Dr. Washington indicated that they suspected that he was gay.

Normally, President Shipley would have responded: "So what?" But this time he listened to the suspicions differently. Just a few months ago, a history professor at Ocean View College, Luis Firenze had died from AIDS. Professor Firenze had made no secret of his sexual preference, and there were always rumors, never substantiated, that students were included among his partners. A confidential memorandum from the vice president for administration indicated that the college's medical insurance carrier had paid nearly $200,000 in medical and hospital bills related to Professor Firenze's treatment. Last week, President Shipley learned that a student is claiming that he contacted AIDS from Professor Firenze and that his parents were planning to sue the college.

President Shipley decided to wait until all the finalists had visited campus and he had received the recommendations of the search committee members.

February 16

The Vice President for Student Affairs and Dean of Students Search Committee has concluded its on-campus interviews of the finalists. The remaining four candidates were good and it appears that they would each do a good job if chosen for the position. However it was obvious to the committee members and to President Shipley that none of them measured up to Dr. Washington in terms of experience, qualifications, and potential to be an outstanding Dean of Students at Ocean View College.

Next week, President Shipley will be attending the annual conference of the Independent Colleges and Universities Association. This conference is attended by presidents and senior administrators of private colleges from across the country. He knows that the president of the college where Josiah Washington is currently employed will also be attending the conference.

Questions

1.   President Shipley came to you for advice. Should he extend a job offer to Dr. Washington?

2.   What is your assessment of the college's affirmative action attempts to recruit African American candidates?

3.   Is it an appropriate recruitment strategy for the college to target minority candidates?

4.   President Shipley is faced with a dilemma. How should he respond to perceptions and rumor?

5.   Are the concerns about Dr. Washington's sexual preference a valid consideration? Should President Shipley discuss the search committee's suspicions with Dr. Washington's current employer?

6.   Are there any legal ramifications of President Shipley's decision?

7.   How should an employer balance a job candidate's individual privacy rights against potential financial considerations?

MOUNTAIN STATE CONSTRUCTION

Mountain State Construction recently opened a new factory. The factory employs 500 people. The labor market in the community is as follows:

45%   Female
17%   African American
5%   Asian
6%   Native American
6%   Hispanic

The human resource department has gathered the following demographic data about the employees working at the new factory:

Number	Male	Female
Recruited	800	400
Selected	300	200

Number	White	African American	Asian	Native American	Hispanic
Recruited	820	200	40	60	80
Selected	328	88	20	24	40

Assignment

In this exercise, you are required to determine if there is disparate impact in the employment practices of Mountain State Construction at the new factory. To make this determination, you need to do the following:

1.   Using the 4/5ths rule, compare the percentage of each protected class recruited to 4/5ths of their percentage representation in the community.

2.   Compare the selection rates of males versus females, and whites versus each of the other racial and ethnic groups by using 4/5ths of the "majority" group rates.

3.   Determine "bottom line" disparate impact by comparing the percentage of each protected class selected to 4/5ths of their percentage representation in the community.

4.   What do the calculations indicate about the factory's equal employment results? Do you anticipate any problems with the factory's employment procedures?

Chapter 6

Implementing Equal Employment

CHAPTER OBJECTIVES

1. Discuss the two types of sexual harassment and how employers should respond to complaints.

2. Give examples of three sex-based discrimination issues besides sexual harassment.

3. Identify two age discrimination issues.

4. Discuss the major requirements of the Americans with Disabilities Act.

5. Describe two bases of EEO discrimination in addition to those listed above.

6. Identify typical EEO record-keeping requirements and those records used in the EEO investigative process.

7. Discuss the contents of an affirmative action plan (AAP).

SUMMARY OF THE CHAPTER

The days are past when employers can manage their workforces in any manner they wish. Federal, state, and local laws prohibit discrimination against individuals on a variety of bases.

Title VII of the Civil Rights Act of 1964 prohibits discrimination in employment on the basis of sex. Other laws and regulations are aimed at eliminating sex discrimination in specific areas.

The EEOC has issued guidelines to curtail *sexual harassment*, which refers to actions that are sexually directed, unwanted, and subject the worker to adverse employment conditions or that create a hostile work environment. There is a growing awareness of sexual harassment and less toleration of it, both among employers and those affected by it. The victims of sexual harassment are more likely to bring charges and take legal action against employers and harassing individuals than they were in the past.

Although over 90% of the sexual harassment charges have involved harassment of women by men, some cases have been filed by men against women managers and supervisors.

The two types of sexual harassment have been defined as *quid pro quo*, where a condition of employment is linked to the granting of sexual favors, and *hostile environment*. In the landmark case of *Meritor Savings Bank v. Vinson*, the Supreme Court ruled that creation of a hostile work environment due to sexual harassment is illegal even if the complainant suffered no loss of earnings or job loss.

Employers generally are held responsible for sexual harassment unless they take appropriate action in response to a complaint. With the passage of the Civil Rights Act of 1991, the costs to employers of being found guilty of sexual harassment likely will increase as a result of jury trials with punitive damages being awarded. Employers need to take positive action to eliminate sexual harassment from their workplaces. It is imperative that every employer have a policy on sexual harassment, and that this policy be communicated to all employees.

Other areas of sex discrimination which affect the employment and employment conditions of women include:

Pregnancy Discrimination - The *Pregnancy Discrimination Act* was passed in 1978 and requires employers to treat maternity leave as other personal or medical leaves. The *Family and Medical Leave Act* of 1993 requires that individuals be given up to 12 weeks of family leave without pay.

Compensation Issues - The *Equal Pay Act* requires employers to pay similar wage rates for similar work without regard to gender.

According to the concept of *pay equity*, jobs requiring comparable levels of knowledge, skills, and ability should be paid similarly even if actual duties differ significantly. Although some state and local governments, and some Canadian provinces, have mandated pay equity, U.S. federal courts have ruled that the existence of pay differences between jobs held by men and jobs held by women is not sufficient to prove that illegal discrimination has occurred.

With regard to benefits coverage, the *Arizona Governing Committee v. Norris* decision held that, regardless of longevity differences, men and women who contribute equally to pension plans must receive equal monthly payments.

Sex Discrimination in Jobs and Careers - Generally employer anti-nepotism policies have been upheld by courts, in spite of the concern that they discriminate against women more than men. One result of the increasing number of women in the workforce is the movement of women into jobs traditionally held by men, including welders, railroad engineers, utility repair specialists, farm equipment sales representatives, sheet metal workers, truck drivers, and carpenters.

The right of employers to reassign women from hazardous jobs to others that may be lower paying because of health-related concerns led some employers to institute *reproduction and fetal protection policies*. However, the U.S. Supreme Court ruled that such policies are illegal.

The *glass ceiling* refers to discriminatory practices that have prevented women and other protected-class members from advancing to executive-level jobs. A related problem is that women have tended to advance to senior management in a limited number of functional areas such as human resources and corporate communications. Limits that keep women from progressing only in certain fields have been referred to as "glass walls" or "glass elevators." Some firms have established mentoring programs to break down these barriers.

The *Age Discrimination in Employment Act* of 1967, amended in 1978 and 1986, makes it illegal for an employer to discriminate in compensation, terms, conditions, or privileges of employment because of an individual's age. The act provides protection for all individuals above the age of 40.

The *Americans with Disabilities Act* (ADA), passed in 1990, expands the scope and impact of laws and regulations on the discrimination against individuals with disabilities. The ADA defines a disabled person as someone who has a physical or mental impairment that substantially limits that person in some major life activities, who has a record of such an impairment, or is regarded as having such an impairment. The U.S. Supreme Court has ruled that an employer cannot discriminate against an individual who had a contagious disease. This has been interpreted as providing protection for AIDS-afflicted employees.

The ADA requires that employers identify for all jobs the essential job functions, and to provide reasonable accommodation for disabled individuals. Accommodations can sometimes be expensive, but the ADA offers only general guidelines on when an accommodation becomes unreasonable and places undue hardship on an employer.

Although the original purpose of the Civil Rights Act of 1964 was to address race discrimination, other laws and regulations have, from time to time, concerned discrimination based on national origin and citizenship, religion, sexual orientation, appearance (including obesity and facial hair), conviction and arrest records, veteran status, and seniority.

Employers must comply with all EEO regulations and guidelines. Managers should be aware of what specific administrative steps are required and how charges of discrimination are investigated. All employers with 15 or more employees are required to keep records that can be requested by the EEOC.

Since the potential areas for discrimination are quite broad, it is important that organizations carefully review their application blanks and interview questions to insure that unlawful pre-employment inquiries are not made. Once the applicant is hired, otherwise forbidden inquiries and medical examinations may be made for insurance and other legitimate purposes. However, such data may need to be maintained in a separate HR records system in order to avoid its use when making appraisal, discipline, termination, or promotion decisions.

Employers with federal contracts are sometimes required to have an *affirmative action plan* (AAP) to take affirmative action to overcome the effects of past discriminatory practices. The Secretary of Labor has been given the power to cancel the contract of a nonconforming contractor or blacklist a non-conforming employer from future government contracts.

STUDY QUESTIONS

Matching Questions

Match the key term from the list below with its most appropriate definition.

a.	Hostile environment harassment	i.	Reasonable accommodation
b.	Tester	j.	Glass ceiling
c.	Equal Pay Act	k.	Disabled person
d.	Undue hardship	l.	Essential job functions
e.	Utilization analysis	m.	*Quid pro quo* harassment
f.	Sexual harassment	n.	Glass walls
g.	Availability analysis	o.	*Arizona Governing Committee v. Norris*
h.	Pay equity		

___ 1.   Identifies the number of protected-class members available to work in the appropriate labor market in given jobs.

___ 2.   Refers to actions that are sexually directed, unwanted, and subject the worker to adverse employment conditions or that create a hostile work environment.

___ 3.   Has the effect of unreasonably interfering with work performance or psychological well-being or when intimidating or offensive working conditions are created.

___ 4.   Identifies the number of protected-class members employed and the types of jobs they hold in an organization.

___ 5.   Forbids employers to pay lower wage rates to employees of one sex than to the other sex for equal work performed under similar working conditions.

___ 6.   A protected-class member who poses as an applicant to determine if employers discriminate in their hiring practices.

___   7.   A modification or adjustment to a job or work environment that enables a qualified individual with a disability to enjoy equal employment opportunity.

___   8.   When making a reasonable accommodation for individuals with disabilities would pose significant difficulty or expense for an employer.

___   9.   Requires that jobs with comparable levels of knowledge, skills, and ability should be paid similarly even if actual duties differ significantly.

___   10.   A employer's deferred compensation plan violated Title VII because female employees received lower monthly benefits payments than men upon retirement despite the fact that women contributed equally to the plan.

___   11.   Discriminatory practices that have prevented women and other protected-class members from advancing to executive-level jobs.

___   12.   The fundamental job duties of the employment position that an individual with a disability holds or desires, but they do not include marginal functions of the position.

___   13.   Limits that keep women from progressing only in certain fields.

___   14.   Someone who has a physical or mental impairment that substantially limits that person in some major life activities, has a record of, or is regarded as having, such an impairment.

___   15.   An employer or supervisor links specific employment outcomes to the individual's granting sexual favors.

True/False Questions

___ 1. A hostile environment occurs when a supervisor links specific employment outcomes to the individual's granting sexual favors.

___ 2. It is legal to designate job categories as "male" or "female" when advertising position openings.

___ 3. Under the ADA, reasonable accommodation is restricted to actions that do not place an "undue hardship" on an employer.

___ 4. The Age Discrimination in Employment Act makes it illegal to discriminate against persons over 40 years of age.

___ 5. Dress codes are not a form of discrimination so long as they are applied uniformly.

___ 6. All seniority systems are invalid if they perpetuate the effects of past discrimination.

___ 7. The courts have ruled that it is legitimate for employers to discriminate against job candidates with arrest records.

___ 8. Employers generally are held responsible for sexual harassment unless they take appropriate action in response to a complaint.

___ 9. An employer of 15 or more employees is required to keep employment records required by EEOC.

___ 10. The Pregnancy Discrimination Act requires employers to provide maternity benefits, including unpaid leave, for pregnant employees.

___ 11. Anti-nepotism policies that restrict the hiring of relatives of employees are illegal because they generally discriminate against women.

___ 12. Racial data is permitted on application blanks or other pre-employment records only if it is not used in the selection process.

___ 13. Affirmative action occurs when an employer sets specific numbers of protected-class members that must be hired.

___ 14. Company policies that exclude women from hazardous jobs because of health-related concerns are illegal.

___   15.   A U.S. Supreme Court case held that it is illegal to discriminate against a person because of a concern that the employee has a contagious disease.

___   16.   The Equal Pay Act requires that jobs with comparable levels of knowledge, skill, and ability should be paid similarly even if actual duties differ significantly.

___   17.   As defined by the ADA, pregnancy is not a disability.

___   18.   The EEOC permits an employer to use a "visual" survey of a person's race provided it is not used in the selection process.

___   19.   The EEOC requires an employer to maintain records on the distribution of minority individuals in the workforce.

___   20.   The contents of an affirmative action plan must be available for review by managers and supervisors within the organization.

Idea Completion Questions

1.   The two types of sexual harassment are called:
_____ , and _____ .

2.   An employer's sexual harassment policy should address such issues as:
_____ ,   _____ ,   _____ ,
and _____ .

3.   Items which may be considered discriminatory in a pre-employment inquiry include:
_____ ,   _____ ,   _____ ,
_____ ,   _____ ,   _____ ,
_____ ,   _____ , and_____ .

4.   According to the ADA, a disabled person is someone who
_____ ,   _____ ,
and _____ .

5.   An employer with at least _____ employees and over $_____ in government contracts must have a written affirmative action plan (AAP).

Multiple Choice Questions

___   1.   The EEOC guidelines and court decisions on sexual harassment
   a.   define the range of sexual harassment from innuendo and lewd remarks to physical actions.
   b.   require employers to have specific policies prohibiting sexual harassment.
   c.   pertain only to harassment of female employees by male supervisors.
   d.   all of the above.
   e.   only a and b above.

___   2.   The EEOC guidelines define *quid pro quo* Harassment as
   a.   actions that are sexually directed that create a hostile working environment.
   b.   occurring when an employer or supervisor links specific employment outcomes to the individual granting sexual favors.
   c.   providing different terms of employment for women than for men.
   d.   all of the above.
   e.   both a and b above.

___   3.   Which question cannot legally be asked during pre-employment interviews?
   a.   Are you a Veteran?
   b.   Are you married?
   c.   What are your career goals for the next five years?
   d.   How long did you hold your last job?
   e.   None of the above can be legally asked.

___   4.   A right-to-sue letter is issued if
   a.   the EEOC is going to sue an employer on behalf of a complainant.
   b.   the EEOC is not going to sue an organization on behalf of an individual.
   c.   the district court finds the organization not guilty of discrimination.
   d.   the complainant has the right to bring suit.
   e.   both b and d above.

___   5.   _____ was the landmark case decided by the U.S. Supreme Court that ruled that the creation of a hostile work environment may constitute sexual harassment.
   a.   Meritor Savings Bank v. Vinson.
   b.   State of Washington v. AFSCME.
   c.   Mejia v. New York Sheraton Hotel.
   d.   U.S. v. Georgia Power Company.
   e.   Bundy v. Jackson

___   6.   The "glass ceiling" refers to discriminatory practices that
a.   have prevented protected-class minorities from advancing to executive-level jobs.
b.   have prevented women from advancing to executive-level jobs.
c.   promote reverse discrimination.
d.   all of the above.
e.   both a and b above.

___   7.   The Family and Medical Leave Act of 1993
a.   prevented employers from granting special privileges to female employees that were not made available to male employees.
b.   required employers to treat maternity leave the same as other personal or medical leaves.
c.   requires that employees be given up to 12 weeks family leave without pay upon the birth or adoption of a child.
d.   all of the above.
e.   both a and b above.

___   8.   The Supreme Court case dealing with religious discrimination ruled that
a.   persons may not be required to work on religious holidays of their faith.
b.   employers must make reasonable accommodation of an employee's religious beliefs.
c.   employers should not hire persons if their religious beliefs cause a scheduling hardship on other employees.
d.   all of the above are true.
e.   only a and b above.

___   9.   Which of the following would not be classified as disabled by the ADA?
a.   a person with AIDS
b.   an obese individual
c.   a deaf person
d.   homosexual and bisexual individuals
e.   none of the above are excluded from coverage

___   10.   An affirmative action plan must
a.   be available for review by managers and supervisors within the organization.
b.   contain a specified table of contents.
c.   specify goals and timetables for achieving equal employment opportunities for protected-class personnel.
d.   all of the above.
e.   only a and c above.

___   11.   The Pregnancy Discrimination Act of 1978
         a.   requires maternity leave be treated as any other personal or medical leaves.
         b.   requires that individuals be given up to 12 weeks family leave without pay.
         c.   protects women by requiring that they be excluded from hazardous jobs during pregnancy.
         d.   provides for all of the above.
         e.   both a and b above

___   12.   Which of the following information, which represents illegal pre-employment inquiries, is legal to obtain after the applicant has been hired?
         a.   age and race
         b.   photograph
         c.   national origin and ancestry
         d.   all of the above
         e.   only a and c above

___   13.   Employers must file an annual report with the EEOC if they meet which of the following conditions:
         a.   have 100 or more employees.
         b.   have no federal contracts.
         c.   have employees under age 16.
         d.   all of the above.
         e.   only a and b above.

___   14.   Regarding the use of conviction and arrest records in employment practices, the courts have generally held that
         a.   conviction records can be used if the offense is recent and job related.
         b.   multiple convictions are grounds for nonemployment.
         c.   arrest records may not be used since they may have adverse impact on certain minority groups.
         d.   all of the above.
         e.   only a and c above.

___   15.   To help employers protect themselves from sexual harassment charges, the EEOC guidelines suggest:
         a.   developing a policy regarding sexual harassment.
         b.   disciplining offenders.
         c.   transferring employees who make complaints to a new supervisor.
         d.   all of the above.
         e.   a and b only.

Essay Questions

1. How has sexual harassment been defined by the EEOC and the courts? Describe the issues that should be addressed in a sexual harassment policy.

2. Discuss the concepts of nepotism, glass ceiling, and glass walls and glass elevators. Explain how and why these concepts tend to adversely affect women more than men.

3. List three questions that cannot be legally asked in an employment interview and explain why each is not legally allowed.

4. Explain the existing court opinion on seniority systems as they relate to discrimination.

5. What are the major implications of the Americans with Disabilities Act of 1990 for the practice of human resource management?

6. Which employers are required to have an affirmative action plan (AAP)? What should be contained in an AAP?

ANSWER KEY

Matching

1. g	2. f	3. a	4. e	5. c
6. b	7. i	8. d	9. h	10. o
11. j	12. l	13. n	14. k	15. m

True/False

1. F	2. F	3. T	4. T	5. T
6. F	7. F	8. T	9. T	10. F
11. T	12. F	13. F	14. T	15. T
16. F	17. T	18. T	19. T	20. T

Idea Completion

1. *quid pro quo*
   hostile environment

2. instructions on how to report complaints
   assurances of confidentiality and protection against retaliation
   a guarantee of prompt investigation
   a statement that disciplinary action will be taken against sexual harassers

3. | | | |
   |---|---|---|
   | maiden name | age | race or color |
   | national origin & ancestry | sex and family composition | creed or religion |
   | language | reference from pastor | name or address of relatives |
   | arrest record | height and weight | social organization memberships |
   | handicapped status | financial status | photographs |

4. has a physical or mental impairment that substantially limits that person in some major life activities
   has a record of such an impairment
   is regarded as having such an impairment

5.   50
     50,000

Multiple Choice

1. e	2. b	3. b	4. e	5. a
6. e	7. c	8. b	9. d	10. d
11. a	12. d	13. a	14. e	15. e

DEAR PLANT MANAGER

MEMORANDUM

January 2, 19XX

TO: C. Tavistock, Plant Manager

FROM: Marge Hopkins

RE: Happy New Year

Dear Plant Manager,

I have just read your plant-wide E-Mail memo, dated December 30, in which you wished us all a "happy new year" and asked us to go the "extra mile" as we enter a difficult new year. You referred to the unfavorable economy, challenging new government regulations, and the entry of foreign competitors into our market. You regretted that there was no "holiday" bonus this year (when did we stop calling it a "Christmas bonus?"), and that pay increases would be minimal. Nevertheless you asked us to restrict overtime, to work harder during regular hours, to be thrifty when ordering supplies, and to look for ways to cut expenses.

My response is not just "No" but "HECK NO!"

If you checked my personnel file, you would learn that I came to work here twenty-six years ago. My husband had been killed in Vietnam leaving me with a six year-old daughter. I had very little money, so moved back to live with my parents in their small two bedroom apartment. And I looked for a job.

Mr. Collingwood offered me a job in the typing pool. There were three other girls in the typing pool, all younger than me and unmarried. I worked hard. I took Trixie to school every morning and was at work by 8:30. Mom would pick her up after school, and I would leave the plant around 5 pm., but would stay later if I was working on a rush job. Mr. Collingwood must have liked my work because after I had been working just over four years, he asked me to be his secretary. His previous secretary was retiring.

I was ecstatic - Secretary to the Plant Manager. The girls in the typing pool were a bit jealous, but I guess that I had earned the promotion. My wages increased slightly, and I had many more responsibilities. In addition to my secretarial duties, I organized Mr. Collingwood's schedule, made his travel arrangements, entertained the head office directors when they were in town (made hotel reservations, prepared lunch, ordered drivers, etc.), and I planned the annual Christmas party and family picnic. I never left the office before 5 o'clock and often stayed late if there was something that needed to be done. Mr. Collingwood never hesitated to call me on the weekend if he was in the plant and needed something. I was probably eligible for overtime, but never asked for it. I was glad to have the job, I loved my job, and wanted to do the best job I could. That was the way I was raised.

I saved all the money I could. I wanted to get a home of my own so that Trixie could have her own room. Just before Trixie became a teenager, I decided to buy a house. The company provided low interest mortgages to employees after five years service, so I applied to the Personnel Department for a housing loan. I figured that with my savings, and an employee loan, I could buy a modest three bedroom home. I would pay off the loan over 25 years. However, when I went to speak with the Personnel Manager, he told me that the company would not be doing me a favor by lending me the money. I still remember his words: "You would be better off staying with your parents. Now if you had a husband, things would be different." I was so upset. I went to the bank and applied for a regular mortgage and bought a house. I have never missed a payment.

At times my office seemed to be the social center of the plant. Whenever anyone (employee, director, customer, sales rep.) came to see you, they stopped by my desk to say "Hi." I tried to be friendly, I always had a fresh pot of coffee brewing and a jar of home made candies on my desk. I remembered everyone's birthday and have made countless birthday cakes over the years. I viewed the plant as our little community. We were a big, happy family, looking out for one another's interests.

I cried the day Mr. Collingwood retired five years ago. It was a sad day for us all. He had been a good boss. Although he rarely gave me praise for my work (he was quiet and reserved), I could tell that he appreciated all I did. I got a significant pay increase each year, and he sent me flowers on my birthday.

Rather than promoting one of the supervisors to plant manager, head office hired you from a factory in the north-east. I welcomed you to town, introduced you to people in the plant and to our customers and reps, and showed you how our system worked. I arranged for a realtor to meet your family when they visited and introduced you to the school superintendent. It was strange having a new boss, but I tried hard to please you and to make you feel welcome.

I must admit there were two incidents which upset me during your first years here. When my mother died I was off work for nearly two weeks. When I returned to the office, you asked me if I wanted the time-off to count towards my vacation time or whether I wanted it leave-without-pay. Mr. Collingwood would have told me to take off as much time as I needed to take care of my mother's things. And he would have paid me, no questions asked.

Then my furnace died right in the middle of winter. I found a tradesman to install a new one for $3,000, but he wanted $2,000 in advance so that he could buy the equipment. I applied for a home improvement loan at the bank. They told me the paperwork would take three weeks for approval. I was desperate, so I asked you if the company would give me a salary advance for three weeks so that I could have the new furnace installed immediately. You advised that it was against company policy to make personal loans to employees below the rank of supervisor. Fortunately Mr. Weiner came to my rescue. He personally loaned me $2,000 which I repaid when the bank loan was approved.

Things were a bit hectic when you had that heart attack two years ago. I held the fort during your ten week absence. I must admit that I was a bit concerned when you returned to work. You seemed a little less friendly, and more demanding and critical. But then I assumed that your heart attack was quite a shock for you and your young family.

Last January it was my turn. I had suffered from back aches for years and my doctor recommended surgery to repair some disks. Although this surgery was covered by our medical insurance, I still needed to pay over $1,000 in deductibles and co-payments. Luckily, the company's disability insurance permitted me to take three month's paid leave. Although I was able to return to work after three months, I needed a wheelchair for another two months until I was able to walk with a cane.

You can imagine how shocked I was when you came to visit me at home just days before I returned to work. The purpose of your visit, you said, was to advise me that when I returned to work, I would be working in the typing pool. You had decided that the temporary secretary you hired during my disability would now become permanent.

My shock turned to anger in the weeks after I returned to work. I was now the junior member of the typing pool, a position I had held twenty-six years ago when I first came to work here. Your new secretary was not only thirty years younger than me, she was attractive, and didn't need a wheelchair to get around. The other typists treat me like a pariah. The supervisors rarely give me any work to do. They seem uncomfortable around me. It is as though they feel I must be guilty of something, otherwise you wouldn't have demoted me so mercilessly.

I have very little work to do, but I am at my desk by 8:30 every morning and leave at precisely 5 pm. I spend most of my days reading and doing crosswords. But my real question is "Why?" Why after all these years am I back where I started? Why am I treated like a pariah? Why, on Christmas eve, did you come by the typing pool, shake hands with each of the typists to wish them "happy holidays" but ignored me? I felt invisible. You didn't even seem to notice that I was there. Why? What did I do to deserve this?

Which brings me back to your memo. Will I be willing to "go the extra mile?" NO! NO! NO! I will come to work every day, and do only what I am asked. No more. No less. I turn sixty-five in just four years. I can't wait until retirement. And don't bother giving me the traditional retirement luncheon, because I won't show up.

Happy New Year to you, too.

PS: I wish I had the nerve to send you this memo, but I must admit I feel so much better for having written it.

Questions

1.   If you were Marge Hopkins, would you send this memo to the plant manager, or would you destroy it? Why?

2.   Do you think Mr. Collingwood was an effective manager of human resources? Why or why not?

3.   Has C. Tavistock violated any employment laws? Which ones?

4.   If Ms. Hopkins is a victim of unlawful discrimination, what action can she pursue? What remedies should she seek?

5.   Would the company be able to defend itself? How? What would it need to prove?

6.   If you were the corporate HR manager and you learned about this treatment of Marge Hopkins, what action would you take?

7.   Assume that you are a friend of Marge Hopkins and she shared this story with you. What advice would you offer Marge?

PRE-EMPLOYMENT INQUIRIES

Part I

Analyze the application for employment presented on the following pages and list below all the items that you feel constitute illegal pre-employment inquiries.

1. _____   6. _____

2. _____   7. _____

3. _____   8. _____

4. _____   9. _____

5. _____   10. _____

Part II

What additional information could legally be included on the application for employment that would improve the selection process?

1. _____   6. _____

2. _____   7. _____

3. _____   8. _____

4. _____   9. _____

5. _____   10. _____

APPLICATION FOR EMPLOYMENT

Name	Date

Position Desired	Attach Recent
Minimum Salary Required	Photograph
Date Available	
Present Address	Here

Present Employer	How Long Employed? _____yrs _____mos

Age	Date of Birth	Height	Weight	Sex	Marital Status

Are you a U.S. citizen? If not, state type of visa

Name of Spouse	No. of Dependents

Name and address of relative not living with you

Are you pregnant?

List any serious illness, accident, or operation within last 10 years

Are you presently under the care of a doctor? If yes, explain.

Give full details of any disabilities which could prevent you from performing specific kinds of work.

Have you ever been arrested?	If yes, give full details

Languages you speak, read, or write fluently.

APPLICATION FOR EMPLOYMENT   **page 2**

Education - Circle highest grade completed
1   2   3   4   5   6   7   8   9   10   11   12

Name of colleges attended	Dates	Degree earned

Previous employment - start with present or most recent

Employer	Address	Dates	Title	Reason for leaving

Briefly state why you seek a change in employment

Are you a union member? If yes, which one?

Personal references - list 3 persons not related to you

Name	Address	Occupation
1.		
2.		
3.		

I acknowledge that all the statements made by me in this application are true and complete to the best of my knowledge. I authorize the company to verify any information that I have provided. I understand that any false statements will void this application.

Signed: _____   Date: _____

Chapter 7

Job Analysis

CHAPTER OBJECTIVES

1. Define *job analysis*, *job description*, and *job specification*.

2. Discuss three behavioral aspects of job analysis.

3. Explain how job analysis is used to comply with the Americans with Disabilities Act (ADA) and other legal requirements.

4. Identify how job analysis information is used in four other HR activities.

5. List and explain four job analysis methods.

6. Identify the five steps in conducting a job analysis.

7. Write a job description and the job specifications for it.

SUMMARY OF THE CHAPTER

Job analysis is a systematic way to gather and analyze information about the content of jobs, the jobs' human requirements, and the context in which jobs are performed. Job analysis is useful in improving productivity and in providing important data for "right-sizing" organizations. It also is used in other human resource activities including HR planning, recruitment, selection, performance appraisal, compensation, training and development, career planning, health and safety, and union activities.

Job analysis is particularly critical for legal compliance with many government laws and regulations, including the Americans with Disabilities Act (ADA). The ADA requires that organizations identify the *essential functions* of jobs. Job analysis is the heart of all means used to identify these essential functions.

Job analysts must be aware of a number of behavioral issues as they conduct job analyses. Employee fears, resistance to change, an overemphasis on the current employees in the job, and "inflated" job significance are some of the behavioral aspects which analysts must address.

There are four commonly used methods in gathering data about jobs. They include:

1.   observation,
2.   interviewing,
3.   questionnaires, and
4.   specialized methods.

The latter approach includes the Position Analysis Questionnaire, Functional Job Analysis, Dictionary of Occupational Titles, Computerized Job Analysis, and specialized methods for conducting managerial job analysis.

The process of conducting a job analysis includes five basic steps:

1.   identify the jobs and review existing documentation,
2.   explain the process to managers and employees,
3.   conduct the job analyses,
4.   prepare job descriptions and job specifications, and
5.   maintain and update job descriptions and job specifications.

Ultimately, job analysis serves as the basis for preparing *job descriptions* - a summary of the tasks, duties, and responsibilities in a job, and *job specifications* - a list of the knowledge, skills, and abilities an individual needs to perform the job satisfactorily.

STUDY QUESTIONS

Matching Questions

Match the key term from the list below with its most appropriate definition.

a.   Job analysis   e.   Position

b.   Job description   f.   Functional Job Analysis

c.   Job specification   g.   DOT

d.   Performance standard   h.   Job

___   1.   A systematic investigation of the tasks, duties and responsibilities required in a job, and the necessary skills knowledge, and abilities someone needs to perform the job adequately.

___   2.   A summary of the tasks, duties, and responsibilities in a job.

___   3.   A collection of tasks, duties, and responsibilities performed by one person.

___   4.   A method that analyzes jobs by building standardized statements and job descriptions to be used in a variety of organizations.

___   5.   Dictionary of Occupational Titles.

___   6.   Lists the various skills, knowledge, and abilities an individual needs to do the job satisfactorily.

___   7.   A grouping of similar positions having common tasks, duties, and responsibilities.

___   8.   Tells what the job accomplishes and what performance is considered satisfactory in each area of the job description.

True/False Questions

___   1.   The enactment of the ADA increased the importance of job analysis.

___   2.   Job specifications are guides to be used in recruiting and selection.

___   3.   A job and a position have the same HR meaning.

___   4.   Work sampling requires observing an entire work cycle and each detailed job action in it.

___   5.   Job descriptions can be used as excuses for employees to limit their work.

___   6.   The interview method of job analysis is very useful because it takes little time to complete.

___   7.   Job analysis data is of little value in identifying hazardous jobs and working conditions.

___   8.   A major advantage of the questionnaire method of analyzing jobs is that information on a large number of jobs can be collected in a relatively short period of time.

___   9.   The observation method of job analysis is best for repetitive type jobs.

___   10.   The Dictionary of Occupational Titles is an outgrowth of the Positions Analysis Questionnaire.

___   11.   In order to be complete, the job specifications should reflect the skills of the person currently holding the job.

___   12.   Performance standards must be developed before a job description can be written.

Idea Completion Questions

1.   Using the Dictionary of Occupational Titles, functional definitions of what is done in a job can be generated by examining the fundamental components of:
_____, _____, and _____.

2.   The PAQ is divided into six divisions. These divisions are:
_____, _____, _____,
_____, _____, and_____.

3.   _____ is the systematic investigation of tasks, duties, and responsibilities of a job and the necessary skills, and abilities someone needs to perform the job adequately.

4.   The two end uses of job analysis are:
_____, and _____.

5.   The four major job analysis methods are:
_____, _____, _____,
and _____.

Multiple Choice Questions

___   1.   Which of the following is not a component of FJA?
   a.   things
   b.   technology
   c.   people
   d.   data

___   2.   The behavioral implications that managers should consider in the job analysis procedure include all the following except:
   a.   employees' fears of the process.
   b.   resistance to change.
   c.   legal constraints.
   d.   over emphasis of the current job holder's qualifications.
   e.   inflated job significance.

___   3.   The major limitation to the interview method of job analysis is
   a.   it is less accurate.
   b.   it is very time consuming.
   c.   it is a very complex process.
   d.   none of the above are major limitations.

___   4.   The fundamental job duties of the employment position that an individual with a disability holds or desires are known, according to ADA, as
   a.   essential functions.
   b.   knowledge, skills, and abilities statement.
   c.   PAQs.
   d.   DOTs.

___   5.   According to ADA the essential functions statements in a job description
   a.   can be listed in any order.
   b.   must be listed in order of importance.
   c.   must be listed in order of time spent.
   d.   are not addressed by the ADA.

___   6.   A statement of the qualifications necessary to satisfactorily perform the job is a
　　　　　a.   job specification.
　　　　　b.   job analysis.
　　　　　c.   job description.
　　　　　d.   performance standard.

___   7.   Of the following jobs, which one would be the most difficult to write a job description for?
　　　　　a.   camp counselor
　　　　　b.   assembly line worker
　　　　　c.   gas station attendant
　　　　　d.   key punch operator

___   8.   A good job description usually contains all but
　　　　　a.   precise action verbs.
　　　　　b.   a general summary statement broadly describing the job.
　　　　　c.   an identification section.
　　　　　d.   precisely what the current employee does.

___   9.   In a typical job analysis interface, the HR unit would be responsible for all of the following except:
　　　　　a.   prepare job descriptions.
　　　　　b.   prepare job specifications.
　　　　　c.   identify performance standards.
　　　　　d.   coordinate job analysis procedures.

___   10.   A good job specification will describe key qualifications in which of the following areas?
　　　　　a.   knowledge
　　　　　b.   skills
　　　　　c.   abilities
　　　　　d.   all of the above

Essay Questions

1.   Do you agree with the following statement? Explain your answer.

      Job analysis is the most basic function of human resource management. Everything else is dependent upon job analysis.

2.   What use could a company make of job descriptions and job specifications?

3.   Define and discuss four job analysis methods.

4.   What would you expect to find in a well-written job description?

5.   Describe the five steps in conducting a job analysis, emphasizing the major components of each step.

6.   Discuss the specific impacts ADA has had on conducting job analyses and on writing job descriptions and specifications.

ANSWER KEY

Matching

1. a	2. b	3. e	4. f	5. g
6. c	7. h	8. d		

True/False

1 . T	2. T	3. F	4. F	5 . T
6. F	7. F	8. T	9. T	10. F
11. F	12. F			

Idea Completion

1.   data
      people
      things

2.   information input
      mental process
      work output
      relationships with others
      job context
      other

3.   Job analysis

4.   job descriptions
      job specifications

5.   observation
      interviewing
      questionnaires
      specialized methods

Multiple Choice

1. b   2. c   3. b   4. a   5. b

6. a   7. a   8. d   9. c   10. d

ROO BURGERS

Mick Ballard, a native of Australia, and a recent MBA graduate of one of the leading universities in the southwest, decided to open a restaurant. This was not his original career plan, but the idea evolved during his two years in graduate business school. An outdoorsman, Mick took every opportunity to go hunting, fishing, and camping. He also loved to cook and his camping companions were fascinated by his concoctions. Mick's specialty was hamburgers seasoned with a special sauce. He claimed that the sauce was a family recipe containing a secret combination of herbs, spices, and vegetable juices. He called them "roo burgers" and boasted that he imported kangaroo meat especially for the burgers. (In fact, he used regular hamburger patties, and marinated them overnight in his special sauce.)

Mick's camping companions encouraged him to open a restaurant and market these "roo burgers." They offered to back him financially and to use their collective education to provide Mick with all the advice he might need in the formative years. Thus the "Roo Burger" was born.

Four years ago Mick Ballard opened a small restaurant in Austin, Texas. He located a suitable building not far from the university campus, obtained sufficient financing from his friends and a bank loan, rented kitchen equipment and furniture, and planned the usual menu of burgers, fries, salads, and soft drinks. His main competitors were the franchise restaurants such as McDonald's and Pizza Hut.

The human resource policies of the Roo Burger Restaurant could be best described as highly unstructured. Before opening the restaurant, Mick placed advertisements in the college newspaper and hired a cook, two waiters/cashiers, and a janitor. He explained to the new employees that he wanted everyone to pitch-in and do whatever needed doing to cook the food, serve the customers, and keep the restaurant clean. He did much of the cooking himself in addition to all the management functions.

The restaurant usually opened at 11:00 a.m. and remained open until midnight, and Mick would be there most of the time. Terry Cantrell was the first employee Mick hired and serves as manager when Mick is not at work. Terry is 34, had dropped out of college during his freshman year, and had held a number of bartender and waiter jobs before working at Roo Burger.

As business grew and more staff were needed, Mick would encourage the current employees to tell their friends that he was hiring. He did all the hiring himself. This usually involved talking to the applicant over a cup of coffee and if the "chemistry was right" he made a job offer on the spot. He was up-front with the applicants he decided not to hire. He told them at the end of the interview that he was sorry but could tell that the person would not "fit in." There were no application forms to fill-out, and no job descriptions. Mick kept only minimal records for payroll purposes.

Today Roo Burger employs two cooks, seven waiters/cashiers, and two janitors. The employees are expected to be able to perform all the jobs in the restaurant, and to assist other employees as needed. Training consisted of on-the-job training with either Mick or Terry showing the new employees what to do.

Mick has no dress codes, preferring that the employees wear clothes they are comfortable in, which normally means jeans or shorts, T-shirts, and gym shoes. In addition, many of the employees have long hair.

Each Friday, Mick posts the schedule of shifts for the next week. However, this schedule is flexible. Mick permits the employees to find their own substitutes, provided that each category of job is covered each shift. Turnover at Roo Burger has been low, unusual for the fast food industry. Mick firmly believed that the low turnover was a direct result of the personal interest he took in all of his employees, coupled with his flexible management style.

The employees liked working for Mick. Most of them were in their early twenties. One employee who had been at Roo Burger from the beginning described Mick as flexible, fun to be around, working side-by-side with his employees, and never acting like a boss.

This past summer, Mick took his first vacation since opening Roo Burger. While hiking through the mountains, he reflected on the success of his enterprise. He had repaid the bank loan, purchased the furniture and equipment which he had initially rented, and his partners were pleased with their share of the profits. In fact, Mick's partners were encouraging him to expand.

Mick knew that he would have no difficulty in obtaining another bank loan. One partner had suggested that Mick relocate to a larger site close by his present restaurant. Another had suggested that he open a second restaurant in another part of town.

But Mick didn't want to lose the personal touch that he enjoyed with his employees. He feared that with a larger business he would not be able to have such a close relationship with all the employees.

Upon reflection, Mick realized that he had been so busy during the past four years building and managing the business, that he had left no time for planning. Did he need a more formal organizational structure? Should he write an employee manual? Is it practical to treat all the employees as friends? He resolved to discuss these questions with Terry Cantrell when he returned from the mountains.

Questions

1. Should Mick Ballard continue the present unstructured informal human resource policy if he did not expand?

2. How would expansion affect this policy?

3. Assume that Mick decides to expand and to formalize the HR function. Also, assume that he has sought your advice regarding the human resource function. What would you recommend? What should Mick do first?

A SAMPLE JOB ANALYSIS

After reading chapter seven, you should have a basic understanding of what is involved in conducting a job analysis and writing job descriptions and job specifications. This exercise provides you with an opportunity to "practice" the processes described.

Assignment

1. Select a job you might like to have. Gather data about the job by interviewing a person who currently holds such a job and perhaps by observing the person actually performing some of the duties of the job.

2. Identify the essential functions of the job.

3. Use the job analysis information to write a draft job description from the suggestions given in chapter seven of the text. Refer to the sample job description and specifications for the Human Resources Assistant (Figure 7-7) for format ideas.

4. Draft job specifications for the job in a form similar to those in Figure 7-7.

5. Have another student and/or your instructor review the draft, then make necessary changes and give the completed exercise to the individual from whom you obtained the information.

6. Is the job description defensible in light of ADA compliance?

Chapter 8

Recruiting

CHAPTER OBJECTIVES

1. Define *recruiting* and discuss three strategic recruiting issues.

2. Discuss why more employers are using flexible staffing.

3. Outline a typical recruiting process and identify legal considerations affecting recruiting.

4. Compare internal and external sources of candidates.

5. Identify three internal sources of candidates.

6. List and briefly discuss five external recruiting sources.

7. Discuss three factors to consider when evaluating recruiting efforts.

SUMMARY OF THE CHAPTER

Recruiting is the process of generating a pool of qualified applicants for organizational jobs. A strategic approach to recruiting has become more important as competitive pressures shift. Employers compete in a variety of labor markets which are the external groupings and areas from which organizations attract employees.

In order to understand the environment in which recruiting takes place, it is important to differentiate among three groups: the labor force population, the applicant population, and the applicant pool. Increasingly organizations are opting for flexible staffing arrangements utilizing recruiting sources and workers who are not employees. These arrangements use independent contractors, temporary workers, and employee leasing.

There are pros and cons associated with both promoting from within and using outside sources to fill openings. Some of the advantages of internal sources include better employee morale, better assessment of abilities, lower cost for some jobs, and a motivator for good performance. However, there are also advantages to using external sources including bringing in "new blood," bringing in industry insights, and the fact that it may be less costly than having to train professionals internally. Since each method had both advantages and disadvantages most organizations use a combination of internal and external sources.

Sources of applicants can be divided into two categories: *internal sources* including present and former employees and previous applicants, and *external sources* such as educational institutions, employment agencies, labor unions, trade and competitive sources, and temporary help agencies. Some special types of recruiting include the use of the mass media (newspapers, magazines, television, and radio), recruiting on college campuses, and executive searches which utilize both personal contacts and search firms. Other relatively new phenomena in the area of recruiting are the use of employee leasing firms and external computerized databases of resumes and computerized matching services.

Evaluation of recruiting efforts and sources is an important HR activity because evaluation helps to identify whether or not the recruiting process has been cost effective in terms of time and money spent. In evaluating the recruiting efforts the HR manager should analyze the quantity and quality of applicants generated, the cost per applicant hired, and whether EEO goals have been met. Selection rates, yield ratios, and elapsed time from contact to hire are additional computations that are useful for evaluating recruiting effectiveness. When doing cost/benefit analysis, both direct and indirect costs should be considered.

STUDY QUESTIONS

Matching Questions

Match the key term from the list below with its most appropriate definition.

a.   Employee leasing

b.   Internal recruiting sources

c.   External recruiting sources

d.   Job posting

e.   Labor force population

f.   Yield ratios

g.   Flexible staffing

h.   Recruiting

i.   Applicant population

___   1.   The process of generating a pool of qualified applicants for organizational jobs.

___   2.   A method of evaluating a recruiting program.

___   3.   Utilizes present employees, promotions, and/or transfers as a means of recruiting.

___   4.   Having a special company handle all the paperwork, recruiting, and tax liabilities of staffing your organization.

___   5.   Utilizes schools, colleges and universities, employment agencies, and/or labor unions as sources for recruiting.

___   6.   Notifying employees of all job vacancies before any external recruiting is done.

___   7.   All individuals who are available for selection if at all possible recruitment strategies are used.

___   8.   The use of recruiting sources and workers who are not employees.

___   9.   A subset of the labor force population that is available for selection using a particular recruiting approach.

True/False Questions

___   1.   The applicant population will tend to be about the same regardless of the recruiting method used.

___   2.   To avoid many of the employment regulations and taxes, a business should declare that most of its service workers are independent contractors.

___   3.   Flexible staffing arrangements use independent contractors, temporary workers, and employee leasing.

___   4.   Cost per applicant hired provides a method for evaluating recruiting.

___   5.   The objective of recruiting is to provide a pool of applicants so that the most qualified can be selected.

___   6.   A labor market can be defined as individuals with similar skills or experience.

___   7.   The recruiting process is started by the submission of a requisition to the HR unit.

___   8.   Recruiting a diverse work force may require some modification of the regular recruiting process.

___   9.   Leasing employees is one way a small business can deal with the increasingly complex employment regulations.

___   10.   Job posting is an excellent external source of recruitment.

___   11.   Organizations that operate in rapidly changing environments should place a heavier emphasis on promotion from within.

___   12.   Job posting usually should be done before external recruiting efforts are undertaken.

___   13.   Employers have a better assessment of applicants' abilities when they hire primarily from external sources.

___   14.   An increase in the unemployment rate would likely make it more difficult to find qualified applicants.

___   15.   Recruiting only through current employees can be viewed as a violation of equal employment regulations.

Idea Completion Questions

1.   General areas for proper evaluation of recruiting include:

_____, _____, _____,

and _____.

2.   The nature of the applicant population is affected by:

_____, _____, _____,

and _____.

3.   Four internal recruiting sources are

_____, _____, _____,

and _____.

4.   _____, _____, _____,

and _____ are four of the general external sources of applicants.

5.   Some major advantages of promoting from within include:

_____, _____, _____,

and _____.

Multiple Choice Questions

___   1.   Friends of employees can be considered what type of recruiting source?
   a.   media source
   b.   competitive source
   c.   external institutional source
   d.   internal source

___   2.   Advantages of internal recruiting would include all but:
   a.   better morale of current employees.
   b.   better assessment of abilities of a person.
   c.   cheaper than training professionals.
   d.   have to hire at entry level only.

___   3.   Internal recruiting would include:
   a.   putting a vacancy notice up on the employee bulletin board.
   b.   putting a vacancy notice up on the company billboard by an interstate.
   c.   putting a vacancy notice at a labor union hall.
   d.   putting a vacancy notice in the daily newspaper.

___   4.   A _____ is a comparison of the number of applicants at one stage of the recruiting process to the number at the next stage.
   a.   selection ratio
   b.   yield ratio
   c.   selection rate
   d.   base rate

___   5.   The _____ includes all individuals available for selection if all possible recruitment strategies are used.
   a.   labor force population.
   b.   applicant population.
   c.   applicant pool.
   d.   none of the above.

6.   All persons who are actually evaluated for selection make up the
    a.   labor force population.
    b.   applicant population.
    c.   applicant pool.
    d.   none of the above.

7.   In the recruiting interface the line manager typically does which of the following?
    a.   forecasts recruiting needs
    b.   plans and conducts recruiting efforts
    c.   determines qualifications and anticipates needs
    d.   audits and evaluates recruiting activities

8.   Internal sources of recruitment include all of the following except:
    a.   former employees.
    b.   present employees.
    c.   friends of employees.
    d.   temporary help firms.

9.   Executive search firms which charge a fee only after a candidate has been hired by the client company are called:
    a.   contingency firms.
    b.   retainer firms.
    c.   network firms.
    d.   contract firms.

10.   A procedure for moving employees into other positions within the organization is called
    a.   job enrichment.
    b.   job modification.
    c.   job switching.
    d.   job posting and bidding.

11.   Which of the following is the major advantage of external recruiting?
    a.   better employee morale
    b.   better assessment of abilities
    c.   brings "new blood" to the organization
    d.   shorter adjustment time

___   12.   Which of the following is a major disadvantage of internal recruiting?
         a.   the need for a strong management development program
         b.   the possible morale problems of those who are not promoted
         c.   it may cause "inbreeding"
         d.   all of the above are disadvantages

___   13.   Which of the following is **NOT** an advantage of hiring older workers?
         a.   They have lower absenteeism.
         b.   They provide better service to customers.
         c.   They have fewer interpersonal conflicts.
         d.   They have more current skills.

___   14.   In the recruiting interface, the HR unit typically does which of the following?
         a.   determine qualifications and anticipate needs
         b.   identify and monitor career plans of employees
         c.   determine management succession
         d.   audits and evaluates recruiting activities

___   15.   State employment agencies differ from private agencies in which of the following ways?
         a.   State agencies do not charge a fee but private agencies do.
         b.   State agencies deal in only one type of position whereas private agencies cover all types of positions.
         c.   State agencies are more likely to assure you of qualified applicants.
         d.   None of the above are actual differences.

___   16.   To effectively recruit persons with disabilities, an organization should
         a.   examine jobs to ensure that accommodations could be made for persons with disabilities.
         b.   use the same sources as used for other recruiting.
         c.   contact associations that specialize in representing individuals with disabilities.
         d.   all of the above.
         e.   both a and c above.

Essay Questions

1. Discuss the concept of employee leasing and identify the advantages and disadvantages of this concept.

2. Compare and contrast the concepts of labor force population, applicant population, and applicant pool.

3. Identify four means of internally recruiting personnel and how those means can be used.

4. Select a typical position for which you might apply. Discuss how recruiting efforts are normally done, and indicate some other sources that also could be used.

5. You are the vice president of marketing for your firm, and you are faced with filling a vacancy of western regional sales managers. What factors must you consider in deciding whether to promote from within or recruit externally?

6. What legal issues should be considered when developing a recruitment strategy?

ANSWER KEY

Matching

1.	h	2.	f	3.	b	4.	a	5.	c
6.	d	7.	e	8.	g	9.	i		

True/False

1.	F	2.	F	3.	T	4.	T	5.	T
6.	T	7.	T	8.	T	9.	T	10.	F
11.	F	12.	T	13.	F	14.	F	15.	T

Idea Completion

1.   quantity of applicants
       quality of applicants
       cost per applicant hired
       EEO goals met

2.   the recruiting method
       the recruiting message
       applicant qualifications required
       administrative procedures

3.   former employees
       previous applicants
       job posting and bidding
       current employees

4.   schools
       colleges and universities
       employment agencies
       temporary help firms
       labor unions
       media sources
       trade and competitive sources

5.   morale of employee promoted
      better assessment of abilities
      lower cost for jobs that don't require training
      motivator for good performance
      causes a succession of promotions
      have to hire only at entry level

Multiple Choice

1. d	2. c	3. a	4. b	5. a
6. c	7. c	8. d	9. a	10. d
11. c	12. d	13. d	14. d	15. a
16. e				

RECRUITING AT SAINT GEORGE'S COLLEGE

Saint George's College is a four-year Church affiliated college and has an enrollment of about 1,500 students. Its business and economics department has a faculty of seven full-time instructors. In addition, part-time instructors are used as needed. Currently about 600 students are majoring in business or economics. The college is located in a medium-sized community of 70,000.

Most of the faculty recruiting is done by one person, the department head. Prospective faculty are usually identified in one of three ways:

1. The department head lists a position vacancy at one of the various professional meetings held during the summer or fall. If the department head cannot attend a meeting, he or she is represented by another instructor from the business and economics department. Candidates are interviewed at the meeting.

2. Advertisements are placed in *The Chronicle of Higher Education* during the spring. If possible, the candidates responding to an advertisement are invited to meet with the department head or representative at one of the professional meetings held during the summer or fall.

3. The college also receives unsolicited letters inquiring about possible job vacancies throughout the year.

Projections are that enrollment at Saint George's will increase 25% in the next five years. Most of the increase is expected in the business and economics majors. The ideal faculty size would be about 12 full-time instructors to handle the load and to eliminate the need for part-time instructors. Most of the full-time instructors currently in the Department of Business and Economics hold either an MA or MBA degree from various Church affiliated colleges. The exception is for accounting instructors who often are CPAs with BBA degrees.

Salary scales and benefits are considered to be slightly lower than the compensation available at similar colleges in the region. In addition to any increase in faculty members needed due to enrollment increases, three replacements are needed for next fall in the business and economics area to replace individuals who have gone elsewhere.

Saint George's College has a recruiting policy that requires final approval of candidates by the department head, the dean of the faculty, and the vice-president for academic affairs. In addition, school policy requires that at least two candidates be invited to the campus before any job offers can be extended. This is so that adequate screening can take place. Often the result is a waiting period of three months between initial contact, application, and campus interview for most applicants.

Some other small colleges in the area pay full travel expenses for potential candidates, while the majority of the others pay at least half. Saint George's does not pay any travel expenses. However, if the candidate accepts a position at Saint George's, the college pays a lump-sum relocation allowance which is usually sufficient to cover both travel and moving expenses. The payment is included in the new faculty member's first pay check.

In the past, Saint George's has not been very successful in filling empty positions. The president is concerned and wants to evaluate the recruiting program so that a better one can be designed.

Questions

1. If you were seeking a teaching position at the college level, would you consider Saint George's College? List the reasons for and against.

2. Evaluate the recruiting process used by Saint George's College.

3. Is the approval procedure for applicants appropriate? Why or why not?

4. Describe an ideal candidate for instructor in the Department of Business and Economics at Saint George's College.

5. Design a recruiting system that you believe would be more appropriate for Saint George's College.

RECRUITMENT STRATEGIES

Consider the following positions. Outline the recruitment strategy you would recommend in each situation. Justify your recommendations.

1.   Your secretary has just resigned. You have decided to recruit within your organization.

2.   You need an electronic engineer. External sources will be used.

3.   You are chief financial officer for an insurance company and you need to hire a controller.

4.   You are Dean of the College of Business at a nationally ranked state university. You need eight new assistant professors for next fall in the following departments:

      4 in accounting,
      2 in management information systems,
      1 in business law,
      1 in finance.

5.   You are chairman of the presidential search committee at a prestigious, Church affiliated university. Your committee's assignment is to recruit a new university president. The Board of Trustees will make the final hiring decision.

6.   You are Vice-President for Human Resources at a Fortune 500 company. You need to appoint three HR specialists for college recruiting.

7.   You have been assigned the task of recruiting management trainees for an east-coast grocery store chain. Applicants must be college graduates.

Chapter 9

Selecting Human Resources

CHAPTER OBJECTIVES

1. Define *selection* and explain several reasons for having a specialized employment unit.

2. Diagram a typical selection process in sequential order.

3. Discuss the reception and application form phases of the selection process.

4. Identify two general and three controversial types of tests.

5. Discuss three types of interviews and six key considerations in the selection interview.

6. Construct a guide for conducting a selection interview.

7. Explain how legal concerns affect background investigations of applicants.

8. Discuss why medical examinations, including drug testing, may be useful in selection.

SUMMARY OF THE CHAPTER

After a pool of applicants has been recruited, the next function is to select the most appropriate candidate.

Selection is the process of picking individuals who have the relevant qualifications to fill jobs in an organization. The selection process can be depicted as a seven-step process, including initial reception, screening interview or a job preview/interest screen, application form, testing, in-depth selection interview, background investigation, and medical examination/drug test. At each step, as more information is obtained, a determination is made as to whether or not there is still a "match" between the requirements of the job and the job-related skills and abilities of the candidate.

In order to insure that the selection process is effective it is important that the organization define its selection criteria accurately, and identify a valid and reliable set of factors which can be used to predict how likely it is that a candidate can meet the selection criteria.

The first step of the selection process, *reception*, is important because first impressions of the organization often are made at this time. Although some organizations allow all applicants to complete an application form, others prefer to conduct a brief initial screening interview first. Its purpose is to determine if there is any advantage to be gained by either the applicant or the organization in pursuing contact. A structured interview form is used, comprised of a list of questions that require simple, short answers. Computerized or other electronic interviewing techniques are now widely used to conduct initial screening interviews.

The *application form* serves four purposes:

1.   a record of the applicant's desire to obtain a position,
2.   a profile of the applicant,
3.   a basic personnel record for applicants who become employees, and
4.   a basic research tool to evaluate the effectiveness of the selection process.

Care must be taken in designing application-form questions to insure that they conform to EEO guidelines and that they are valid predictors of job-related behaviors. Since the Immigration Reform and Control Act requires that employers verify the eligibility of persons to work in this country, many organizations include the completion of I-9 forms as part of the application-form step in the selection process.

If the applicant shows no obvious disqualifications after the initial screening interview and a review of the application form data, he or she can either be scheduled for testing or for an in-depth interview.

Tests may be divided into two general types: aptitude and ability tests, and general personality and psychological tests. A major concern with the use of tests is whether they are valid indicators of future performance on the job. Personality and psychological tests are somewhat difficult to validate; however, -

proficiency tests can be correlated easily with job performance and a high degree of validity can be established. In choosing and using selection tests, it is important to be sure that tests are both valid and reliable, and that those evaluating the test results are properly trained.

The *in-depth selection interview* is designed to integrate all information from the application form, reference checks, and tests. The interview data, like other tools in the selection process, must be a valid predictor of future job success and therefore meet the same standards of job relatedness and non-discrimination. There are several basic types of interviews: structured, situational, behavioral description, non-directive, and stress interviews. Each type has advantages and disadvantages of which the interviewer must be aware.

A good interviewer must plan in advance in order to insure that adequate information is obtained in a reasonable length of time. Questions should be phrased in such a manner so as to elicit informative answers rather than just "yes" or "no" responses. After the interview it is important to promptly record interview data so the information can be re-evaluated later for consistency or to determine the need for further information. In some interviews realistic job previews are used to provide job applicants with an accurate picture of the job.

Additional information can be obtained through *background investigations.* Background references can be any one of several kinds including academic references, prior work references, financial references, law enforcement records, and personal references. Recently a number of legal considerations have impacted the background investigation process. On the one hand, concerns about an applicant's right to privacy, as protected by both federal and state laws, must be balanced against the employers' need to know information necessary to insure they are not liable for negligent hiring practices.

The final step in the selection process is the *medical examination.* The American with Disabilities Act prohibits the use of pre-employment medical exams except for drug testing. Given current concern over drug abuse, drug testing is increasingly being used as part of the selection process, even when physical exams *per se* are not given.

The selection process can thus be viewed as a sequential set of steps, each providing additional information to insure that the most suitable candidate actually is selected.

STUDY QUESTIONS

Matching Questions

Match the key term from the list below with its most appropriate definition.

a.   Selection   h.   Structured interview

b.   Initial screening interview   i.   Nondirective interview

c.   Weighted application form   j.   Stress interview

d.   Testers   k.   I-9 form

e.   Proficiency test   l.   Listening responses

f.   Cultural noise   m.   Realistic job preview

g.   Polygraph   n.   Assessment center

_____   1.   A document used to verify a person's eligibility for employment.

_____   2.   An employee selection and development device composed of a series of evaluative exercises and tests.

_____   3.   Nodding, pausing, echoing, and mirroring are example of these.

_____   4.   An interview using a set of standardized questions that are asked of all applicants for a job.

_____   5.   The process of picking individuals who have relevant qualifications to fill jobs in the organization.

_____   6.   A mechanical device that measures the galvanic skin response, the heart and pulse rate, and the breathing rate of a person.

_____   7.   A brief interview to see if the applicant is likely to match any available jobs in the organization.

_____   8.   Individuals who apply for employment that they do not intend to accept for the sole purpose of uncovering unlawful discriminatory hiring practices.

___ 9. An interview designed to create anxiety and put pressure on the applicant.

___ 10. The process of providing a job applicant with an accurate picture of a job.

___ 11. Numeric values are placed on different responses to application form items.

___ 12. A typing test given to a secretarial applicant would be an example of this type of test.

___ 13. An interview in which the applicant is asked general questions designed to have the applicant discuss himself or herself.

___ 14. Responses a job applicant believes are socially acceptable rather than false.

True/False Questions

___ 1. Poor selection generally would result from establishing a specialized employment office because of the lack of coordination with operating managers.

___ 2. Public relations is an important aspect of the reception stage of selection.

___ 3. The Halo Effect occurs when the interviewer allows some prominent characteristic to overshadow other evidence.

___ 4. Because application forms are not tests, they need not be validated for EEO purposes.

___ 5. Research indicates that applicants are usually careful not to overstate or misrepresent their qualifications on application forms.

___ 6. A structured format is more useful in a screening interview than an unstructured format.

___ 7. A typing test is an example of an aptitude test.

___ 8. Drug testing is seldom a part of the medical exam in the selection process.

___ 9. The situational interview is a form of nondirective interview.

___ 10. Cultural noise refers to the physical setting in which an interview is conducted.

___ 11. Asking applicants questions that can be answered "yes" or "no" is recommended as a way to increase the amount of information an interviewer can obtain.

___ 12. Research indicates that the interview, although widely used, is probably one of the weakest tools for predicting future job performance.

___ 13. Personal references have been found to be very useful in the selection process.

___ 14. Given the current concern with both applicant privacy and liability for negligent hiring it is wise to require applicants to sign releases authorizing reference checks.

___ 15. The Americans with Disabilities Act prohibits the use of pre-employment medical exams except for drug testing.

Idea Completion Questions

1. Six reasons for centralizing the selection process in a specialized unit include:
   _____, _____, _____,
   _____, _____, and_____.

2. The first step in the selection process, applicant reception, is important because _____
   _____.

3. It is important to remember in choosing a selection test that the instrument be both
   _____ and _____.

4. The five basic types of selection interviews are:
   _____, _____, _____,
   _____, and _____.

5. A realistic job preview is useful because _____
   _____.

Multiple Choice Questions

___ 1. An application form
      a.   provides a record of the applicant's desire to work for the company.
      b.   provides basic personal information for applicants who become employees.
      c.   provides the interviewer with a profile of the applicant.
      d.   all of the above.
      e.   Only a and c above.

___ 2. Which of the following statements is **NOT** correct?
      a.   Weighted application forms put a weight or numeric value on different responses.
      b.   Weighted applications can remain the same once they are developed.
      c.   Weighted application forms are more job related.
      d.   All are correct.

___ 3. A typing test is an example of a(n)
      a.   psychological test.
      b.   aptitude test.
      c.   ability test.
      d.   none of the above.

___ 4. To minimize EEO concerns with interviewing it is suggested that interviewers do which of the following?
      a.   Identify objective criteria.
      b.   Put criteria in writing.
      c.   Have multiple levels of review of decisions.
      d.   All of the above.
      e.   Only a and c above.

___ 5. Employers tend to feel the most important selection tool is (are)
      a.   the interview.
      b.   reference checks.
      c.   tests.
      d.   physical exams.

___   6.   An EGAD question refers to all but the applicant's
          a.   abilities.
          b.   expectations.
          c.   aspirations.
          d.   goals.

___   7.   To enhance the value of the in-depth interview, the interviewer should use
          a.   questions that can be answered by a simple "yes" or "no" in order to save time.
          b.   questions that require interviewees to talk about themselves.
          c.   leading questions, so that interviewees can be "tested" to see if they give the right answers.
          d.   personal bias to ensure that no misfits are hired.

___   8.   An assessment center is
          a.   a step in the typical selection process.
          b.   a place where selection tests are performed.
          c.   a means of selection composed of a series of evaluative exercises and tests.
          d.   all of the above.
          e.   only a and b above.

___   9.   Maintaining job relatedness in the questions is a major problem with which type of interview?
          a.   structured
          b.   nondirective
          c.   stress
          d.   both a and b above

___   10.   Which of the following questions are permissible to ask a disabled person?
          a.   Do you have any physical limitations?
          b.   Have you ever filed for or collected workers' compensation?
          c.   How many times were you absent due to illness in the past two years?
          d.   None of the above.
          e.   Only b and c above.

___ 11.   In responding to reference requests, you should do all of the following except:
   a.   fully document all released information.
   b.   answer the rehire question if asked.
   c.   give information such as attendance record and type of job responsibilities.
   d.   release only general types of information such as dates of employment and salary history.

___ 12.   Which type of reference is least valuable in the selection process
   a.   academic references
   b.   prior work references
   c.   personal references
   d.   financial references

___ 13.   Of the following, the weakest tool for predicting an applicant's job performance is the
   a.   application form.
   b.   interview.
   c.   proficiency test.
   d.   prior work reference.

___ 14.   Answers to questions which are socially acceptable are referred to as
   a.   EGAD factors.
   b.   halo effects.
   c.   biased effects.
   d.   cultural noise.

___ 15.   The types of questions in a situational interview are
   a.   hypothetical.
   b.   related to knowledge.
   c.   related to requirements.
   d.   all of the above.
   e.   only b and c above.

Essay Questions

1. Assume you are applying for a job as a credit analyst at a large regional bank. Describe what you would believe to be a total selection process that would give you a fair opportunity to demonstrate your abilities and potential.

2. Discuss the usefulness, limitations, and EEO considerations associated with application forms and how some of these limitations can be overcome.

3. Discuss the relationship of testing and test validity to equal employment opportunity.

4. What are some of the advantages and limitations of the interview as a selection device?

5. As an employer you want to check an applicant's work references. What procedure would you use?

ANSWER KEY

Matching

1.	k	2.	n	3.	l	4.	h	5.	a
6.	g	7.	b	8.	d	9.	j	10.	m
11.	c	12.	e	13.	i	14.	f		

True/False

1.	F	2.	T	3.	T	4.	F	5.	F
6.	T	7.	F	8.	F	9.	F	10.	F
11.	F	12.	T	13.	F	14.	T	15.	T

Idea Completion

1.   it is easier for the applicant because there is only one place to apply for a job

it coordinates contact with outside sources of applicants because issues pertaining to employment can be cleared through one central location

it frees the operating managers to concentrate on their operating responsibilities

it can provide for better selection because selection is done by specialists trained in staffing techniques

the applicant is more assured of consideration for a greater variety of jobs

selection costs may be cut because duplication of effort is avoided

people who know the government regulations will be handling a major part of the process

2.   the person's attitudes about the organization and even the products or services it offers can be influenced

3.   valid
      reliable

4.   structured interviews
      situational
      behavioral descriptive
      non-directive interviews
      stress interviews

5.   it presents the job applicant with an accurate picture of the job, thus reducing unrealistic expectations
      and employee disenchantment

Multiple Choice

1. d	2. b	3. c	4. d	5. a
6. a	7. b	8. c	9. b	10. d
11. b	12. c	13. b	14. d	15. d

WHAT SHOULD I SAY?

Margaret Jones is an attorney specializing in labor law. Last night she had dinner with Carolyne Phillips, a friend from high school. Carolyne had got married during her senior year, and just weeks after graduation, gave birth to a daughter, Melissa. When Melissa was about four years old, she fell off a slide at the city playground. Melissa suffered severe back and head injuries, and the diagnosis was that she would not be able to walk again. Soon after the accident, Carolyne's husband deserted her and their child. Having very little money, Carolyne moved back to live with her parents.

About two years after her husband left, Carolyne gave birth to a son, Charles. Carolyne was miserable and lonely - no job, no husband, no home of her own, a handicapped daughter, and now a son. Carolyne's parents suggested that she continue her education, and, with the assistance of various government programs, Carolyne enrolled at a community college. Three years later, she transferred to Northwest State University. She continued to live with her parents who helped her financially and took care of the children. In fact they had exhausted much of their savings paying Melissa's medical bills.

Three months ago, Carolyne graduated from college with a BBA degree. Her major was marketing.

Margaret and Carolyne had remained in touch over the years and had gone out together for dinner last night. Carolyne, obviously frustrated with her job search, had shared the following with Margaret:

"I've really made a mess of my life, haven't I? I don't know where Melissa's father is. I don't know who Chuck's father is. I'm 31 and still living at home ....

"When I graduated last summer, I dreamed of a new beginning. At last I would be able to get a real job. Anything is better than waiting tables at a college bar. A job would give me some independence. Maybe I could get an apartment, give the kids a better family life. More than anything, I want a job that provides health insurance and maybe even some child care ....

"The problem is, I've got a history. And not one I'm proud of. But is it anybody's business? Especially an employer's? Just last week, I went for an interview at Sterling & Co. It was for a position in their PR department. I had originally met their college recruiter on campus at a career fair. Following the interview, the PR manager asked me if I had plans for lunch. When I said "No," he asked his secretary to take me to the staff cafeteria. Over lunch, she asked me several personal questions - Was I married? How many children? Do I plan to have any more kids? When? I got the impression that she had been instructed to ask me the questions that the firm was unable to ask me legally. What a sneaky approach ....

"But this wasn't the first time I had faced such questions. At one interview, the sales manager asked what my husband would say if he knew that I worked in a section where all my co-

workers were eligible bachelors. In describing the amount of travel required by sales represen-tatives, he joked about whether he could trust his salesmen to behave themselves when traveling out-of-town with such a pretty woman. I couldn't believe it ....

"Then at Consolidated Paper, the receptionist started talking to me about the cost of prescription medicines. She confided that she had three children, and that the health insurance plan is one of the reasons she likes working at Consolidated. I think that she was trying to get me to talk about my family situation ....

"I have encountered many enquiries, usually indirect, about child-care, family responsibili-ties, disabilities, health, "my husband's" career. Do they ask men the same questions? ....

"So what am I to do? Should I evade the questions, or just not tell the truth? Even though I know I'd be a very reliable worker, I know that if I tell the truth, especially about Melissa's medical needs, I will never get a job. So I've decided, next time some jerk asked me a whole lot of personal questions, I'll reply that I'm unmarried, dating nobody, and never plan to have any children. Once I get the job, what can they do?"

Margaret Jones kept thinking about her friend's experiences. She wanted to help her get a job and maybe offer some advice.

Questions

1.   What information does an employer need to know about a candidate for employment?

2.   If you were a campus recruiter and a 31-year-old, female recent graduate applied for a position, what questions would you want to ask? What questions can you ask?

3.   Are the employers justified in asking these personal questions? Why or why not? If they don't ask a job candidate, can they find out this information from other sources?

4.   Should Carolyne be honest with her interviewers when confronted with these inquiries? Should she respond that it is none of their business? Should she lie? What would be the possible consequences of each response?

5.   If an interviewer were to ask if Carolyne had worked while in college, should she tell them about her job at the bar?

6.   What responsibilities do employers have to accommodate the personal needs of their employees?

QUESTIONS TO ASK

The ability to be a good interviewer is not an innate skill, but requires training and experience. You have the opportunity to begin developing some necessary skills to improve your interviewing ability, especially those regarding question formulation.

You have just received the resume of William Alexander which is printed on the next page. One hour from now, you will conduct an in-depth interview with Mr. Alexander, who is a finalist for the position of sales coordinator with your firm.

Suggestions for Analysis and Discussion

1. Evaluate this resume and list the limitations and possible discrepancies that you might want to pursue during the interview.

2. Develop a set of questions you would use to clarify the items you have listed.

3. Does the resume provide you with any information that EEO guidelines would prevent you from asking in an interview?

4. What information would you like to know about Mr. Alexander that you cannot legally ask?

William P. Alexander

Qualifications

Ambitious ... Proven Leader ... Self Motivated ... Strong Interpersonal Skills ... Superior Sales Record

Objective

A progressive management assignment in line with my past accomplishments.
A challenging assignment with the opportunity to increase a company's sales and profits.

Education

University of North Carolina, Greensboro, NC. Class of 1984. Major: Interpersonal Communication

College Activities

Work study assistant in the Office of the Dean of Students
Assistant Editor of the campus newspaper, senior year
Member of Young Democrats all four years
Social Chairman, Zeta Zeta Zeta Fraternity, junior year

Work Experience

1985-1987	Woods Grocery, Management Trainee
1988-1989	Self employed in a family business and consultant to small business firms.
1989-1993	Ajax Corporation, Administrative Assistant in marketing department. Assisted with marketing research, sales forecasting, product development.
1993-present	Home Products Corp, Marketing Director. Sales have increased annually by over 50 percent. Extensive exposure to all functional areas of marketing.

Self Development

Completed management development courses in personal selling, time management, and supervisory skills.
Member of International Toastpersons

Personal

Age 35, single, 2 dependents, excellent health

Chapter 10

Orientation and Training

CHAPTER OBJECTIVES

1. Define *training* and discuss its legal aspects.

2. Describe four characteristics of an effective orientation system.

3. Discuss the major phases of a training system.

4. Identify three ways to determine training needs.

5. List and discuss at least four training methods.

6. Discuss at least four learning principles that relate to training.

7. Give an example for each level of training evaluation.

8. Identify three designs used in evaluating training.

SUMMARY OF THE CHAPTER

The strategy an organization is following impacts the nature of training in which it engages. *Training* is a learning process whereby people acquire skills or knowledge to aid in the achievement of goals. This broad definition encompasses the aspects of skill training and developmental training. Current interest in TQM and cultural diversity of the workforce have added new dimensions to the overall domain of training.

Training has legal implications concerning who is selected for training, the criteria used for selection, pay differences based on training, and the use of training when making promotion decisions. Since fair employment laws apply to training, employers must be aware of their implications throughout the training process.

The first type of training an employee receives in the organization is orientation. *Orientation* is the planned introduction of employees to their jobs, their co-workers, and their organizations. The orientation process has several important purposes, including:

1. creating a favorable impression of the organization and its work,
2. easing the employee's entry into the work group, and
3. reducing turnover.

In order that orientation be as effective as possible, a coordinated, systematic approach should be taken. First, both the supervisor and the HR unit should be prepared to receive the employee. This includes informing co-workers that the new employee is arriving. Next, the organization needs to determine what information the new employee needs to know, and how and when that information should be presented. The final step, evaluation and follow-up, is to determine if the employee needs any reorientation and to provide input to future orientation programs.

There are three major phases in a training process:

1. the assessment phase,
2. the implementation phase, and
3. the evaluation phase.

Once training needs and objectives are determined, the implementation phase or actual training effort can begin. Training methods or techniques can be classified into several major groups including on-the-job training, simulation training, cooperative training, behaviorally-experienced training, and classroom and conference training.

A number of training media can be used in conjunction with the aforementioned training methods, such as programmed instruction, computer-assisted instruction, and audiovisual aids.

To be an effective trainer requires knowledge of the basic learning principles including intention to learn, whole learning, reinforcement, behavior modification, immediate confirmation, active practice, learning patterns, behavior modeling, and transfer of learning.

The evaluation phase of training compares post-training results to the objectives expected by managers, trainers, and trainees, and can be evaluated at four levels:

1.   the reaction level,
2.   the learning level,
3.   the behavior level, and
4.   the results level.

Since evaluation provides feedback on how well training is meeting its desired objectives, the evaluation phase is both the end and the beginning of the systems approach to training.

STUDY QUESTIONS

Matching Questions

Match the key term from the list below with its most appropriate definition.

a.   Orientation

b.   Behavior Modeling

c.   Training

d.   Positive reinforcement

e.   Negative reinforcement

f.   Punishment

g.   Extinction

h.   Immediate confirmation

i.   Spaced Practice

j.   Whole learning

k.   On-the-job training

l.   Cooperative training

m.   Behaviorally-experienced training

n.   Training media

o.   Reaction level evaluation

p.   Learning level evaluation

q.   Behavior level evaluation

r.   Results level evaluation

____   1.   The planned introduction of employees to their jobs, co-workers, and their organizations.

____   2.   Action taken to prevent the person from repeating the undesired action.

____   3.   Training or practice which is distributed over a period of hours or days.

____   4.   A type of job-experiential training using internships or apprenticeships as a training means.

____   5.   Measures how well trainees have learned facts, ideas, concepts, theories, and attitudes.

____   6.   This concept of training suggests it is better for a trainee to see the "big picture" of what he or she will be doing before going into the specifics.

____   7.   Measures how the people liked the training.

___ 8. A learning concept which suggests that people learn best if reinforcement is given as soon as possible after the training response.

___ 9. Attempts to measure the effect of training on job performance.

___ 10. Occurs when an individual works to escape an undesirable "reward."

___ 11. A learning process whereby people acquire skills or knowledge to aid in the achievement of goals.

___ 12. An attempt to change behavior by not giving the trainee any reinforcement or confirmation whatsoever.

___ 13. A type of training usually done by the manager and/or other employees.

___ 14. A type of training which utilizes role-playing and/or business games as learning experiences.

___ 15. Measures the result of training on the achievement of organizational objectives.

___ 16. Aids in presenting training information such as computer-assisted instruction and audiovisual aids.

___ 17. A learning principle which simply involves copying someone else's behavior.

___ 18. A method of changing behavior by providing rewards desired by the employee.

True/False Questions

___   1.   The "in basket" process is an example of behaviorally-experienced training.

___   2.   Simulated training is a type of behaviorally-oriented training.

___   3.   Giving trainees a questionnaire that asks them how they liked their training and their instructor is an example of a results level measure of training effectiveness.

___   4.   Comparing a sales representative's sales before and after training gives a reaction level measure of training effectiveness.

___   5.   Even if learning does not occur, training can still be effective.

___   6.   Cross-cultural training is necessary only for employees being sent overseas.

___   7.   Individuals tend to continue behavior which is not positively reinforced.

___   8.   Suspending an employee from work for violating a work rule is an example of an extinction response.

___   9.   There are very few legal consequences associated with training.

___   10.   Apprentice training is a type of simulated training.

___   11.   The HR office is primarily responsible for conducting on-the-job training.

___   12.   Positive and negative reinforcement, extinction, and punishment collectively are known as behavior-modification strategies.

___   13.   Information overload specifically refers to having an employee handbook that is too long.

___   14.   Orientation is basically finished after the first week a new employee has been on the job.

___   15.   Modeling is one of the most elementary ways in which people learn and one of the best.

Idea Completion Questions

1. The three purposes of orientation are:
    _____, _____, and_____.

2. The components of an effective orientation system are:
    _____, _____, _____,
    _____, and _____.

3. Training is defined as _____
    _____.

4. Seven learning concepts associated with training are:
    _____, _____, _____,
    _____, _____, _____,
    and _____.

5. The three phases in a training system are:
    _____, _____, and_____.

Multiple Choice Questions

___   1.   Asking people how they liked the training program would be a _____ level measure of training effectiveness.
     a.   reaction
     b.   learning
     c.   behavior
     d.   results

___   2.   Comparing a salesman's dollar sales volume before and after training is a _____ level measure of training effectiveness.
     a.   reaction
     b.   learning
     c.   behavior
     d.   results

___   3.   Training media would include all of the following except:
     a.   programmed instruction.
     b.   role playing instruction.
     c.   computer assisted instruction.
     d.   audiovisual aids.
     e.   all of the above are training media.

___   4.   When learning or skill level increases rapidly at first and then slows down, the learning pattern is referred to as a(n)
     a.   decreasing returns pattern.
     b.   increasing returns pattern.
     c.   S-shaped curve pattern.
     d.   plateau pattern.

___   5.   In a typical training interface, the HR unit does all of the following except:
     a.   monitor training needs.
     b.   prepare training materials.
     c.   coordinate training efforts.
     d.   conduct or arrange for off-the-job training.

___ 6. Internships and apprentice training are examples of
   a. cooperative training.
   b. job instructional training (JIT).
   c. simulated training.
   d. conference training.

___ 7. A training program that involves simply copying someone else's behavior is
   a. behavior modification.
   b. spaced practice.
   c. modeling.
   d. active practice.

___ 8. The HR unit is usually responsible for all of the following aspects of orientation except:
   a. placing an employee on the payroll.
   b. designing a formal orientation program.
   c. developing an orientation checklist.
   d. introducing the new employee to co-workers.

___ 9. Guided self-learning and immediate confirmation are a part of
   a. apprentice training.
   b. internships.
   c. programmed instruction.
   d. JIT.

___ 10. A written test would be a _____ level measure of training effectiveness.
   a. reaction
   b. learning
   c. behavior
   d. results

___ 11. Work group approval, recognition, promotion, and merit increases are examples of
   a. job enrichment.
   b. positive reinforcement.
   c. extinction.
   d. exigency.

___   12.   A situation in which no response is given to the trainee describes
a.   punishment.
b.   negative reinforcement.
c.   avoidance.
d.   extinction.

___   13.   Gestalt learning refers to
a.   active practice.
b.   whole learning.
c.   plateau learning.
d.   group therapy.

___   14.   An employee makes sure he is never late to work so as to avoid criticism by the supervisor. This is an example of
a.   negative reinforcement.
b.   punishment.
c.   positive reinforcement.
d.   extinction.

___   15.   The most common type of training at all levels in an organization is
a.   apprentice training.
b.   on-the-job training.
c.   classroom instruction.
d.   programmed instruction.

Essay Questions

1.   Discuss the purpose of orientation and several components of an effective orientation program.

2.   Define and explain the following learning concepts:

   a.   behavior modification,

   b.   whole learning,

   c.   plateaus.

3.   Identify the three phases of a training system and explain the thrust of importance of each phase. Also, describe how the three phases are related to each other.

4.   Identify the following training methods and media:

   a.   modeling,

   b.   internship,

   c.   classroom and conference training,

   d.   programmed instruction.

5.   List and discuss the four levels at which training can be evaluated.

ANSWER KEY

Matching

1.	a	2.	f	3.	i	4.	l	5.	p
6.	j	7.	o	8.	h	9.	q	10.	e
11.	c	12.	g	13.	k	14.	m	15.	r
16.	n	17.	b	18.	d					

True/False

1	T	2.	F	3.	F	4.	F	5.	F
6.	F	7.	F	8.	F	9.	F	10.	F
11.	F	12.	T	13.	F	14.	F	15.	T

Idea Completion

1.   create a favorable initial impression of the organization and its work
enhance interpersonal acceptance
reduce turnover

2.   prepare for new employees

determine information new employees want to know

present information about the normal workday, the nature of the organization, and organizational policies, rules and benefits

determine how to present the information

evaluation and re-orientation

3.   a learning process whereby people acquire skills or knowledge to aid in the achievement of goals

4.   intention to learn
     whole learning
     reinforcement
     immediate confirmation
     practice
     learning curves
     transfer of training

5.   the assessment phase
     the implementation phase
     the evaluation phase

Multiple Choice

1.	a	2.	d	3.	b	4.	a	5.	a
6.	a	7.	c	8.	d	9.	c	10.	b
11.	b	12.	d	13.	b	14.	a	15.	b

TURNOVER OF AN ACCOUNTANT

Mark Jacobs appeared to have everything going for him. A senior accounting major with an "A" average from a leading state university, he was courted by three of the "Big Six" national accounting firms in addition to several "Fortune 100" corporations. He read their glossy literature, interviewed with their college recruiters, visited their offices, stayed at classy hotels, dined in elegant restaurants, and met the senior executives and partners.

After receiving five attractive offers, which were accompanied by regular phone calls from executives and partners, he finally made a decision, and accepted a position with one of the accounting firms as a staff accountant.

Following graduation, he was eager to begin his professional career. He arrived at work early on his first day and the office receptionist told him to wait in the conference room. Over the next half-hour twenty other new employees, including seventeen accounting graduates, two typists, and a graphic artists, were shown to the conference room. Mark made small talk with some of the new employees. The conversations centered on enquiries as to the location of a bathroom, and a desire for a cup of coffee.

After a while, the HR partner entered the conference room. Mark was glad when he saw that she was accompanied by an assistant pushing a cart containing coffee and donuts. The partner welcomed the new employees, invited them to have some coffee and donuts, and then distributed several forms that needed to be filled out. Mark completed his forms in about 20 minutes and spent the next 30 or 40 minutes waiting for the others to finish theirs. After collecting all the forms, the HR partner described the firm's benefit programs, no smoking policy, and dress codes. Then she showed a video which highlighted the history and current operations of the firm. When it was time for lunch, the HR partner gave the location of some nearby restaurants and dismissed the new employees with a reminder that no drinking was permitted during business hours.

After lunch the accountants returned to the conference room while the other new employees met with their new supervisors. Various staff members addressed the accountants throughout the afternoon reviewing different aspects of their jobs, which ranged from describing the training course they would begin the following week, to outlining the firm's policy regarding reimbursement of business-related expenses.

Late in the afternoon, the Senior Partner came to the conference room to greet the new accountants. After congratulating them on their decisions to join the firm, he invited them to join him for cocktails in his suite.

The following morning, Mark met his new supervisor and spent the rest of the week assisting her. Mark then spent two weeks at the firm's residential educational center where he, and several hundred other newly hired accounting graduates, received extensive training to prepare him for his new job as an auditor.

Following the training course, Mark returned to his office ready to start work. He has given his first assignment …. to count toilet seat covers in a client's inventory. He soon discovered that newly hired accounting graduates usually spend their first two years living out of suitcases, staying at "family" (that is, lower priced) hotels, doing basic clerical work assisting in audits - one staff accountant among many, not the prestigious professional position he had expected. He suffered from "reality shock."

Mark Jacobs continued to work for the firm, but he became more and more disillusioned before quitting after two years.

At his exit interview he told the HR partner that he had been offered a better position at an industrial company with a significant increase in salary. The firm was sorry to see him go, and wanted to try to prevent good employees from quitting in the future.

Questions

1. What is the *real* reason why Mark Jacobs quit? Why didn't he tell the HR partner?

2. The firm is concerned that their better hires seem to be the first to leave. How can they discover the real reason for the turnover of staff accountants?

3. Assume that Mark Jacobs told them about the reality shock he experienced. Design an orientation program that will better prepare newly-hired accountants for the jobs they actually encounter.

EVALUATING CLASSROOM TRAINING

Chapter 10 of your text suggests that the evaluation phase of training is an often neglected, but very important, part of any training program. Since this course you are taking is, in essence, a training system in HR management, it too should be evaluated.

Questions for Analysis and Discussion

1. Identify two examples of measuring classroom training for each of the following evaluation levels:

    a.   Reaction level,

    b.   Learning level,

    c.   Behavior level,

    d.   Results level.

2. Are tests really a good measure of learning level evaluation? If not, is the training process or the testing process at fault? Explain your answer.

3. Is the behavior level of evaluation relevant to the college classroom training situation? Justify your answer.

4. Is it really possible to evaluate classroom training at the results level? Explain your answer.

5. Is the reaction level of evaluation really that important to the classroom training situation? Why or why not?

6. Design an evaluation system which would be appropriate for college classroom instruction (or training).

Chapter 11

Human Resource Development and Careers

CHAPTER OBJECTIVES

1. Define *human resource development*, and explain how it differs from training.

2. Describe the development process.

3. List and describe at least four on-the-job and four off-the-job development methods.

4. Discuss specific advantages and problems associated with assessment centers.

5. Differentiate between organization-centered and individual-centered career planning.

6. Explain how dual-career ladders for engineers and scientists function.

7. Identify how dual-career marriages affect career paths and strategies of individuals and organizations.

SUMMARY OF THE CHAPTER

Development is different from training in that it is often the result of experience and the maturity that comes with it. *Development* involves efforts to improve employees' ability to handle a variety of assignments.

There are two essential conditions that must be recognized for successful employee development: top management support and the appropriate relationship of development to other HR activities. Development planning must begin with the overall strategic plan of the organization. Key components of this planning include succession planning and development needs analysis. The latter may include the use of assessment centers, psychological testing, and performance appraisals.

The goals of an effective development program may be people-oriented, job specific (technical) or planning and conceptual. Different techniques serve these difficult goals and can be categorized broadly as either on-the-job methods or off-the-job methods. *On-the-job* methods provide an opportunity to learn by doing, and include coaching, committee assignments, job rotation, and "assistant-to" positions.

Off-the-job techniques provide individuals the opportunity to get away from the job and concentrate solely on what is to be learned. The various off-the-job methods include classroom courses, human relations training, case studies, role playing, simulation games, sabbaticals, and outdoor training. Organizations should recognize that the various techniques have both advantages and disadvantages and a particular program should be selected based on the development goal to be fulfilled.

Three areas of special interest concerning management development are managerial modeling, management coaching, and mentoring. The idea of *modeling* simply suggests that much of management is learned by copying the behavior of other managers. Managerial *coaching* combines observations with suggestions. Like modeling, it is a very natural way for humans to learn.

Development is also facilitated through the *mentoring* process in which a relationship develops between a new young manager and a manager at the mid-point of his or her career. Mentoring is a process of four stages defined as: initiation, cultivation, separation, and redefinition.

A number of mistakes and problems are associated with human resource development. However, many of these problems result from inadequate planning and narrow thinking about coordinated employee development.

Encapsulated development occurs when an individual learns new methods and ideas in a development course, but is not provided the opportunity to implement them in the work unit.

A *career* is the sequence of work-related positions a person occupies throughout life. As the employee work role becomes more complex and career plans are changed due to corporate retrenchment and downsizing, more employers are providing career planning and guidance, including retirement planning. Career planning can be organization centered, which involves career paths that are the logical progression of people between jobs within the organization; or individual centered which focuses on expanding the individual's goals and skills.

An important part of career planning is the development of *dual-career ladders* for technical people such as engineers and scientists.

With increasing numbers of professional women in the workforce, an important part of career planning must include the concerns of dual-career couples regarding recruitment, transfer, and family issues.

A final aspect of career planning is the issue of *moonlighting*, that is working outside one's regular employment for twelve or more hours per week.

STUDY QUESTIONS

Matching Questions

Match the key term from the list below with its most appropriate definition.

a.   Development   f.   Mentoring

b.   Encapsulated development   g.   Replacement charts

c.   On-the-job methods   h.   Organization-centered career planning

d.   Off-the-job methods   i.   Individual-centered career planning

e.   Assessment center   j.   Career

_____   1.   Efforts to improve employees' ability to handle a variety of assignments.

_____   2.   A type of planning which focuses on jobs and constructing career paths that provide for logical progression of people between jobs in an organization.

_____   3.   A tool to ensure the right individual is available at the right time with sufficient experience to handle the job.

_____   4.   A relationship in which a manager in the mid-point of his or her career aids a young adult in the first stage of a career.

_____   5.   Planning which focuses on an individuals' careers rather than organizational needs.

_____   6.   May involve coaching, committee assignments, and job rotations.

_____   7.   A development technique which helps in selection and promotion decisions as well as identifying areas in employees that need development.

_____   8.   Examples include classroom courses, human relations training, and simulations.

_____   9.   The sequence of work-related positions occupied throughout a person's life.

_____   10.   Employee learns new methods and ideas in a development course but cannot apply them to the work situation due to old attitudes and methods.

True/False Questions

___   1.   Role playing is an off-the-job development method.

___   2.   The primary advantage of simulations is their realism.

___   3.   The goal of a development program should be people oriented rather than job specific or technically oriented.

___   4.   Moonlighting is a career development strategy for some professionals.

___   5.   The purpose of succession planning is to stockpile talent until it can be used.

___   6.   Delegation and participation in decision making could be rightly seen as part of top management support for developmental activities.

___   7.   Development can be a viable substitute for good selection. If a new employee lacks the capacity to do the work, a good development program can rectify that.

___   8.   Self-awareness of abilities and interests is an objective of organization-centered career planning.

___   9.   Dual-career couples have more to lose when faced with a job transfer.

___   10.   Career paths are best represented as the linear track a person follows while moving upward in an organization.

___   11.   Managerial modeling refers to "shaping" a manager through "imitating" other managers.

___   12.   Good career planning at the individual level first requires that a person accurately know himself/herself.

___   13.   Assessment centers have two distinct uses: selecting managers, and identifying areas in employees that need development.

___   14.   Studies indicate that assessment centers are poor predictors of managerial success.

___   15.   Encapsulated training is defined sufficiently as the learning an individual receives in a concentrated off-the-job course.

Idea Completion Questions

1.   The four stages in a mentor/learner relationship are:

_____,   _____,   _____,

and _____.

2.   Individual career planning focuses on _____,

rather than on _____.

3.   On-the-job methods of human resource development include:

_____,   _____,   _____,

and _____.

4.   Some off-the-job methods of employee development include:

_____,   _____,   _____,

_____,   _____,   _____,

and _____.

5.   Managerial modeling is _____

_____.

Multiple Choice Questions

___   1.   A form of training which resulted from the Hawthorne studies is called
     a.   human relations training.
     b.   case study training.
     c.   role playing.
     d.   sabbaticals.

___   2.   Which of the following is an off-the-job training and development method?
     a.   assistant-to positions
     b.   case study
     c.   committee assignments
     d.   coaching

___   3.   Which of the following is an on-the-job training and development method?
     a.   coaching
     b.   sabbatical
     c.   simulation
     d.   psychological testing

___   4.   Individual-centered career planning would include all but
     a.   the identification of personal abilities and interests.
     b.   the assessment of alternative career paths outside the organization.
     c.   planning life and work goals.
     d.   the audit and development of a career system for the organization.
     e.   all of the above are individual-centered career planning.

___   5.   An advantage of on-the-job training is that
     a.   it uses basically one method.
     b.   employees can "learn by doing."
     c.   the employee's development is influenced only by top management.
     d.   it is standardized and uniform for all employees.

6. Shifting employees from one position to another describes
    a. committee assignments.
    b. critical incident.
    c. coaching.
    d. job rotation.

7. The _____ is suggested as one solution to the dilemma of how to provide advancement for technical people who do not want to move into management.
    a. assistant-to position
    b. replacement chart
    c. dual-career ladder
    d. assessment center

8. An advantage of classroom training is that
    a. students do not have to participate or come prepared.
    b. people are familiar with classroom methods.
    c. success depends on the size of the group and the ability of the instructor.
    d. employees can learn while on the job.

9. Passive listening and lack of participation are disadvantages of
    a. classroom courses.
    b. assistant-to positions.
    c. managerial modeling.
    d. simulation.

10. A person's career choice is affected by
    a. interests.
    b. self-image.
    c. personality.
    d. social background.
    e. all of the above.

___ 11. The term _____ describes the situation in which women fail to progress to top management positions.
  a. glass ceiling
  b. adverse impact
  c. encapsulated development
  d. territoriality
  e. glass walls

___ 12. Assessment centers have proven to be useful because
  a. they help identify areas in employees that need development.
  b. they assist managers in assessing the performance of their employees.
  c. they help organizations select the managers.
  d. all of the above.
  e. a and c.

___ 13. Development-need assessment methods used by organizations include all of the following except:
  a. assessment centers.
  b. psychological testing.
  c. performance appraisals
  d. replacement charts.
  e. only a and c are necessary.

___ 14. To ensure that the right individual is available at the right time to fill a job, organizations utilize
  a. depth charts.
  b. replacement charts.
  c. organization charts.
  d. assessment charts.

___ 15. _____ occurs when a trainee is unable to apply newly learned methods to the job in the work unit.
  a. Inadequate training
  b. Fragmental development
  c. Encapsulated development
  d. None of the above occurs.

Essay Questions

1.   Define human resource development and explain why it is an important HR activity.

2.   What is an assessment center? How is it useful in staffing organizations?

3.   Describe the following on-the-job development methods:

    a.   coaching,

    b.   assistant-to positions,

    c.   committee assignments,

    d.   job rotation.

4.   Discuss the usefulness and limitations of the following off-the-job development methods:

    a.   human relations training,

    b.   classroom courses,

    c.   psychological testing,

    d.   sabbaticals.

5.   How do people choose careers? Explain how life stages parallel career stages.

6.   Discuss the problems associated with managerial moonlighting and suggest appropriate HR strategies for dealing with those problems.

ANSWER KEY

Matching

1.	a	2.	h	3.	g	4.	f	5.	i
6.	c	7.	e	8.	d	9.	j	10.	b

True/False

1.	T	2.	F	3.	T	4.	T	5.	F
6.	T	7.	F	8.	F	9.	T	10.	F
11.	T	12.	T	13.	T	14.	F	15.	F

Idea Completion

1. initiation
   cultivation
   separation
   redefinition

2. individuals
   jobs

3. coaching
   committee assignments
   job rotation
   "assistant-to" positions

4. classroom courses
   psychological testing
   human relations training
   case studies
   role playing
   simulation or business games
   sabbaticals

5. management learned by modeling the behavior of other managers

Multiple Choice

1. a	2. b	3. a	4. d	5. b
6. d	7. c	8. b	9. a	10. e
11. a	12. e	13. d	14. b	15. c

SHENANDOAH NATIONAL BANK

Pete Lugar, Director of Human Resources at the Shenandoah National Bank and Trust, is becoming increasingly concerned over the rate of teller turnover. In the past year, over 40% of the bank's tellers have quit, and Pete doesn't know why. The tellers are well paid, starting at about $8.00 an hour which is slightly above that paid by other financial institutions in the state. Shenandoah National Bank is the largest bank in the state with over 100 branches employing about 1,450 tellers.

In an attempt to get at the causes of the problem, Pete arranged for a meeting of the managers of the branches having the highest rate of teller turnover. *"I've asked for this meeting to see if we can discover why our tellers are quitting,"* Pete began. *"When I add up the costs of recruitment, selection, and training, I find that it costs us over $9,000 every time a teller leaves."*

"The problem is obvious to me," one manager began. *"If your department would send us qualified tellers who are motivated and well trained, our turnover troubles would be over."*

"That's right," added a second. *"Young people today just aren't motivated. They just want an easy job, with no responsibility. But they all want good pay and plenty of time off."*

"I see it differently," responded another branch manager. *"Some are so eager to get ahead that they get frustrated and quit if we don't promote them fast enough. There are just not enough opportunities for promotion, and the young people are impatient."*

Still another manager commented, *"I think they are just not responsible enough. Take this teller, Dixie Miller. She'd been in my branch for about a year. She was cheerful and rarely made errors. Then last week a customer complained that Dixie had been rude to him. I called her into my office to ask her to be more polite to the customers. She refused to accept the criticism and just walked out."*

After the meeting, Pete Lugar felt he was not much closer to finding the cause of the problem. He decided that he would try to talk to some tellers who had recently quit, hoping that they would shed some light on the problem. Remembering the comments made regarding Dixie Miller, he studied her employment file and then made an appointment to talk with her. From the employment file, Pete learned that Dixie was 20 years old. She had graduated from high school three years earlier, and after working as a cashier at a suburban grocery store, had joined the bank as a teller. Her annual performance review was a good one.

Dixie was surprised when Pete Lugar called on her. After hearing that he was genuinely interested in why she had resigned, she talked freely:

"I was working in this grocery store. The pay was OK, but the work was boring. One day when I was at the bank I saw a notice about tellers being needed, so I talked to the

manager. He seemed so pleased to see me and was very friendly. He told me that the job was challenging and had plenty of variety and that I would get to meet many interesting people. I was really impressed when I saw the computer terminals in the teller cages. I asked him about career opportunities and learned that most bank managers began as tellers. He told me that he had begun as a teller and within a year and a half was an assistant manager, and then five years later became a branch manager. Opportunities seemed endless. The only discouraging factor was that I would be earning less as a teller than I had in the grocery store, but since he explained that pay raises were good if you performed well, I was willing to take the cut in pay.

"He told me he would send my application to the HR Department at the main office and I would hear from them. Well, I was called in for an interview and given a simple math test. Then I got the job.

"First off, I spent three weeks in a teller training class at the main office. I didn't realize that there was so much to learn - rules, procedures, different transactions, and so on. One thing that impressed me was the number of women in senior positions at the main office. The bank seemed to encourage women to excel.

"After the training, I was sent to the branch near my home where I had originally applied. When I arrived everyone seemed pleased to see me, but were too busy to spend much time showing me around. I spent the first two days watching one of the older tellers and on the third day was assigned to a teller cage of my own.

"At first I was really confused. I kept asking for advice, but everyone was usually too busy. Still, I managed and after a month or so, I settled into a routine. The manager always seemed to be standing around watching to see if anyone made a mistake, but he didn't try to be too helpful when I needed assistance or advice.

"Just this last month or so I began to get fed up. The work had become so routine that I really didn't have to think about what I was doing. I balanced almost every day, more often than most tellers, but no one seemed to notice. When the manager gave me my annual performance review recently, he said I was doing fine, and I got a five percent pay raise, just the same everyone else got. I asked him about the possibility of a promotion, and he sort of smiled, and said his branch has just one senior teller and that six people had been there longer than I had. Besides, the senior teller wasn't planning on leaving. So I asked him about the management training program and was stunned to hear that you can't enter management training unless you have a college degree. I felt I had been cheated.

"Last Tuesday was the last straw. This customer came in with a social security check to be cashed. The bank rules say that we must ask for identification for all government checks. So I asked. He objected, saying that he had banked here for 20 years and had never been asked for identification before. I told him that I was sorry but it is a bank rule *and I could not cash his check without proper identification. He then stormed into the manager's office.*

"Later that day, the manager called me in and asked why I had been rude to a customer. I told him that I had not been rude, but that I had asked for identification. He didn't seem to care what I said. He just told me that in the future I had to be more courteous and not upset the customers.

"Well, that did it. I told him that if he didn't care about me, I didn't care about his bank. So I quit. Wouldn't you?"

Questions

1.   What factors may be contributing to the turnover of tellers?

2.   Why did Dixie Miller take the job at the bank? Why did she quit?

3.   What is your assessment of the bank's training programs? Would you recommend any changes?

4.   What is your assessment of the bank's human resource development efforts?   Would you recommend any changes?

5.   Pete Lugar needs help. What advice would you give him?

6.   Dixie Miller needs some career advice. What would you suggest?

CAREER PLANNING

William Jenks

On his forty-fifth birthday, William Jenks became depressed. He felt that his career had peaked. There did not seem to be any possibility of promotion and he did not expect his salary to increase significantly beyond annual cost-of-living adjustments. Furthermore, he had been looking through employment advertisements and believed that he had little or no chance of getting a more interesting job. He moaned "I feel trapped - twenty more years until retirement. Twenty more years doing the same job. Where did I go wrong?"

William graduated from college with a BS in chemical engineering. He received several attractive job offers, and accepted a position at an oil refinery. He enjoyed his job, worked hard, and received above-average salary increases. At age 26, he enrolled in a part-time MBA program. But the pressure of work and family, he was married with two children, forced him to drop-out at the end of his second semester. He had asked his supervisor for time-off to study for finals, but this was denied. He found that the tuition put quite a strain on the family budget, even though his company reimbursed him for fifty percent of the tuition upon successfully completing each semester.

By the time he was 37, William had relocated six times, as the company transferred him to different refineries. Each transfer was accompanied by a salary increase, but this in itself did not compensate his family for the upheaval of moving. Mrs. Jenks had her career interrupted, and their children had to change schools and make new friends. Soon after his 37th birthday, William was offered another transfer and promotion to plant superintendent. William felt that he had to decline the promotion explaining that his wife had recently been promoted at her job and that the children were at critical stages of their education. Ever since, William has wondered if this was a mistake.

Maria Jenks

Maria Jenks graduated from college with an accounting degree one year after William. They were married a week after her graduation. Over the years she has held a variety of jobs, mostly at schools and colleges. Ten years ago, following William's last transfer, she accepted a position in the business office of a private college. After just two years she was promoted to comptroller.

Sometimes she wonders if she had been selfish when she refused to move eight years ago. But she didn't want to leave a job where, for the first time, she was doing "real accounting" and not just clerical work.

Analysis and Discussion

1.   Analyze William's career. Has he been successful? A failure? Did the company's actions help or hinder his career?

2.   Analyze Maria's career. Was she selfish in refusing to move?

3.   As you begin your career, you can either abdicate your career to your employer(s), or else you can control its outcomes. Set a goal for where you want to be at ages 25, 35, 45, 55, and 65. Now outline an individual career development program to help you reach these goals. This program may include formal education, training and development activities, job assignments, etc. How important is it that you find a mentor at each stage of your career?

4.   How will you determine if your career has been successful? Where do family and off-the-job activities fit into your plans?

5.   Are your career goals dependent upon remaining single or being married? Having children or no children?

Chapter 12

Performance Management and Appraisal

CHAPTER OBJECTIVES

1. Distinguish between job criteria and performance standards and discuss criterion contamination and deficiency.

2. Identify the two major uses of performance appraisal.

3. Explain several rater errors by giving examples of them.

4. Describe both the advantages and disadvantages of multi-source (360°) appraisal.

5. Identify the nature of behavioral approaches to performance appraisal and management by objectives (MBO).

6. Discuss several concerns about appraisal feedback interviews.

7. Identify the characteristics of a legal and effective performance appraisal system.

SUMMARY OF THE CHAPTER

Human resource performance is an important part of the strategy most organizations must follow to achieve their goals. *Performance management systems* attempt to monitor, measure, report, improve, and reward employee performance.

Job criteria are the dimensions of a job on which performance is measured. Criteria can be classified as trait-based, behavior-based, and results-based. Criteria must be relevant, that is, they must measure important elements of the job. Otherwise the criteria will be considered deficient and/or contaminated. Before performance appraisal can be conducted, a standard, the expected level of performance, must be established for each job criterion. The various criteria also should be weighted to reflect the relative importance of each.

Performance appraisal determines how well employees do their jobs and communicates that information to them. Performance appraisals serve two potentially conflicting roles in organizations: administrative uses including compensation, promotion, dismissal, downsizing, and layoff decisions, and developmental uses including identifying strengths and areas for growth, development planning, and coaching and helping with plans.

Performance appraisal can be done by supervisors, subordinates, team members, outside raters, self, or a combination of raters referred to as 360 ° appraisals. Regardless of who is doing the rating, a method is necessary. Appraisal methods can be categorized into four major groups: category methods, comparative methods, narrative methods, and special systems.

Category methods, which include graphic rating scales, and checklists that basically require the rater to evaluate the employee by marking a level of performance on a form.

Comparative methods such as ranking, paired comparisons, and forced distribution all require that the rater compare performances of employees against each other.

In the *narrative methods* including critical incident, essay, and field review, the rater provides documentation and descriptive comments about the employee's performance.

Two *special methods*, behavioral rating approaches and management by objectives (MBO), attempt to overcome the problems associated with the above three methods.

Raters should be aware that there are many sources of error in performance appraisal, including:

1.   varying standards - different standards and expectations used for different employees performing similar jobs;

2.   recency effect - evaluation based on performance during a recent period rather than entire appraisal period;

3.   rater bias - rater's values, beliefs, or prejudices distort ratings; and

4.   rater patterns - inter-rater and intra-rater inconsistencies. These include the central tendency error, leniency errors, the halo effect, and the contrast error.

The appraisal process is not complete until the results of the appraisal have been communicated back to the employee. To insure a successful performance appraisal interview, the manager should prepare adequately for the interview; involve the employee in a discussion rather than simply "lecturing" on his or her strengths and weaknesses; focus on performance development not on salary or placement decisions; and determine specific future performance targets so the employee knows the acceptable performance to continue, as well as the deficiencies to overcome.

The major legal concern is that performance appraisals be job-related and non-discriminatory. The EEOC and numerous court decisions provide guidelines for designing a legal appraisal system.

The effectiveness of a performance appraisal system lies not in the specific methods used, but rather it depends upon managers' understanding of its purposes. Training of appraisers and guarding against "number magic" are important aspects of an effective appraisal system.

STUDY QUESTIONS

Matching Questions

Match the key term from the list below with its most appropriate definition.

a.   Performance appraisal   g.   Varying standards problem

b.   Graphic rating scales   h.   Recency effect

c.   Job criteria   i.   Central tendency error

d.   Paired comparisons   j.   Halo effect

e.   Forced distribution   k.   Performance management systems

f.   Critical incident   l.   MBO

___   1.   The elements of the job to be evaluated during performance appraisal.

___   2.   A situation in which the rater uses different standards and expectations for employees performing similar jobs.

___   3.   Specifies the performance goals an individual hopes to attain within an appropriate length of time.

___   4.   Type of appraisal method in which the rater checks the appropriate place on the scale for each duty listed.

___   5.   Attempts to monitor, measure, report, improve, and reward employee performance.

___   6.   Type of rater pattern in which appraiser rates all employees within a narrow range.

___   7.   Keeping a written record of highly favorable and unfavorable actions in an employee's performance is an example of the _____ appraisal method.

___   8.   Determining how well employees do their jobs compared to a set of standards and communicating that information to them.

___   9.   Type of appraisal method which assumes that the "bell-shaped curve" of performance exists in a given group.

___   10.   Occurs when an employee is rated high or low on all items because of one characteristic.

___   11.   Type of appraisal method in which the rater compares each employee with each other employee in the rating group.

___   12.   Occurs when performance appraisal is affected by the most recent period of time or work.

True/False Questions

___   1.   Managers usually enjoy the performance appraisal process because they can "play God" and make judgmental decisions.

___   2.   Because of the advantages of subordinates rating superiors, it is fairly widely used in industry.

___   3.   Multisource feedback recognizes that the manager is no longer the sole source of performance appraisal information.

___   4.   One voiced advantage of MBO is that employees involved in setting and planning objectives may work harder to insure that they are met.

___   5.   The timing for performance appraisals and pay discussions should be different.

___   6.   Appraisal takes place only if a formal system is established.

___   7.   The primary use of performance appraisal is as a basis for pay decisions.

___   8.   To meet legal requirements, a performance appraisal system must demonstrate absence of adverse impact and presence of job relatedness.

___   9.   Most organizations do formal performance appraisals three times per year.

___   10.   Because they focus on behaviors, behaviorally anchored rating scales (BARS) take less time to develop.

___   11.   A BARS system is very specific about what a rating is and how it is determined.

___   12.   The BARS system, by spelling out the behavior associated with each level of performance, causes more problems than it solves.

___   13.   Peer ratings have been used widely in both military training and in industrial situations.

___   14.   The forced-distribution method is a type of category, not comparative, method.

___   15.   The successes of MBO have revealed that it is useful in most organizations and with most employees.

Idea Completion Questions

1.   The two major uses of appraisals are:
_____, and _____.

2.   The major legal implications of performance appraisals are that they must be
_____, and _____.

3.   Four rater errors associated with performance appraisal are:
_____, _____, _____, and _____.

4.   Eight appraisal methods used by supervisors to rate subordinates are:
_____, _____, _____,
_____, _____, _____,
_____, and _____.

5.   Post appraisal interviews can be improved if the supervisor
_____, _____, _____,
_____, and _____.

Multiple Choice Questions

___ 1. The most commonly used method of superior ratings of subordinates is
   a. check list.
   b. graphic rating scale.
   c. essay.
   d. ranking.

___ 2. Keeping a record of all employees and listing significant successes and failures of each describes which method?
   a. critical incident
   b. MBO
   c. essay form
   d. field review

___ 3. The appraisal method that would require a rater to place only a certain percentage of employees in each quartile would be an example of
   a. a field review.
   b. paired comparisons.
   c. forced distribution.
   d. a checklist.

___ 4. Using the paired comparison method, a rater who must appraise 8 employees on 6 different criteria would have to make how many separate one-to-one comparisons?
   a. 48
   b. 60
   c. 96
   d. 168

___ 5. Performance appraisal is useful in all but
   a. making seniority determinations.
   b. making placement decisions.
   c. making decisions about pay raises.
   d. determining weaknesses in employees' training.

___   6.   A problem with the appraisal process is
       a.   a rater's values, beliefs, and prejudices cannot be used in the ratings.
       b.   performance ratings may be significantly influenced by the most recent period rather than over the entire evaluation period.
       c.   all supervisors tend to rate employees using the same standards.
       d.   managers rate employees differently on all dimensions, thus avoiding the halo effect.

___   7.   An advantage of the subordinate rating approach is
       a.   the supervisor rather than managing will become a "nice-guy."
       b.   most supervisors enjoy being evaluated by subordinates.
       c.   its use in identifying supervisors who interact well with employees.
       d.   subordinates can "get even" with supervisors they dislike.

___   8.   Job criteria which look at what the employee has done or accomplished are known as
       a.   trait-based criteria.
       b.   behavior-based criteria.
       c.   results-based criteria.
       d.   none of the above.

___   9.   An effective performance appraisal system will be all of the following except:
       a.   consistent with the strategic mission of the organization.
       b.   useful as an administrative tool.
       c.   useful as a developmental tool.
       d.   viewed as generally fair by employees.
       e.   different for protected groups of employees.

___   10.   MBO has been most successful with which of the following groups?
       a.   assembly line workers
       b.   research scientists
       c.   managers
       d.   equally successful with all groups

___   11.   If one supervisor interprets performance standards differently from another supervisor, what type of appraisal error is likely to occur?
a.   recovery problem
b.   rater bias
c.   halo effect
d.   rater pattern

___   12.   Which is not a drawback to the graphic rating scale?
a.   separate traits or factors are grouped together yet the rater is given only one box to check
b.   descriptive words have different meanings to different people
c.   supervisors can still write comments following each factor rated
d.   all of the above are drawbacks

___   13.   The essence of management by objectives is operationalized by the
a.   manager setting the objectives he expects his subordinates to meet and making sure they meet them.
b.   manager deciding who will do what and when.
c.   employee himself deciding what he should do, and how it should be done, and then doing it.
d.   manager and employee mutually agreeing upon the objectives to be accomplished.

___   14.   In preparing for the appraisal interview, the manager should
a.   call employees in to discuss their appraisal, without allowing time for the employee to prepare, so as to minimize defensive behavior.
b.   review all documents and records relating to the employee's performance.
c.   "ad lib" the session.
d.   avoid all of the above.

___   15.   In a typical appraisal interface the HR unit would do all of the following except:
a.   design and maintain the formal system.
b.   make sure reports are in on time.
c.   review appraisals with employees.
d.   train raters.

Essay Questions

1.   Discuss how appraisals and appraisal information is related to at least three other HR activities.

2.   Give short explanations of each of the following supervisor rating methods:

    a.   graphic rating scale,

    b.   checklist,

    c.   ranking,

    d.   paired comparison,

    e.   field review.

3.   What is MBO? Discuss the MBO process and some of the advantages and disadvantages associated with it. How can MBO help overcome some of the problems associated with traditional approaches to performance appraisal?

4.   Describe four key considerations that would be useful in making post-appraisal interviews more effective and explain why those considerations would be useful.

5.   Briefly describe the steps involved in developing a BARS appraisal system. How can BARS overcome some of the problems associated with the more traditional methods of appraisal?

ANSWER KEY

Matching

1. c	2. g	3. l	4. b	5. k
6. i	7. f	8. a	9. e	10. j
11. d	12. h			

True/False

1. F	2. F	3. T	4. T	5. T
6. F	7. F	8. T	9. F	10. F
11. T	12. F	13. F	14. F	15. F

Idea Completion

1.   feedback for development
     administrative decisions

2.   job related
     nondiscriminatory

3.   contrast error
     recency problem
     rater bias
     rater patterns
     halo effect

4.   graphic rating scale
     check list
     ranking
     paired comparison
     forced distribution
     critical incident
     essay
     field review

5.   prepares in advance
      focuses on performance
      is specific
      mutually decide on specific steps for improvement
      reinforces desired behavior

Multiple Choice

1.	b	2.	a	3.	c	4.	d	5.	a
6.	b	7.	c	8.	c	9.	e	10.	c
11.	d	12.	c	13.	d	14.	b	15.	c

WHO GETS THE AXE?

Henry Donaldson is a department head at Statewide Insurance Company. He has been with the company for 30 years and knows his way around quite well. He has two subordinates Tom Smith and Melody Watson:

Tom Smith, a white male, has been employed by the company for 15 years. He has always been cooperative, loyal, dependable, but not an especially good supervisor. Recently Henry noticed that Tom has begun to "slip" on the performance of some of his duties.

Melody Watson, an African American, has worked at Statewide Insurance for about six years. She is a very ambitious, energetic, and dependable supervisor who grasps problems quickly and easily.

Henry has to complete performance appraisal forms on both individuals semi-annually. Last quarter he did his appraisal reviews with a great deal of displeasure since he hated to face the unpleasantness of a negative appraisal-feedback interview. As a result, he rated both employees "above average" on most dimensions. In the feedback interviews, both supervisors appeared to be satisfied with the ratings they had received. He recommended that they both receive standard cost-of-living salary increases.

Because business had begun to fall off as a result of the general economic down-turn, a reduction in force has been put into effect. This week, after a number of other people were laid off or demoted, Henry was instructed to move either Tom Smith or Melody Watson from the position of supervisor to that of a clerk in the processing section until business picked up. Henry wants to keep Melody in the supervisory job, but on the basis of the appraisals there is no difference between the two. In the past when two employees have had the same ratings, the person with the most seniority receives priority.

Henry's superior wants his recommendation today.

Questions

1.   What mistakes has Henry made in his appraisal activities?

2.   Is there the possibility of a legal challenge if he chooses to demote Tom? Melody? On what basis?

3.   Given the current situation, what would you do? Why?

4.   As HR director, what suggestions would you make so that Henry could improve his handling of performance appraisals?

MBO AT MARIO'S PIZZA

Although MBO is used primarily for appraising managers, the process can also be useful when appraising employees at other levels of the organization. Because most of you will be familiar with the job of a pizza delivery person, that job will be used to illustrate the MBO process.

Mario's Pizza is located in a college town. It has no restaurant facilities. All orders are either "take-out" or are delivered by Mario's drivers. Mario's advertises that orders to college housing will be delivered within 30 minutes of the order being phoned in, or else the customer will receive a $10 coupon towards another order.

Since it takes about 15 minutes to cook a pizza, the drivers have 15 minutes for delivery. The drivers also collect the money from the customers for the pizzas. The drivers split all tips 50/50 with the cooks.

The delivery supervisor has prepared the following performance evaluation for driver Emily Polaski:

EMILY POLASKI

Dimension	Measure	Performance Evaluation Present Level
On-time	Time clock Cost	90% on-time delivery $10 per late delivery
Collections	Quantity	98% of the customers pay on delivery
Tips	Quantity	tips average 8%

Assignment

Role play the appraisal interview. Your instructor can assign certain class members to assume the roles of Emily Polaski and the delivery supervisor. Use the information from the above evaluation to plan your approach.

Use the information from the evaluation to role play the MBO process of job review and objective setting. Use the following form to record your agreements:

EMILY POLASKI

Dimension	Measure	MBO Objective	
		Desired Level	Time Frame

Questions for Analysis and Discussion

1.   What difficulties did you face in conducting the appraisal interview?

2.   What potential problems do you see in establishing and implementing the MBO objectives?

3.   Discuss the effectiveness and legality of the MBO process as depicted in this exercise.

Chapter 13

Compensation

CHAPTER OBJECTIVES

1. Identify the three types of compensation and discuss two compensation philosophies.

2. Discuss different bases for compensation.

3. Describe three equity considerations and how organizational justice is related to compensation.

4. Identify the basic provisions of the Fair Labor Standards Act.

5. Define *job evaluation* and discuss four methods of performing it.

6. Outline the process of building a wage and salary administration system.

7. Discuss how a pay-for-performance system is established.

SUMMARY OF THE CHAPTER

Compensation serves the function of allocating people among employers based on the attractiveness of jobs and compensation packages.

There are three specific types of compensation: pay, incentives, and benefits.

Pay is the basic compensation an employee receives, usually as a wage or salary.

An *incentive* is compensation that rewards an employee for efforts beyond normal performance expectations.

A *benefit* is an indirect reward given to an employee or group of employees as a part of organizational membership.

There are three bases for compensation. The *time basis* pays employees for the amount of time they are on the job. Wages are pay amounts directly calculated on the amount of time worked. Salary is payment that is consistent from period to period. The *productivity basis* ties pay to performance or productivity. A common example of this compensation basis is a piece-rate system. The third basis for compensation is the *skill basis*. In a skill-based pay system, employees are paid for the skills or competencies they have, rather than for specific tasks being done.

In most every organization a compensation program should address three objectives: legal compliance, cost effectiveness, and equity.

Organizational justice is a growing issue in organizations. Two kinds of justice are procedural and distributive. *Procedural justice* is the perceived fairness of the process and procedures used to make decisions about employees, including their pay. *Distributive justice* refers to the perceived fairness of the amount given for performance.

There are a number of legal constraints which must be considered in developing a compensation system. The major law is the *Fair Labor Standards Act* first passed in 1938. This act established a minimum wage floor, encouraged limits on the number of weekly hours employees work through overtime payments, and discouraged the oppressive use of child labor.

The *Equal Pay Act* passed in 1963 as a major amendment to the Fair Labor Standards Act, prohibits paying different wage scales to men and women performing substantially the same jobs.

The *Walsh-Healey Act* of 1936 requires companies with federal supply and service contracts exceeding $10,000 to pay a "prevailing wage."

The *Davis-Bacon Act* of 1931 requires that firms engaged in federal construction projects pay the "prevailing wage" rate. Compensation also is influenced by various state and local laws.

The development, implementation, and ongoing maintenance of a base pay system is described as *Wage and Salary Administration*. The process begins with the determination of the overall organizational pay policies. In addition to legal considerations, pay policy decisions also are affected by other factors including whether or not the organization is unionized, what the employer can afford to pay, and what prevailing wage rates are in the area.

Once pay policies have been determined, the actual development of a pay system begins. In order to choose an appropriate compensation method and determine equitable pay rates, differences in jobs must be determined. *Job evaluation*, the systematic determination of the relative worth of jobs within an organization, is a useful approach in determining job differences. This can be done by comparing: (1) the relative importance of the job, (2) the skills needed to perform the job, and (3) the difficulty of the job compared to other jobs. There are a number of methods for conducting job evaluations, including ranking, classification, the point method, and factor comparison.

The U.S. has had a long history of classifying jobs, at least implicitly, as "male" or "female" jobs. It has been claimed that the traditionally "female" jobs are routinely paid less than the traditionally "male" jobs. *Comparable worth*, also called *pay equity*, requires that jobs with comparable knowledge, skills, and abilities be paid similarly.

While job evaluation provides the basis for insuring the internal equity of a pay system, external equity is an equally important consideration. A pay survey is a means of gathering data on existing compensation rates for workers performing similar jobs in other organizations. Once the data to insure internal and external equity are derived, the organization is in a position to develop a pay structure which establishes pay ranges and pay grades.

Once pay ranges have been developed, adjustments to individual pay must be considered for persons whose pay currently falls outside established ranges. On an ongoing basis, pay increases can be based on seniority, cost-of-living adjustments, performance, or a combination of these approaches.

STUDY QUESTIONS

Matching Questions

Match the key term from the list below with its most appropriate definition.

a.	Pay		k.	Point method
b.	Incentives		l.	Benchmark job
c.	Benefits		m.	Pay survey
d.	Compensatory time		n.	Garnishment
e.	Fair Labor Standards Act		o.	Pay compression
f.	Equal Pay Act		p.	Market pricing
g.	Walsh-Healey Act		q.	Pay grade
h.	Davis-Bacon Act		r.	Non-exempt
i.	Red-circle rate		s.	Job evaluation
j.	Comparable worth		t.	Green-circle rate

_____   1.   Requires that the prevailing wage rate be paid on all federal construction projects.

_____   2.   Rewards available to an employee or group of employees as a part of organizational membership.

_____   3.   A court action in which a portion of an employee's wages is set aside to pay a debt owed a creditor.

_____   4.   Assumes that the pay set by other employers is an accurate reflection of a job's worth.

_____   5.   Requires companies with federal supply contracts exceeding $10,000 to pay a prevailing minimum wage.

_____   6.   A group of individual jobs having approximately the same job worth.

___ 7. Requires that jobs with comparable knowledge, skills, and abilities be paid similarly.

___ 8. A job in which the incumbent is paid above the range set for the job.

___ 9. Breaks down jobs into various identifiable components and places weights on these components.

___ 10. A job in which the incumbent is paid below the range set for the job.

___ 11. The basic compensation employees receive.

___ 12. A means of gathering data on existing compensation rates for employees performing similar jobs in other organizations.

___ 13. The first major law establishing minimum-wage levels and overtime payments.

___ 14. Employees in this classification must be paid overtime.

___ 15. The systematic determination of the relative worth of jobs within an organization.

___ 16. A job performed by several individuals with similar duties that are relatively stable, requiring similar KSAs, and found in many other organizations.

___ 17. Occurs when pay differences between individuals become small.

___ 18. Rewards designed to encourage and reimburse employees for efforts beyond normal performance expectations.

___ 19. Time-off given in lieu of payment for time worked.

___ 20. Prohibits pay differentials on the basis of sex.

True/False Questions

____   1.   All salaried employees are covered by the overtime provisions of the Fair Labor Standards Act.

____   2.   The U. S. Civil Service System uses the classification method of job evaluation.

____   3.   Even though job evaluation is a systematic look at jobs and their worth, subjectivity still enters in, no matter which method is used.

____   4.   The ranking method of job evaluation considers jobs as total entities instead of jobs and their components.

____   5.   A four-day/10-hour work schedule would require no overtime payment under the Fair Labor Standards Act.

____   6.   Under the Equal Pay Act jobs must be identical, otherwise pay differentials can be used.

____   7.   A firm with a federal construction contract of $1,000 would have to comply with the Davis-Bacon Act.

____   8.   A compa-ratio is a pay level divided by the mid-point of the pay range.

____   9.   Broad banding involves using fewer pay grades having a broader range than traditional compensation systems.

____   10.   Persons hired as independent contractors must be paid the same benefits as regular employees.

____   11.   Generally speaking, an open pay system will not work as well if employee performance can be specifically and directly measured.

____   12.   Pay compression occurs when an employer's pay adjustments increase more rapidly than the labor market pay levels.

____   13.   A major disadvantage of the factor comparison method is its complexity.

____   14.   Pay surveys are concerned with external, as opposed to internal, equity.

____   15.   A red-circle rate is a job whose pay rate is out of grade.

Idea Completion Questions

1.   The three major objectives of a compensation program are:
_____, _____, and_____.

2.   The three major objectives of the Fair Labor Standards Act are:
_____, _____, and_____.

3.   The four major federal laws that affect compensation are:
_____, _____, _____,
and _____.

4.   The three bases used in computing employees' pay are:
_____, _____, and_____.

5.   The four major job evaluation methods are:
_____, _____, _____,
and _____.

Multiple Choice Questions

___   1.   Which method of job evaluation is the most difficult to use?
a.   factor comparison method
b.   ranking method
c.   classification method
d.   point method

___   2.   Know-how, problem solving, and accountability are factors in the
a.   Hay Plan.
b.   ranking system.
c.   classification system.
d.   none of the above.

___   3.   A green-circle job is
a.   a job whose current occupant is paid less than the pay grade.
b.   a job for which current pay is lower than that paid by other employers as revealed by a pay survey.
c.   a way of denoting piece-rate employees.
d.   the rate paid probationary employees just starting with an employer.

___   4.   In a typical division of compensation responsibilities, the HR unit does all of the following except:
a.   develops and administers compensation system.
b.   conducts job evaluations and wage surveys.
c.   recommends pay rates and pay increases.
d.   develops wage/salary structures and policies.

___   5.   Mary, who is employed by a firm with a $2 million federal supply contract, works directly with fulfilling the contract. She worked 10 hours Monday, 6 hours Tuesday, and 8 hours each day on Wednesday, Thursday, and Friday. Her regular rate of pay is $6.00/hour. Her total pay for the week is
a. $228.
b. $240.
c. $246.
d. $252.

___ 6. Gross pay under the Fair Labor Standards Act for an employee paid $5.00/hour who worked 12 hours on Monday, 10 hours on Tuesday, 12 hours on Wednesday, and 8 hours on Thursday would be _____ for the week.
   a. $175
   b. $200
   c. $215
   d. $235

___ 7. The job evaluation method that requires that key (benchmark) jobs be determined is the
   a.   factor comparison method.
   b.   point method.
   c.   classification method.
   d.   ranking method.

___ 8. Which of the following evaluation methods breaks down jobs into various components, and places weights on these components?
   a.   factor comparison method
   b.   point method
   c.   classification method
   d.   ranking method

___ 9. Knowledge and skill-based pay systems have which of the following organization-related outcomes?
   a.   greater workforce flexibility
   b.   increased effectiveness of work teams
   c.   greater employee skill specialization at non-union firms
   d.   all of the above
   e.   only a and b apply

___ 10. Compensation strategies of the future are likely to reflect which of the following characteristics?
   a.   fewer fixed salaries, more variable pay
   b.   portable benefits
   c.   skill-based career, interim employment
   d.   all of the above.
   e.   only a and b above

___   11.   Which of the following was <u>not</u> a major objective of the FLSA?
- a.   discourage oppressive child labor
- b.   establish a minimum wage
- c.   encourage limits on the number of weekly hours employees work through overtime provisions
- d.   is designed to cover only executive and administrative employees

___   12.   Which act deals specifically with pay on federal construction contracts?
- a.   Fair Payment Act of 1957
- b.   Walsh-Healey Act of 1936
- c.   Davis-Bacon Act of 1931
- d.   Equal Pay Act of 1963

___   13.   Pay compression occurs primarily because
- a.   employers fail to conduct job evaluations.
- b.   organizations fail to conduct pay surveys.
- c.   labor market pay levels increase more than employers' pay adjustments.
- d.   none of the above is the major reason.

___   14.   The "comparable worth" issue is associated most closely with which law?
- a.   Fair Labor Standards Act
- b.   Equal Pay Act
- c.   Walsh-Healey Act
- d.   Davis-Bacon Act

___   15.   The advantages of lump-sum increases include
- a.   heightens employee awareness of what their performance "merited."
- b.   reduces the compounding effect of succeeding years.
- c.   unions generally prefer this type of increase.
- d.   all of the above are advantages.
- e.   only a and b above are advantages.

Essay Questions

1. Discuss some of the advantages and disadvantages associated with time, productivity, and skill as bases of pay.

2. What legal constraints need to be considered when designing a pay system?

3. Explain why job evaluation is useful to organizations.

4. Identify the four basic methods of job evaluation and briefly explain each.

5. Identify and define the following terms:

    a.   pay grades,

    b.   pay compression,

    c.   out-of-range rates.

6. Discuss the concepts of procedural justice and distributive justice as they relate to compensation.

ANSWER KEY

Matching

1.	h	2.	c	3.	n	4.	p	5.	g
6.	q	7.	j	8.	i	9.	k	10.	t
11.	a	12.	m	13.	e	14.	r	15.	s
16	l	17.	o	18.	b	19.	d	20.	f

True/False

1.	F	2.	T	3.	T	4.	T	5.	T
6.	F	7.	F	8.	T	9.	T	10.	F
11.	F	12.	F	13.	T	14.	T	15.	T

Idea Completion

1. legal compliance
   cost effectiveness
   equity

2. establish minimum wages
   overtime provisions
   discourage oppressive child labor

3. Fair Labor Standards Act of 1938
   Equal Pay Act of 1963
   Walsh-Healey Act of 1936
   Davis-Bacon Act of 1931

4. time
   productivity
   skills

5.   ranking
        point
        factor comparison
        classification

Multiple Choice

1. a	2. a	3. a	4. c	5. b
6. c	7. a	8. b	9. e	10. d
11. d	12. c	13. c	14. b	15. e

MY PAY

MEMORANDUM

July 18, 19XX

TO: Celia Van Clief
               Director of Human Resources

FROM: William O'Grady

RE: My Pay

When I began my job search during my senior year at North Central Tech, I used the college's placement office to do a salary survey. I checked the starting pay of computer science graduates hired by a cross section of business and government organizations in the mid-west. I found that the range was $28,000 - $36,000.

I then checked through the data routinely collected by the college placement office and learnt that recent computer science graduates of NC Tech received offers in the $27,000 - $31,500 range.

Prior to graduation I received four job offers, including one from Berrington Data Services which I accepted. Berrington's offer was not the best money-wise at $29,200, but I was impressed by the firm's personnel, training program, and the fact that Berrington would pay my relocation expenses and give me a "signing bonus" to help with my rent payments, security deposits, new clothes, etc. So six years ago this month, I started to work here.

Taken as a whole, I have enjoyed working here. I received very valuable training when I began work and attend update seminars every few months. Each year I have received "above average" performance reviews and my annual pay raises have averaged five to six percent. Today my salary is $38,220.

So what's my problem? Yesterday Marian Oertling joined my section, and it was my turn to mentor the new employee and to "show her the ropes." You made a good decision to hire Marian. She graduated last month from a west coast university with a major in computer science. She is bright, eager to learn, and I believe that she will be an outstanding addition to our staff. At lunch I asked Marian why she left the west coast to move to the mid-west. She told me she decided to accept Berrington's offer because she had lived all her life in the Los Angeles area and wanted to sample life elsewhere. She confided that she had been courted aggressively by two west coast firms, both of which offered her much more money that the $38,000 Berrington offered.

When I learnt what you were paying Marian, I was mad. That's only $220 less than I make and I've been here for six years. I know that we are not supposed to discuss our salaries with other employees, a fact that is emphasized each year when we receive our pay adjustment notices. Printed right there at the bottom of the notice is the statement:

> *"The Human Resource Department reminds you that all salary and benefit information at Berrington Data Services is strictly confidential. Any questions should be referred to the Director of Human Resources."*

So I am writing to ask you: Why is Marian Oertling's salary so high? Was she an affirmative action hire? Were you trying to match her other offers? Alternatively, why is my salary so low? Has there been something wrong with my performance to account for my pay level? Is the firm sending me a message?

I'm confused! Do we keep salaries confidential to cover up discrepancies? What must I do to get a pay raise in recognition of my six years' seniority? If I were to quit, and then apply for a new job here, would I come in at a higher salary to account for my six years of experience?

Questions

1.   Should firms require employees to keep their salaries and benefits confidential? Why or why not?

2.   What role does organizational justice play in this case?

3.   Comment on the salary system at Berrington Data Services. Do you see any weaknesses in the system?

4.   As Director of Human Resources, how would you respond to William O'Grady?

AN ATTEMPT AT PAY EQUITY

The President of Central Carolina University is caught in a dilemma. Located in a rural county, it has traditionally enrolled commuter students from low income families. The majority of the students live at home, work part-time, and major in the more practical areas of accounting, civil engineering, and nursing.

As a state university, Central Carolina must make a listing of its monthly pay roll available to the public. It is this policy that has caused President Lennox's dilemma. Last year a delegation of female faculty, primarily from the School of Nursing, presented President Lennox with the following analysis of salary comparisons which clearly showed that male professors, on average, earned more than female professors of the same rank.

FACULTY COMPENSATION

RANK	MALES		FEMALES	
	Number	Average Salary	Number	Average Salary
Professor	53	$52,762	29	$38,567
Associate Professor	13	$34,403	11	$28,894
Assistant Professor	10	$28,374	17	$24,885
Instructor	8	$20,500	9	$20,041

President Lennox agreed that discrimination existed and promised to begin rectifying the discrepancies in the next budget. Last month, President Lennox sent a memo to all female faculty members advising that, due to state budget constraints, it would not be possible to achieve immediate pay equity. However, as an intermediate solution, all female faculty would receive salary increases on July 1, as follows: Professors, $6,000; Associate Professors, $3,000; Assistant Professors, $2,000; Instructors, $200. The president promised to continue such annual salary increases until full pay equity was achieved.

Within days, President Lennox received an angry letter signed by all eighty-four male faculty members objecting to the president's action. They assumed that they would receive no salary increases until the female salaries had been increased to equal those of the male faculty. The letter threatened legal action if they were denied regular, comparable salary increases.

President Lennox responded by scheduling a faculty forum to discuss the pay equity problem.

Instructions

1. Select two teams to debate the issue of pay equity as presented above. One team will represent the male faculty, the second team will represent the female.

2. Use your university library to locate material relevant to this topic. Possible sources will include the newspapers, academic journals, political journals, and weekly news- magazines.

3. In class, both groups will present the arguments that would be used to influence President Lennox's decision.

4. Following the debate, discuss alternative actions that President Lennox could have taken in response to the apparent salary differences.

Chapter 14

Incentives and Executive Compensation

CHAPTER OBJECTIVES

1. Define *incentive* and give examples of three categories of incentives.

2. Identify four guidelines for successful incentive programs.

3. Discuss three types of individual incentives.

4. Define *gainsharing* and explain several types of gainsharing plans.

5. Explain why profit-sharing and employee stock ownership plans (ESOPs) are important as organizational incentive plans.

6. Identify the components of executive compensation.

7. Discuss several criticisms of board compensation committees and long-term incentives for executives.

SUMMARY OF THE CHAPTER

Many organizations feel that it is important to provide compensation beyond that made available to all employees through base pay. An *incentive* provides compensation for those employees who produce beyond normal performance expectations. It attempts to tie compensation as directly as possible to employee productivity. Incentive systems can be set up in three ways: individual, group, and organizational. If an incentive system is to be effective it must recognize organizational culture and resources, tie incentives to desired performance, be kept current, recognize individual differences, and separate incentive plan payments from base pay.

Many different types of individual incentives are available, including piece-rates, differential piece-rates, commissions, and bonuses, but they all attempt to relate individual effort to individual reward. Conditions favoring the use of individual incentive plans are:

1.   individual performance must be able to be identified,
2.   work must be performed independently,
3.   competition between employees is desired, and
4.   the organizational culture must emphasize individual achievements and rewards.

If conditions do not favor the use of individual incentives, organizations may choose group or organizational incentive systems instead of individual incentives. The intent of these types of incentive programs is to promote cooperation and coordinated effort within the group or organization. For group incentives to work it is usually necessary that the tasks require significant coordination, and that the group size be kept small.

There are several types of organizational incentive systems. The most common are gainsharing (including Improshare and the Scanlon and Rucker plans), profit-sharing, and employee stock ownership plans (ESOPs).

The two objectives of *executive compensation* are to tie the executives' compensation to the overall performance of the firm over time, and to insure competitiveness with the compensation packages of other firms. Two components of executive compensation, base pay and benefits, are similar to the compensation provided other employees. Performance-based supplemental compensation in the form of annual bonuses, long term performance rewards, and stock options attempt to tie executive compensation to the long-term growth and success of the organization.

Perquisites ("perks") are special benefits for executives that are usually non-cash items. It is the status enhancement value of perks that is important to many executives, in addition to their substantial tax savings.

STUDY QUESTIONS

Matching Questions

Match the key term from the list below with its most appropriate definition.

a.   Incentive   f.   ESOP

b.   Piece-rate   g.   Gainsharing

c.   Commission   h.   Stock option

d.   Draw   i.   Perquisites

e.   Scanlon plan   j.   Golden parachute

____   1.   Employees receive incentive compensation for reducing labor costs.

____   2.   The sharing of greater than expected gains with employees, either profits or productivity.

____   3.   A severance benefit that provides protection and security to executives who may be affected if they lose their jobs or if their firms are acquired by another firm.

____   4.   Wages determined by multiplying the number of units produced by the rate for one unit.

____   5.   A stock bonus plan whereby employees gain ownership in the firm.

____   6.   Special benefits for executives that are usually non- cash items.

____   7.   Additional compensation related to performance.

____   8.   Compensation computed as a percentage of sales.

____   9.   An employee is given the right to buy stock in the company, usually at a fixed price for a period of time.

____   10.   An amount advanced to an employee which is paid from future commissions due the employee.

True/False Questions

____   1.   The main purpose of incentives is to tie employees' rewards closely to their achievements.

____   2.   Improshare is an organizational incentive system similar to individual peace-rate systems.

____   3.   Individual incentive systems may be either group- or organization-based.

____   4.   Separating incentive pay from base pay reinforces the idea that part of an employee's pay must be "re-earned" in the next performance period.

____   5.   In a differential piece-rate system, the rate for each piece does not change regardless of the number of pieces produced.

____   6.   Major purposes of special incentive programs, such as merchandise and travel awards for salespersons, are to focus attention on specific products or obtaining new accounts.

____   7.   Despite its incentive value, the piecework system is difficult to use.

____   8.   In a straight commission system, a salesman would receive no salary if no sales are made.

____   9.   Unions strongly favor individual incentive systems because they reward the highly motivated competent workers.

____   10.   Group incentive systems seem to work better if the group is small and highly interdependent.

____   11.   The Scanlon plan is a profit-sharing incentive system.

____   12.   A major objective of executive compensation administration is to insure that the total compensation given key executives is competitive with the compensation packages in other firms.

____   13.   One disadvantage of incentive stock options is that the executive is tied to the company with "golden handcuffs."

____   14.   Major criticism of executive compensation has focused on disparities between total compensation received and corporate performance.

____   15.   It is the status enhancement value of perks that is important to many executives.

Idea Completion Questions

1.   Three types of individual incentives are:
     _____, _____, and_____.

2.   _____, _____, _____,
     _____, and _____ are five types of group or
     organizational incentives.

3.   Five guidelines for effective incentive systems are:
     _____, _____, _____,
     _____, and _____.

4.   Four components of most executive compensation systems are:
     _____, _____, _____,
     and _____.

5.   The two main features of the Scanlon plan are:
     _____, and _____.

Multiple Choice Questions

___   1.   Which of the following statements dealing with individual incentives would be incorrect?
           a.   Employee competition for incentives may provide undesirable results.
           b.   Employees are not rewarded for their achievements.
           c.   Unions may resist individual incentive programs.
           d.   All statements are correct.

___   2.   Profit-sharing plans would include which of the following?
           a.   employee stock ownership plan
           b.   gainsharing
           c.   Scanlon plan
           d.   all are profit-sharing plans

___   3.   Direct Compensation plans include:
           a.   salary.
           b.   incentive systems.
           c.   executive compensation plans.
           d.   all of the above.
           e.   a and c only.

___   4.   Individual incentive systems include all but
           a.   differential piece-rate.
           b.   commissions.
           c.   Scanlon plan.
           d.   bonuses.
           e.   all are individual incentive systems.

___   5.   An amount advanced to an employee which is repaid from future commissions due the employee is a
           a.   draw.
           b.   deposit.
           c.   straight commission.
           d.   salary-plus.

___   6.   Sales and productivity contests, conducted so that individual employees receive something extra in the way of compensation, are examples of
  a.   organizational incentives.
  b.   the Scanlon plan.
  c.   special incentive programs.
  d.   individual incentives.
  e.   c and d only.

___   7.   An ESOP is
  a.   a profit-sharing plan.
  b.   a stock option plan for executives.
  c.   an employee stock ownership plan.
  d.   all of the above.
  e.   a and c only.

___   8.   Advantages of an ESOP include all except:
  a.   the firm receives highly favorable tax treatment of the earnings earmarked for use in the ESOP.
  b.   the employees' retirement benefits are dependent upon the performance of the firm.
  c.   an ESOP gives employees a "piece of the action."
  d.   all of the above are advantages.

___   9.   Which of the following are not components in most executive compensation packages?
  a.   base pay
  b.   benefits
  c.   stock options
  d.   perquisites
  e.   all of the above are components

___   10.   Research has shown that salaries average about _____ of top executives' total compensation.
  a.   26%
  b.   78%
  c.   92%
  d.   50%

___ 11.   Drawbacks to profit-sharing plans include
   a.   expensive financial information disclosure is necessary.
   b.   profits are often beyond the control of employees.
   c.   payoff is too far removed from employee efforts.
   d.   all of the above.

___ 12.   A severance benefit designed to protect non-executive employees is known as a
   a.   golden parachute.
   b.   silver parachute.
   c.   golden handcuff.
   d.   perk.
   e.   none of the above.

___ 13.   The basic concept underlying the Scanlon plan is that
   a.   profits should be shared by all employees.
   b.   efficiency depends on teamwork and plant-wide cooperation.
   c.   unions inhibit profitability.
   d.   employees are more motivated if they share ownership of the firm.

___ 14.   With incentive stock options, an executive
   a.   is given stock in the firm as an incentive.
   b.   has the option to sell corporate stocks.
   c.   has the right to buy stock in the company at a fixed price.
   d.   establishes a pension plan that buys corporate stock options.

___ 15.   Most firms include generous perquisites in their executive compensation package because
   a.   it is their status enhancement that is valued by many executives.
   b.   perks provide substantial tax savings to executives.
   c.   perks are less costly to the firm than pay increases.
   d.   all of the above.
   e.   a and b only.

Essay Questions

1. What are some advantages and disadvantages associated with the use of each of the following:

    a.   individual incentives,
    b.   group incentives,
    c.   organizational incentives.

2. Identify and discuss some key considerations to be remembered when designing and managing an incentive system.

3. Describe the various stock option plans available to employees. Are they useful as incentives for both executives and lower-level employees? Explain.

4. Compare and contrast Scanlon Plans and Rucker Plans.

5. "Executive compensation must be viewed as a total package." Why?

ANSWER KEY

Matching

1.	e	2.	g	3.	j	4.	b	5.	f
6.	i	7.	a	8.	c	9.	h	10.	d

True/False

1.	T	2.	T	3.	F	4.	T	5.	F
6.	T	7.	T	8.	T	9.	F	10.	T
11.	F	12.	T	13.	F	14.	T	15.	T

Idea Completion

1. piece-rate
    commission
    bonus

2. Scanlon plan
    profit sharing
    Improshare
    Rucker plans
    ESOPs

3. recognize the organizational culture and resources
    tie incentives to desired performance
    keep the system current
    recognize individual differences
    separate incentive plan pay from base pay

4. base pay
    benefits
    performance based supplemental compensation
    perquisites

5.   committees to evaluate all cost saving suggestions
       direct incentives to all employees to improve efficiency

Multiple Choice

1. b	2. a	3. d	4. c	5. a
6. e	7. e	8. b	9. e	10. d
11. d	12. b	13. b	14. c	15. e

TIM'S INCENTIVE

After graduating from New Jersey State University, Tim Cleaver moved to Atlanta to look for a job. He had been a marketing major, and had a reputation at college for being a fast talker. So Tim looked for a sales job.

Within a few weeks, Tim was offered a sales job at Georgia Business Products, Inc., an Atlanta-based firm which specialized in printing business forms. Tim was hired on a salary-plus-commission basis. His starting salary was $15,000 plus 5% commission on gross sales, including re-orders. Tim's supervisor told him that most sales representatives earned between $1,000 and $2,000 each month in commissions. Of course, Tim had to pay his own expenses (car, entertainment, phone, etc).

Tim was assigned a territory and his supervisor suggested that he concentrate on hotels, bars, and restaurants which always needed checks, bills, statements, etc. For the first few months, Tim worked day and night visiting small business owners, and gained some new accounts for Georgia Business Products. But he wasn't satisfied and began to look for contacts in some large businesses.

Seven months after moving to Atlanta, Tim got his first good break. While attending the Christmas Party honoring New Jersey State alumni living in the Atlanta area, Tim met a fellow alumnus who was purchasing manager for International Airlines which was headquartered in Atlanta. The alumnus, class of '54, was impressed by Tim's ambition and wanted to help him get started in his career. He invited Tim to stop by his office to prepare a proposal for printing the documentation for the airline's on-line reservation system, including tickets, boarding passes, and itineraries.

The alumnus found Tim's proposal to be very competitive and the quality of the work was better than that of their other suppliers. International Airlines placed a large order with Georgia Business Products, and assured Tim that there would be more business in the future.

Tim was delighted to obtain the airline's account, and after a few months, his commission checks exceeded those of the other sales representatives. In fact, his total income was higher than that of the Marketing VP at Georgia Business Products.

When Tim received his annual performance review, his supervisor congratulated him on a very successful first year. The supervisor told him that, as recognition of his outstanding performance, Tim would be promoted to senior sales representative. This position came with a salary of $45,000 plus a generous expense account, but no further commissions.

Tim is now pondering his success and the subsequent "reward."

Questions

1. What do you think will be the impact of Georgia Business Products' incentive system?

2. Is it fair for a sales representative to earn more than his or her manager?

3. Should Tim be pleased with his promotion and reward for good performance?

4. What options does Tim have as a result of his supervisor's action?

5. What advice would you give to Tim?

SUPERVISORS' INCREASES

You were hired as a division manager at Regional Manufacturing Inc. a year ago. The management executive committee has recently allocated a total of $15,000 as pay increases for the eight production supervisors in your division. This committee has asked you to make the salary increase recommendations for each of these supervisors, with the suggestion that raises be in the four to ten percent range. However you may deviate from this range in special circumstances. The consumer price index (CPI) increased by five percent during the past year.

Although the company does not have a formal performance appraisal system, you have made some notes about each of the eight production supervisors:

Jose Martinez

Jose is not, as far as you can tell, a good performer. You have checked your view with others, and they do not believe that he is effective either. However, you happen to know he has one of the toughest work groups to manage. His subordinates have low skill levels, and the work is dirty and hard. If you lose him, you are not sure whom you could find to replace him. His present salary is $25,000.

Dave Maroney

Dave is single and seems to live the life of a carefree bachelor. In general, you feel that his job performance is not up to par, and some of his "goofs" are well known to his fellow employees. His present salary is $22,500.

Ron Fox

You consider Ron one of your best employees. However, it is quite apparent that other people don't consider him to be an effective manager. Ron has married a rich wife, and as far as you know he doesn't need additional money. His present salary is $26,000.

Joshua Irving

You happen to know from your personal relationship with "Josh" that he badly needs more money because of certain personal problems he is having. As far as you are concerned, he also happens to be one of the best of your employees. For some reason, your enthusiasm for him is not shared by your other employees, and you have heard them make joking remarks about his performance. His present salary is $23,000.

Barbara Ferraro

Barbara has been very successful so far in the tasks she has undertaken. You are particularly impressed because she has a hard job. She needs money more than many of the other people, and you are sure that they also respect her because of her good performance. Her present salary is $19,500.

Jack Smith

Jack has turned out to be a pleasant surprise to you. He has done an excellent job, and it is generally accepted among the others that he is one of the best. This surprises you because he is frivolous and doesn't seem to care much about money and promotion. His present salary is $22,000.

Rosemary Johnson

To you, "Rocket" just isn't cutting the mustard. Surprisingly enough, however, when you check with others to see how they feel about her, you discover that her work is regarded as OK. You also know that she badly needs a raise. She's the only black in your division, was recently divorced, and is finding it extremely difficult to support her house and her young family of four. Her present salary is $22,500.

Ned Owen

You know Ned personally, and he seems to squander his money continuously. He has a fairly easy job assignment, and he doesn't do it particularly well in your view. His present salary is $24,000.

Assignment

1. As an *individual*, indicate the percentage increase you would recommend for each supervisor, the dollar amount of this raise, and his or her new salary. Write your reasons for each decision in the space provided.

2. After you have completed your own decision, discuss these as a *group* and arrive at a consensus regarding the raises for each supervisor.

SUPERVISOR (Present Salary)	Raise		New Salary	Reasons
	Percent	Amount		
MARTINEZ $25,000 . Individual				
. Group				
MARONEY $22,500 . Individual				
. Group				
FOX $26,000 . Individual				
. Group				
IRVING $23,000 . Individual				
. Group				
FERRARO $19,500 . Individual				
. Group				
SMITH $22,000 . Individual				
. Group				
JOHNSON $22,500 . Individual				
. Group				
OWEN $24,000 . Individual				
' . Group				

Questions for Analysis and Discussion

1.   What issues of equity or fairness did you consider? How did the group discussion influence your decisions?

2.   Would your decisions have been any easier if the company had a formal performance appraisal system? Explain. What additional performance data would you require?

3.   The management executive committee has just announced that it plans to adopt an "open pay" policy. Will this cause you to change any of your salary increase recommendations? Explain.

Chapter 15

Employee Benefits

CHAPTER OBJECTIVES

1. Define *benefit* and identify approximate average benefit costs.

2. Identify strategic reasons an employer might choose to offer benefits.

3. Distinguish between mandated and voluntary benefits and list three of each.

4. Describe two security benefits.

5. Explain why health-care cost management has become important and list some methods of achieving it.

6. List and define at least six pension-related terms.

7. Discuss several types of financial and related benefits.

8. Identify typical time-off benefits.

9. Discuss benefits communication and flexible benefits as considerations in benefits administration.

SUMMARY OF THE CHAPTER

Employee benefits are a form of indirect compensation given to employees for organizational membership. Benefits must be viewed by both employees and employers as a critical part of the total compensation package, since they represent an average of about 40.7% of total payroll costs. While benefits attempt to protect employees from financial risks associated with illness, disability, unemployment, old age, and others, they contribute strategic value to the organization in the form of helping to attract and retain employees, elevating the organization's image, and increasing job satisfaction.

Benefits can be grouped into several categories: security, health care, retirement, financial and insurance, social and recreational, and time-off. Security benefits can be subdivided into those that are required by law and those which are voluntary. The most important of the required security benefits are extended health care coverage under COBRA, family and medical leave, workers' compensation, unemployment compensation, and social security. Voluntary benefits include supplementary unemployment benefits (SUB), severance pay, legal insurance, and child/elder care.

A second major benefit category is health care. Common types of benefits in this category include medical, dental, and prescription drug insurance, and vision care. Since health-care cost containment will be a major challenge of the 1990s, many employers are attempting to shift some of these costs to the employees by requiring them to share in the cost through co-payments. Other common cost containment measures include self-funding, requiring the use of preferred provider organizations (PPOs) or health maintenance organizations (HMOs) called "managed care plans," and establishing "wellness" programs within the organization.

Retirement benefits encompass both financial planning and pre-retirement counselling to help employees adjust both financially and psychologically to retirement. Financial retirement benefits may include both pensions and health-care benefits. Organizations are not required to provide pensions, however if they choose to do so, the plans must conform to the requirements of the Employee Retirement Income Security Act (ERISA). Pension plans may be either contributory or noncontributory, and benefits paid are based upon whether the plan is a defined contribution plan or a defined benefit plan. Depending upon a person's type of employment, several individual retirement benefit options are available including IRAs, 401(K) plans, and Keogh plans.

A wide range of financial and other benefits are often provided to round out the benefits package. Included in this category are various types of financial benefits including employee credit unions, purchase discounts on company products, thrift, saving, and stock option plans, and financial planning and counselling. In addition to health insurance, employers often provide other types of insurance including life and disability insurance. Other miscellaneous benefits sometimes provided include educational assistance, and various social and recreational benefits.

The final category of benefits is time-off. Included in this category are holiday pay, vacation pay, leaves of absence including medical leaves, sick pay, military leaves, funeral and bereavement leaves, and jury duty leave.

With the myriad of available benefits and regulations pertaining to them, benefits administration is becoming a very specialized field requiring not only expertise in the systems, but also the ability to communicate benefits in an understandable manner to employees. Many organizations are turning to a type of flexible benefit plan referred to as the "cafeteria-style" plan which allows each employee to select an individual combination of benefits within some overall limits. Also where employees are paying part of their benefit costs, flexible spending accounts allow them to pay for some of their benefits with pre-tax dollars. Flexible benefit plans have the advantage of allowing employees to tailor benefit packages to their needs, helping in cost control, heightening employee awareness of both the cost and the value of benefits, and facilitating the recruitment and retention of employees because of the attractiveness of the plans. Flexible plans, however, have the disadvantage of being complex and thus difficult to keep track of and communicate to employees. There is also the concern that employees will choose inappropriate benefit packages.

STUDY QUESTIONS

Matching Questions

Match the key term from the list below with its most appropriate definition.

a.   Keogh plan   g.   Cafeteria-style benefits

b.   Benefit   h.   PPO

c.   COBRA   i.   Contributory pension plan

d.   Defined benefit plan   j.   Vesting

e.   Workers' compensation   k.   Portability

f.   SUB   l.   ERISA

___   1.   The act which requires most employers to provide extended health-care coverage to certain groups.

___   2.   Provides benefits to any person injured on the job.

___   3.   A health-care provider that contracts to provide health-care services to employees at competitive rates.

___   4.   Allows self-employed individuals to establish individualized pension plans.

___   5.   Supplemental unemployment compensation that is not required by law.

___   6.   Allows employees to move pension benefits from one employer to another.

___   7.   Money for pension benefits is paid in by both employees and employer.

___   8.   Additional compensation given to employees as a reward for organizational membership.

___   9.   Has provided employees increased security through regulation of pension plans.

___   10.   Allows each employee to choose an individual combination of benefits within some limits.

___ 11. Allows employees to be assured of certain pension benefits, provided they have worked a minimum number of years.

___ 12. Provides an employee a pension amount based on age and service.

True/False Questions

___ 1. A contributory plan is one in which the employer makes all the contributions to the pension fund.

___ 2. Non-contributory pension plans are preferred by employees and unions.

___ 3. Mandated benefits of the future are likely to include universal health-care benefits.

___ 4. Since women live longer, they can be required to contribute more to pension plans.

___ 5. Employers are required to provide pay for such established holidays as Labor Day, Memorial Day, Christmas, and Fourth of July.

___ 6. A SUB plan pays an individual compensation only after governmental unemployment compensation runs out.

___ 7. The Family and Medical Leave Act affects only private employers.

___ 8. Military leave, election leave, and jury leave are required by various state and federal laws.

___ 9. HMOs provide health-care services for a group on a prepaid basis for a fixed period of time.

___ 10. A company sponsored bowling team should be classified as a benefit.

___ 11. Both HMOs and PPOs are part of what is known as "managed care plans."

___ 12. Benefits generally are not taxed as income.

___ 13. A worker injured on the job must prove the employer was at fault in order to receive workers' compensation.

___ 14. Now that the Age Discrimination in Employment Act prevents employers from forcing employees to retire, early retirements are projected to decline.

___ 15. The ERISA legislation requires employers to provide retirement protection to employees by establishing pension plans.

Idea Completion Questions

1. A(n) _____ is a managed care plan that provides services for a fixed period on a prepaid basis.

2. A benefits system which allows individuals to select their own package of benefit items is known as the _____ approach.

3. Under the Family and Medical Leave Act, leave may be taken for _____, _____, and_____.

4. _____ is a security benefit offered by some employers to employees who lose their jobs permanently if a plant closes.

5. Health-care cost management strategies include:
    _____, _____, _____, _____, and _____.

Multiple Choice Questions

___   1.   Which of the following benefits is (are) not provided by the Social Security system?
     a.   old age
     b.   disability
     c.   unemployment
     d.   retirement
     e.   all are provided

___   2.   SUBs and severance pay would be examples of which category of benefits?
     a.   required security
     b.   voluntary security
     c.   insurance and financial
     d.   retirement related

___   3.   Unemployment compensation is a(n)
     a.   required security benefit.
     b.   voluntary security benefit.
     c.   time off benefit.
     d.   insurance and financial benefit.

___   4.   Holiday pay, sick leave, and vacation pay are all examples of
     a.   required security benefits.
     b.   time off benefits.
     c.   insurance and financial benefits.
     d.   social benefits.

___   5.   If a pension plan assures that employees will receive benefits provided they have worked a minimum number of years, the plan is
     a.   funded.
     b.   vested.
     c.   contributory.
     d.   portable.

___ 6.   The cafeteria-style benefit system does all of the following but
a.   considers the complex person.
b.   increases employees' awareness of the cost and value of the benefits.
c.   provides management with a relatively easy system to administer.
d.   fits individual life situations.
e.   the system does all of the above.

___ 7.   A _____ allows employees to contribute pre-tax dollars to buy additional benefits.
a.   contributory plan
b.   flexible spending account
c.   defined contribution plan
d.   cafeteria-style plan

___ 8.   A plan allowing workers to move their pension rights from one employer to another is
a.   vested.
b.   trusteed.
c.   portable.
d.   funded.

___ 9.   A _____ is a health-care provider that contracts with an employer to provide employees' health-care services at competitive rates.
a.   health maintenance organization (HMO)
b.   self-funding option (SFO)
c.   preferred provider organization (PPO)
d.   major medical insurer (MMI)

___ 10.   The Arizona Governing Committee v. Norris ruling forced benefit plan administrators to
a.   use "unisex" mortality tables when developing pension plans.
b.   provide maternity leave for pregnant employees.
c.   provide paternity leave for male employees if maternity leave is offered to female workers.
d.   all of the above.

___   11.   A(n) _____ plan allows employees to receive cash or have employer contributions from profit-sharing and stock bonus plans placed into a tax-deferred account.
   a.   Keogh
   b.   401(k)
   c.   IRA
   d.   Rule of 45

___   12.   Some leaves, such as _____ are required by various state and federal laws.
   a.   sick leave
   b.   vacations
   c.   military leave
   d.   all are required
   e.   only a and c are required

___   13.   Employee benefits average about _____ percent of total pay checks.
   a.   23
   b.   41
   c.   49
   d.   55

___   14.   Which of the following is correct? Workers' compensation
   a.   provides benefits to employees only if they were not a fault for the accident.
   b.   costs are borne solely by the employer.
   c.   provides only for reimbursement of medical expense.
   d.   all statements are incorrect.

___   15.   Which of the following is **incorrect** under the Family and Medical Leave Act?
   a.   Employees taking leave must be able to return to the same or equivalent job status.
   b.   Health benefits must be continued while the employee is on leave.
   c.   Leave must be taken in one large block of time.
   d.   Employees can be required to use all paid leave before taking unpaid leave.

Essay Questions

1. What is a cafeteria style of benefit compensation? What are some advantages and disadvantages associated with it?

2. Differentiate between a defined contributions pension plan and a defined benefits pension plan. Discuss the advantages and disadvantages of each to both employers and employees.

3. Benefits represent a significant expenditure from an employer's point of view. Why do you think employers offer such a wide range of benefits?

4. Describe the impact that government legislation and court decisions have had on benefit administration.

5. When you are looking for a job, what three items would you consider most important in a benefits package? Explain.

6. Discuss the requirements and provisions of the Family and Medical Leave Act.

ANSWER KEY

Matching

1.	c	2.	e	3.	h	4.	a	5.	f
6.	k	7.	i	8.	b	9.	1	10.	g
11.	j	12.	d						

True/False

1.	F	2.	T	3.	T	4.	F	5.	F
6.	F	7.	F	8.	T	9.	T	10.	T
11.	T	12.	T	13.	F	14.	F	15.	F

Idea Completion

1.   HMO

2.   flexible or cafeteria-style

3.   birth, adoption, or foster care placement of a child
caring for spouse, child, or parent with a serious health condition
serious health condition of the employee

4.   Severance pay

5.   co-payment
self-funding
PPO
HMO
utilization review

Multiple Choice

1.	c	2.	b	3.	a	4.	b	5.	b
6.	c	7.	b	8.	c	9.	c	10.	a
11.	b	12.	c	13.	b	14.	b	15.	c

ISN'T IT PATERNALISM?

MEMORANDUM

TO: Jack Savage
           VP Human Resources

FROM: Carole Tinsley
           HR Director

Jack,

I just read the memo you sent to the Employee Benefits Committee asking them to look into the possibility of establishing an on-site day care facility for children of our employees. You cite the survey conducted by the National HR Association which found that on-site child-care made recruitment easier, resulted in lower absenteeism among working and single mothers, and improved job satisfaction. In addition, the survey reported that employers had complained that the productivity of female employees with school-age children dropped significantly about 3 p.m. each day. The mothers seemed to spend most of the late afternoon on the phone dealing with family concerns. It is assumed that an on-site facility would relieve this problem,

Maybe I am being callous, but don't we hire people to work a full eight-hour day? We can't ask job candidates about their personal situations, children, child-care arrangements, etc. So why should it be our responsibility to provide for their personal situations after they start work? If they can't do their jobs, or slack off because of their kids, they can just leave. Let's face it, we are a car company, not a charity! We make cars, we don't babysit!

I was twenty-five when I came to work here as a financial analyst. I had just completed my MBA in finance at the University of Michigan. Combined with my undergraduate degree in mechanical engineering, I was a "hot prospect." I was also married with a one-year-old baby. When my daughter was born two years later, I was off work for three weeks, but I used my accumulated sick leave and vacation time. Then my ex left me when Meredith was three.

Babysitting was always a problem, but I managed. It wasn't easy juggling two children and a job. I was often here until late at night and on weekends. When Meredith was in the second grade, I realized that I was missing out on much of Chip's and her life. The babysitters and child-care center knew Chip and Meredith much better than I did. So I made a career change. I asked for a transfer to what was then called the "personnel department." I was a compensation specialist. At least I used some of my analytical skills. My hours were more "regular" and I was relieved of much of the constant stress and excessive travel. But I took a small pay cut and my salary stayed somewhat stagnant for a few years. But my children were better off and I was certainly less stressed-out.

I progressed through the ranks and am now an HR director. Maybe one day I will make VP. But my career has not progressed as far, both in position and salary, as it would have if I had remained in financial analysis. But it was **MY** choice to put family first. I certainly didn't expect the company to give me special treatment. Of course it would have made my life easier, and less expensive, if I could have dropped the kids off at a subsidized on-site child-care center and arranged for the school bus to pick them up at the center and then drop them off there after school. But it wasn't the company's responsibility. It was the same when the kids got sick. I took vacation days to care for them.

I'm proud of my kids. They are both in college, and have kept out of trouble. The company had a loyal and responsible employee, and I have a good job with reasonable pay and benefits.

Which brings me to my concern. What will we cut if we add child-care to our benefits package? The Board has already complained that benefits now exceed 45 percent of total compensation. In '93 we increased the employees' contribution to the health insurance plan to offset the costs associated with complying with the Family and Medical Leave Act. Remember how upset people were - especially the singles and those without children. I estimate that a subsidized on-site child-care facility will cost much more than that.

My point is, when did we stop being a business and start becoming a parent? I managed. I coped. Are the parents of today less capable than I was? Or have they become used to having everything provided for them. That's paternalism, not freedom!

Anyway, I just wanted to express my sentiments.

CAROLE

Questions

1. How would you summarize Carole Tinsley's complaint?

2. Do you agree or disagree with her sentiments? Explain your answer.

3. Why do employers provide so many benefits for their employees? Are they cost effective? Do you think that a new benefit should only be provided if an existing benefit is eliminated or reduced?

4. What should be the role of individuals, employers, and government in accommodating the lifestyle choices of employees?

5. Can you think of any new categories of benefits that employers may offer in the future?

BENEFITS COSTING

AKD Textiles Inc. is a New York-based company which is locating a new plant in Arkansas. This new plant, which will be operated as a profit center, will have 300 employees (250 nonexempt and 50 exempt).

It is estimated that wages will average $9.00 per hour. It has been determined that benefits will equal 30 percent of the hourly wages.

The costs of various benefits are listed below.

Benefit Options

Benefit	Cost
Social Security.............................	6.20 percent
Medicare Care..............................	1.45 percent
Unemployment Insurance......................	6.00 percent
Workers' Compensation.......................	1.50 percent
Pension....................................	5.00 percent
One Holiday................................	3.45 cents
Sick Leave (1 day/month)...................	43.50 cents
Vacation (per day).........................	3.45 cents
Family Dental Care.........................	14.70 cents
Drug Insurance Program.....................	7.35 cents
Life Insurance (3 years salary)...........	7.35 cents
Hospitalization (120 days + major medical).........................	41.85 cents
Christmas Bonus............................	3.30 cents
Long Term Disability Salary Contributions.....................	1.65 cents
Vision Care Insurance......................	3.60 cents
Group Auto Insurance.......................	7.35 cents
Funeral Payment............................	1.35 cents
Employee Meals Provided Free...............	0.15 cents
100% College Tuition Reimbursement........	1.65 cents
Discounts on Company Produced Goods........	1.20 cents
Recreational Program.......................	0.45 cents
Prepaid Legal Services.....................	1.05 cents
Employee Thrift Plan.......................	2.25 cents
Credit Union Facilities...................	0.30 cents
Child Care Center..........................	3.30 cents

Assignment

1.   Which of these benefits are required?

2.   Are there other benefits that AKD Textiles is required to provide by law?

3.   As the new human resource manager you are to determine the benefits package. Which benefits would you recommend in addition to those that are required?

4.   Would you offer a "cafeteria-style" approach to benefits? Why or why not?

5.   What issues should you consider in establishing the benefits package for the new plant?

Chapter 16

Health, Safety, and Security

CHAPTER OBJECTIVES

1. Define *health*, *safety*, and *security* and explain their importance in organizations.

2. Explain how workers' compensation and child labor laws are related to health and safety.

3. Identify basic provisions of the Occupational Safety and Health Act of 1970.

4. Describe the Occupational Safety and Health Administration (OSHA) inspection and record-keeping requirements.

5. Identify and briefly discuss the different approaches to safety that comprise effective safety management.

6. Discuss three different health problems and how employers are responding to them.

7. Discuss workplace violence as a security issue and some components of an effective security program.

SUMMARY OF THE CHAPTER

Organizations have an obligation to provide employees with safe, healthy, and secure work environments. *Health* refers to a general state of physical, mental, and emotional well-being. *Safety* refers to protection of the physical well-being of people. The purpose of *security* is to protect employer facilities and equipment from unauthorized access and to protect employees while on the work premises or work assignments.

Prior to the passage of the first workers' compensation law in 1911, employers believed that safety was the employee's responsibility. Employers once thought that accidents and occupational diseases were unavoidable by-products of work. This idea was replaced with the concept of using prevention and control to minimize or eliminate health and safety risks in the workplace. Recently, increased occurrences of workplace violence and unauthorized access to computer systems have led to growing concern about workplace security.

Workers' compensation coverage is provided by employers to protect employees who suffer job-related injuries and illnesses. The passage of the Americans with Disabilities Act has created new problems for employers who have tried to make accommodations for injured workers. The child-labor laws, found in the Fair Labor Standards Act, sets 18 years as the minimum age for working in a "hazardous" occupation.

The *Occupational Safety and Health Act* of 1971 (OSHA) was passed "to assure so far as possible every working man or woman in the Nation safe and healthful working conditions and to preserve our human resources." To implement the act, numerous specific standards were established concerning equipment and working environments which employers were required to meet. In addition, the "general duty" clause of the act requires that in areas in which no standards have been adopted, the employer has a *general duty* to provide safe and healthy working conditions.

The federal Hazard Communication Standard requires manufacturers, importers, distributors, and users of hazardous chemicals to evaluate, classify, and label these substances. Employers also must make available to employees, their representatives, and health professionals information about hazardous substances.

OSHA established a standard national system for recording and reporting occupational injuries, accidents, and fatalities. The act also provides for on-the-spot inspection by OSHA agents. However, the Supreme Court has ruled that safety inspectors must produce a search warrant if an employer refuses to allow an inspector into the plant voluntarily. The OSHA violations and citation notices issued depend on the severity and extent of the problems and on the employer's knowledge of them. There are basically five types, ranging from minimal to imminent danger.

In the years since its passage, OSHA has been both praised and criticized. Although the effect on injury rates is still somewhat unclear, it appears that OSHA has been able to reduce the number of accidents and injuries in some cases. In addition, OSHA definitely has increased the safety consciousness of employers.

Criticism of OSHA has emerged because many of the standards are so vague and the rules so complicated and technical that it is difficult to know whether or not one is complying. The presence of so many minor standards also hurt OSHA's credibility. Small companies have complained that the cost of correcting violations may be prohibitive. On the other hand, critics have noted that because OSHA has so many work sites to inspect, many employers have only a relatively small probability of being inspected.

Effective safety management begins with organizational commitment to a comprehensive safety effort. This effort should be coordinated from the top level of management to include all members of the organization. Once an organization has made a commitment to safety, three different approaches to safety can be used:

The **organization approach** involves safety policies and discipline, safety training and communications, safety committees, safety inspection and accident investigation, accident research, and evaluation of safety efforts.

The **engineering approach** examines the physical setting of work, the "sick building syndrome," engineering work equipment and materials, ergonomics, and cumulative trauma disorders.

Individual approaches are concerned with behavioral aspects of safety such as accident rates and individuals, accident rates and work schedules, and safety incentives.

Employers are increasingly confronted by the problems associates with employees who have AIDS or other life-threatening illnesses such as cancer. Some employers have policies for dealing with employees with such illnesses. OSHA requires that employers comply with its bloodborne pathogens standards.

Other health-related issues confronting organizations include workplace smoking, substance abuse, and stress. Some organizations now provide an employee assistance program (EAP) which establishes a liaison relationship with a social service counselling agency to provide assistance to employees with a broad range of emotional, physical, or other personal problems.

Unlike EAPs that deal with problems after they have occurred, corporate wellness programs are designed to maintain or improve employee health before problems arise.

Security activities provide protection to employees and organizational premises, equipment, and systems. Many examples can be cited regarding workplace violence, vandalism, theft of organizational and employee property, and unauthorized "hacking" on organizational computers. Organizational responses involve a comprehensive analysis of the vulnerability of the security of the organization, controlling access to the physical facilities, employee security screening and selection, and the use of security personnel.

STUDY QUESTIONS

Matching Questions

Match the key term from the list below with its most appropriate definition.

a.	Health	i.	OSHA
b.	Safety	j.	A *de minimis* violation
c.	Security	k.	Cumulative trauma disorders
d.	Wellness programs	l.	Safety management
e.	Ergonomics	m.	Imminent danger violation
f.	EAP	n.	Stress
g.	Sick building syndrome	o.	General duty clause
h.	Security audit		

___   1.   Occupational Safety and Health Administration.

___   2.   A field which has developed to engineer the work environment.

___   3.   A citation is not issued for this type of violation.

___   4.   A program which provides counselling and other help to employees having emotional, physical, or other personal problems.

___   5.   A general state of physical, mental, and emotional well-being.

___   6.   The absence of guard rails to prevent an employee from falling several stories into heavy machinery would be an example of a(n) _____.

___   7.   A condition in which the physical well-being of people is protected.

___   8.   A cause of emotional illness and alcohol and drug abuse.

___   9.   Begins with organizational commitment to a comprehensive safety effort.

___ 10. Designed to maintain or improve employee health before problems arise.

___ 11. A situation in which employee health problems appear to be linked to time spent in the work building.

___ 12. Employers who know of, or should reasonably know of, unsafe or unhealthy conditions can be cited for violating this.

___ 13. Protection of employer facilities and equipment from unauthorized access and protection of employees while on work premises or work assignments.

___ 14. Muscle and skeletal injuries that occur when employees repetitively use the same muscles to perform tasks.

___ 15. A comprehensive analysis of the vulnerability of the security of an organization.

True/False Questions

___ 1. The "sick building syndrome" is most often caused by poor ventilation or airborne contaminants.

___ 2. To be eligible for workers' compensation, an employee must suffer a work-related injury or illness as the result of employer negligence.

___ 3. An OSHA compliance officer is required to notify an organization at least one day prior to an inspection.

___ 4. OSHA inspectors generally can obtain warrants to enter a firm fairly easily.

___ 5. In areas where no standards have been adopted, the employer still has a general duty to provide safe and healthy working conditions.

___ 6. Stress has been identified as a source of physical problems.

___ 7. Child-labor laws set 18 as the minimum age for working at a hazardous occupation.

___ 8. OSHA standards are voluntary compliance guides.

___ 9. The term "safety" includes both emotional and physical health.

___   10.   The primary safety responsibility in an organization usually falls on the HR department.

___   11.   Worker attitudes must be considered when planning safety efforts.

___   12.   The bloodborne pathogens standard issued by OSHA in 1992 permit employers to dismiss employees with certain blood diseases such as Hepatitis B or HIV.

___   13.   A *de minimis* violation is one that highlights a direct and possibly serious injury situation.

___   14.   Industrial psychologists are concerned with the proper match of people to jobs.

___   15.   The major reason why accident investigation and research is important is to gather information useful in settling workers' compensation and insurance claims.

___   16.   The "right to know" regulations have been held to be standards within the meaning of the Occupational Safety and Health Act.

___   17.   Cumulative trauma disorders (CTD) occur when workers repetitively use the same muscles to perform tasks.

___   18.   The Drug Free Workplace Act of 1988 requires all employers to maintain a drug-free environment for its workers.

Idea Completion Questions

1.   Health refers to _____,
     while safety refers to _____.

2.   The purpose of security is to _____
     _____.

3.   The engineering approach to health and safety studies _____,
     while the behavioral approach emphasizes _____.

4.   When stress related problems become so severe that the employee is unable to function normally,
     the employer should _____.

5.   Typical wellness programs may include:
     _____, _____, _____,
     and _____.

6.   Actions that an organization can take to reduce the risk of workplace violence and improve security
     include:
     _____, _____, _____,
     and _____.

Multiple Choice Questions

___   1.   Accident rates may be affected by
       a.   worker boredom.
       b.   work design.
       c.   worker carelessness.
       d.   all of the above.
       e.   a and c only.

___   2.   A specialized field which engineers the work environment is
       a.   industrial existentialism.
       b.   ergonomics.
       c.   environmentalism.
       d.   engineering design.

___   3.   When a substance abuser is offered a choice between treatment and discipline, the option is referred to as a
       a.   final offer.
       b.   last chance offer.
       c.   firm choice offer.
       d.   least resistance choice.

___   4.   According to the Americans with Disabilities Act (ADA), the prudent employer would be wise to
       a.   consider all substance abusers as disabled.
       b.   consider only illegal substance abusers as disabled.
       c.   consider only legal substance abusers as disabled.
       d.   get a case-by-case medical opinion on what to do.

___   5.   The Occupational Safety and Health Act covers all employers, _____ engaged in commerce.
       a.   having more than 50 employees.
       b.   having more than 10 employees.
       c.   having more than 5 employees.
       d.   having 1 or more employees.

6. A hose left out in an aisle so that someone could trip and get hurt would probably be
   a. a *de minimis* violation.
   b. an other-than-serious violation.
   c. a serious violation.
   d. an imminent danger violation.

7. In Whirlpool v. Marshall, the U.S. Supreme Court ruled that workers _____ if they believe that the job is hazardous.
   a. should try to correct dangerous situations
   b. should call their union
   c. have a right to walk off a job
   d. all of the above.

8. In the typical health and safety interface, the line managers would do all of the following except:
   a. develop safety reporting systems.
   b. monitor employee health and safety daily.
   c. coach employees to be safety conscious.
   d. investigate accidents.

9. Programs which provide help to employees through a social service counseling agency are called
   a. employee detection programs.
   b. employee assistance programs.
   c. drug abuse clinics.
   d. occupational health programs.

10. According to the child labor laws, 16-18 year olds
    a. may be employed in "hazardous" occupations with parental permission.
    b. cannot work in "hazardous" occupations.
    c. cannot work on school days.
    e. none of the above are true.

___   11.   The _____ clause of OSHA requires employers to provide safe and healthy working conditions even in areas where no specific standards exist.
a.   umbrella
b.   universal
c.   general duty
d.   basic provisions

___   12.   Lack of a blade guard on an electric saw would be considered a(n) _____ violation under OSHA rules.
a.   *de minimis*
b.   other-than-serious
c.   serious
d.   willful and repeated
e.   imminent danger

___   13.   Which of the following is **not** a criticism of OSHA?
a.   failed to increase safety consciousness of employers
b.   standards are vague
c.   rules are very complicated and technical
d.   cost of compliance is not realistic in some cases

___   14.   The lack of doors on restroom toilet stalls would constitute a(n) _____ violation.
a.   *de minimis*
b.   other-than-serious
c.   serious
d.   imminent danger

___   15.   _____ is defined as the protection of employer facilities and equipment from unauthorized access and protection of employees while on work premises or work assignments.
a.   Safety
b.   Ergonomics
c.   Violence prevention
d.   Security

Essay Questions

1. Differentiate among health, safety, and security as concepts, and indicate some areas of concern under each.

2. Design a sample AIDS policy for your college, taking into account the needs of both the person with AIDS and the other members of the college community.

3. Discuss why alcoholism and drug abuse are important HR concerns and describe some actions that have been taken to deal with these problems.

4. What is the primary purpose of the Occupation Safety and Health Act?   To what extent has OSHA made workplaces safer?

5. Explain what a systems approach to safety is, and why it is necessary.

6. What actions should an organization take to insure the protection of its employees at work or while on work assignments.

ANSWER KEY

Matching

1.	i	2.	e	3.	j	4.	f	5.	a
6.	m	7.	b	8.	n	9.	l	10.	d
11.	g	12.	o	13.	c	14.	k	15.	h

True/False

1.	T	2.	F	3.	F	4.	T	5.	T
6.	T	7.	T	8.	F	9	F	10.	F
11.	T	12.	F	13.	F	14.	T	15.	F
16.	T	17.	T	18.	F				

Idea Completion

1. a general state of physical, mental and emotional well-being
   protection of the physical well-being of people

2. protect employer facilities and equipment from unauthorized access and to protect employees while they are on work premises or work assignments

3. redesigning the machinery or work area
   the proper match of people to jobs and emphasize employee training in safety methods, fatigue reduction, and health awareness

4. direct the employee to appropriate professionals for help

5. screenings
   exercise programs
   education/awareness programs
   skills programs

6.   security audit/vulnerability analysis
        controlled access
        employee screening and selection
        security personnel

Multiple Choice

1.   d   2.   b   3.   c   4.   a   5.   d

6.   b   7.   c   8.   a   9.   b   10. b

11. c   12. c   13. a   14. a   15. d

THE REBEL

Cheryl Wilkes-Derrick is a rebel. She always believed that rules exist to be broken, authority must be challenged, and stereotypes should be discarded. She was outspoken in her belief that artificial barriers were always being erected to prevent women from working at the best paying jobs. Thus it was no surprise when she went to work at Dayton Precision Equipment, Inc. as an apprentice tool-and-die maker. The work was hard and the factory was noisy. But the pay was good, and it didn't bother Ms. Wilkes-Derrick that she was the only female employee on the shop floor. All the other women employed by Dayton Precision Tools were in the office or the canteen. In fact she enjoyed the notoriety. She was popular with all the shop workers who believed that if she could handle the demands of the job, her gender was irrelevant.

For three years Ms. Wilkes-Derrick enjoyed her work. She had by far the best productivity record of all the apprentices. It was only after the accident that Cheryl's supervisor and other shop managers questioned whether her "independent spirit" was hazardous to her health and well-being.

The accident occurred when she was grinding some metal. A piece of flying metal hit her in the right eye. She was taken to the hospital's emergency room where the metal fragment was removed during surgery. Only minor permanent damage resulted from the accident. Cheryl downplayed the incident and seemed embarrassed by it. It was only after she had begun to receive the medical bills that Cheryl decided to notify OSHA. She charged specifically that the company was negligent in their operation of the workplace.

In response to Cheryl's complaint, an inspection of the factory was made by OSHA. The company answered Cheryl's charges by claiming that it provided safety glasses with side shields for all employees and counter-charged that Ms. Wilkes-Derrick was negligent since she would not wear these glasses. Cheryl explained that she did not like wearing the safety glasses because they didn't fit right and were uncomfortable. She said that somehow she was under the impression that only the toolmakers and diemakers were required to wear the safety glasses, but not the apprentices.

The company showed the OSHA compliance officer a copy of the company safety rules where it was stated quite clearly:

> "Working around high-speed machine tools presents certain dangers, so toolmakers
> and diemakers must follow strict safety procedures. For example, safety glasses with side
> shields and other protective clothing must be worn to protect against bits of flying metal."

The safety rules had been read and signed by Ms. Wilkes-Derrick at the beginning of her employment. At that time she was issued with a pair of safety glasses.

Questions

1. Without having read the specific OSHA standards, do you think the company should receive a citation?

2. How sound is the company's defense?

3. Is the company liable for any of Cheryl Wilkes-Derrick's medical expenses?

4. It appears from the facts that the company did not enforce their safety rules, at least as far as Cheryl Wilkes-Derrick was concerned. Why?

5. As a safety specialist, what would you do to get the employees to use the safety glasses and other protective clothing that are provided for their own protection?

OFFICE INSPECTION

OSHA inspectors often ignore offices while making safety inspections in organizations. However, survey data show that one out of every 22 workers' compensation claims is for an office injury.

Presented on the next two pages is a checklist of items that, if violated, could pose potential safety hazards in an office area.

Using the checklist, conduct a safety inspection of an office at the university or at an organization in which you might be employed. After completing the inspection checklist, answer the questions for analysis and discussion at the end of the exercise.

Questions for Analysis and Discussion

1.   Review the completed checklist and indicate whether or not you believe the office you inspected would pass an OSHA inspection. Explain your reasoning.

2.   What do you consider the most serious violation you encountered?

3.   List other items, not on the checklist, that you believe might present potential hazards in an office.

OFFICE SAFETY CHECKLIST

Item #	Good/ Complete Compliance	Partial/ Occasional Violations	Frequent/ Total Violation
1. Slick floors dry and free of fallen items such as paper clips, rubber bands, etc.			
2. Small waste baskets under desks, out of aisles			
3. See-through glass panels on all doors			
4. Steel file cases bolted together or to floor or wall			
5. Step stools & ladder in good repair (no loose weak or broken rungs)			
6. Safety cover electric extension cords between desks and in aisles			
7. Electric cords and socket connectors in good repair			
8. Desk and file cabinet drawers closed when not in use			

OFFICE SAFETY CHECKLIST   page 2

Item #	Good/ Complete Compliance	Partial/ Occasional Violations	Frequent/ Total Violation
9. Safety cover (or auto turn-off systems) on all open equipment such as typewriters			
10. Written and enforced rules for the following: a. No carrying of large loads of materials that will cut off floor/aisle vision			
b. Limit the amount of supplies carried on stairs so an arm free to grasp handrail			
c. No lifting of heavy, awkward boxes or equipment			
d. All employee owned items (fans, coffee makers, etc.) must be safety approved			

Chapter 17

Employee Rights and Discipline

CHAPTER OBJECTIVES

1. Explain how employee rights and HR policies are interrelated.

2. Identify three exceptions to employment-at-will used by the courts.

3. List elements to consider when developing an employee handbook.

4. Explain the concept of just cause and how it is determined.

5. Discuss the issues and problems associated with drug tests.

6. Identify the major concerns about polygraph and honesty testing.

7. Outline a progressive discipline sequence.

8. Explain three alternative dispute resolution methods.

SUMMARY OF THE CHAPTER

Rights do not exist in the abstract. They exist only when someone is successful in demanding their practical application. A *right* is that which belongs to a person by law, nature, or tradition. Although the U.S. Constitution grants citizens rights to freedom and due process, such rights are not necessarily present in the work place unless specific legislation or labor/management contracts apply.

Rights are offset by *responsibilities*, which are duties or obligations to be accountable for actions. If an employee has a right to a safe working environment, the employer has an obligation to provide a safe workplace. The concept that employment is a reciprocal agreement suggests that both sides have obligations. Employee rights arise in exchange for reciprocal employee responsibilities such as loyalty and service.

Current employee rights, as widely defined under various laws, are divided into three major categories:

1. Rights affecting the employment agreement - These include the employment-at-will doctrine which states that employers have the right to hire, fire, demote, or promote whomever they choose, unless there is a law or contract to the contrary. However, this doctrine is being challenged in the courts. Nearly all states have one or more statutes that limit an employer's right to discharge, in addition to the universal restrictions of race, age, sex, national origin, religion, and handicap.

Wrongful discharge suits require that employers take care to see that dismissals are handled properly and that all personnel management systems are in order. The suits imply that employees have job rights that must be balanced against employment-at-will. Also, due process gives one the right to defend oneself against charges and is guaranteed in the U.S. Constitution. Courts have questioned the fairness of an employer's decision to fire an employee without just cause and due process. An idea becoming popular in medium to large companies is the use of an *ombudsman*, a person outside the normal chain of command, to insure that employees are given a fair hearing.

Like employment-at-will, the idea that an implied contract exists between worker and employer affects the employment relationship. Court cases have led to the conclusion that long service, promises of continued employment, and lack of criticism of job performance imply continuing employment. Similarly, in *Pine River State Bank v. Mettile*, the court concluded that employee handbooks are implied contracts.

Other rights affecting the employment agreement include: the *Worker Adjustment and Retraining Notification Act*(WARN) which requires employers to give a 60-day notice before a "massive layoff" or "plant closing" involving more than 50 people; state laws prohibiting employers from disciplining employees for most off-the-job behaviors; and protection for whistle-blowers - people who report real or perceived wrongs committed by their employers.

2. Employee privacy rights - Employers keep a variety of information about employees. While these records provide excellent sources for doing research inside the organization, there are concerns about the protection of individuals' privacy. The *Privacy Act of 1974* applies only to federal agencies and organizations supplying services to the federal government. However, similar state laws have also been passed. These laws protect the employee's right to access personnel information, to correct erroneous information, and to reasonable precautions assuring the individual the information will not be misused. An employer responding to a request from another employer about a former employee may violate the former employee's privacy rights.

Other privacy rights concern requirements that employees submit to blood tests, urinalysis, polygraph or honesty tests. These tests are increasingly being used to detect chemical dependency and the use of controlled substances, as well as reduce employee dishonesty. Unless state or local laws prohibit testing, employers have a right to require employees to submit to such tests. However, court decisions generally have indicated that random drug testing may be unconstitutional and that public agencies must have "probable cause" to test.

The *Drug-Free Workplace Act of 1988* requires government contractors take steps to eliminate employee drug use. The *Polygraph Protection Act of 1988* prohibits the use of polygraphs for most preemployment screening and for judging a person's honesty while employed.

3. Other employee rights - Other areas of employee rights include those related to workplace investigations, whereby employers investigate employee theft and drug abuse; employee rights to know of potential hazards and unsafe working conditions; employee free speech or whistle-blowing; and notification of plant closings; and security at work.

HR policies, procedures, and rules greatly affect employee rights and discipline. It is important that policies and rules be consistent, necessary, applicable, understandable, reasonable, and distributed and communicated. An *employee handbook* gives employees a reference source for company policies and rules and can be a positive tool for effective management of human resources. However, management should have legal council review the language contained in the handbook.

Employee *discipline* is a form of training that enforces organizational rules. The goal of preventive discipline is to heighten employee awareness of organizational policies and rules. Many times people simply need to be made aware of a rule, and counseling by a supervisor can provide that awareness. Progressive discipline is an approach that uses a verbal caution for a first offense and attempts to get progressively more severe, up to and including dismissal, as the employee continues to show improper behavior. The purpose of discipline is to change an undesirable behavior. Therefore, for discipline to work, it must be focused on a specific behavior not the employee personally. Discipline is also most effective if it is immediate and impersonal.

A common alternative to lawsuits in cases involving employee rights, *alternative dispute resolution*, uses arbitration, peer review panels, and mediation.

STUDY QUESTIONS

Matching Questions

Match the key term from the list below with its most appropriate definition.

a.   Due process   i.   Whistle-blower

b.   Discipline   j.   Employment-at-will

c.   Right   k.   Progressive discipline

d.   Polygraph   l.   Constructive discharge

e.   Ombudsman   m.   WARN Act

f.   Responsibility   n.   Alternative dispute resolution

g.   Policies   o.   Arbitrator

h.   Mediator

____ 1.   That which belongs to a person by law, nature, or tradition.

____ 2.   A common law doctrine stating that employers have the right to hire, fire, demote, or promote whomever they choose, unless there is a law or contract to the contrary.

____ 3.   Gives one the opportunity to defend oneself against charges and is guaranteed in the U.S. Constitution.

____ 4.   Occurs when an employer deliberately makes conditions intolerable in an attempt to get the employee to quit.

____ 5.   A person who reports a real or perceived wrong done by his or her employer.

____ 6.   A form of training that enforces organizational rules.

____ 7.   Attempts to modify behavior get progressively more severe as the employee continues to show improper behavior.

___   8.   Lie detector test.

___   9.   A person outside the normal chain of command who serves as a "public defender."

___   10.   Requires severe fines for employers who do not give workers 60 days notice before massive layoffs or plant closing.

___   11.   Used as an alternative to law suits in cases involving employee rights.

___   12.   Tries to get the two parties to agree on a mutual position to resolve a dispute.

___   13.   Makes a decision to resolve a conflict.

___   14.   General guidelines that regulate organizational actions.

___   15.   A duty or obligation to be accountable for an action.

True/False Questions

___   1.   Due process, which is guaranteed in the Constitution, does not necessarily protect the rights of at-will employees.

___   2.   Employers cannot discharge an employee for just cause based upon the employee's off-the-job activities.

___   3.   The Privacy Act of 1974 protects the individual privacy of all employees.

___   4.   Research shows that substance abusers have no more absences or accidents than non-abusers.

___   5.   Employment-at-will is a common law doctrine that supersedes most union contracts.

___   6.   The courts have held that promises of job security made prior to hiring constitute a contract between employer and employees, even though there is no signed document.

___   7.   Since employee handbooks have been recognized as implied contracts, the recommended legal remedy is to abandon the handbooks as a way to communicate with employees.

___   8.   For unionized employees, due process usually refers to their rights to use the grievance procedures specified in the union contract.

___   9.   Workers now have very little protection from employer HR practices as a result of the decline in the number of union members in the U.S. work force.

___   10.   Rights are sometimes divided into moral and legal categories. Legal rights may not necessarily correspond to certain moral rights.

___   11.   Employment as a reciprocal agreement suggests that employee moral rights arise in exchange for such expectations as loyalty, long-term service, and accountability.

___   12.   The federal government has the primary responsibility for defining employee rights.

___   13.   Federal constitutional rights, such as unreasonable search and seizure, protect an individual only against the activities of the government, not against searches by private employers.

___   14.   Paper-and-pencil honesty tests have generally been shown to be valid.

___   15.   For discipline to work, it should focus on employees' overall attitudes rather than specific behaviors.

___ 16.   Drug testing generally is legal and thus is widely used by major employers seeking to deal with the increasing drug problem at work.

___ 17.   Polygraph tests are widely used to investigate employee theft.

___ 18.   Policies are specific guidelines that regulate and restrict the behavior of individuals.

___ 19.   Procedures are customary methods of handling activities.

___ 20.   Peer review panels, as an alternative dispute resolution method, have worked well to settle contested dismissals and to keep the process out of court.

Idea Completion Questions

1.   Employee rights defined in various state laws are divided into three major categories: _____, _____, and_____.

2.   When developing employee handbooks, three standards that should be observed are: _____, _____, and_____.

3.   When responding to requests from another employer for information about a former employee, lawyers recommend that only employment history such as: _____, _____, and_____ be given.

4.   The five steps in a typical progressive discipline procedure are: _____, _____, _____, _____, and _____.

5.   The three common alternative dispute resolution methods are: _____, _____, and_____.

Multiple Choice Questions

___   1.   Requirements that employees submit to blood tests, or urinalysis are
  a.   becoming much more common.
  b.   unlawful for federal government employees.
  c.   unlawful for employees in the private sector.
  d.   permitted by the Helms-Simpson Act of 1982.
  e.   b and c only.

___   2.   Federal constitutional rights, such as unreasonable search and seizure,
  a.   prevent employees from being subjected to searches at work.
  b.   were reinforced by the U.S. Supreme Court in *Nixon v. Pearson*.
  c.   mean that employers cannot hold employees accountable for their off-the-job conduct.
  d.   protect an individual only against the activities of the government.
  e.   a and b only.

___   3.   Employment _____ suggests that employee rights arise in exchange for such employee responsibilities as loyalty and service.
  a.   of non-unionized workers
  b.   as a reciprocal relationship
  c.   of union members
  d.   -at-will

___   4.   The _____ is a person outside the normal chain of command who serves as a "public defender" or problem solver for management and employees.
  a.   ombudsman
  b.   personnel consultant
  c.   executive director
  d.   shop steward

___   5.   Several courts have held that an implied employment contract exists, and the employer has lost the right to terminate at will, if the employer
  a.   hires someone for an indefinite period.
  b.   promises job security.
  c.   gives specific procedures for discharge.
  d.   all of the above.
  e.   a and b only.

___ 6. In the landmark *Pine River State Bank v. Mettile* case, the Minnesota Supreme Court ruled that

   a.   employees are also bound by implied employment contracts limiting their right to leave at any time.

   b.   employers are required to abide by the grievance procedures outlined in the union contract.

   c.   a personnel handbook is part of an employee's contract of employment.

   d.   all of the above.

   e.   only a and c above.

___ 7. The constitutional guarantee of due process

   a.   prevents dismissal for just cause.

   b.   encourages constructive discharge.

   c.   gives one the opportunity to defend oneself against charges.

   d.   requires fair and impartial investigations.

___ 8. The Privacy Act of 1974

   a.   regulates the dissemination of personnel records among private employers.

   b.   applies only to federal agencies and organizations supplying services to the federal government.

   c.   forbids drug and polygraph testing of employees.

   d.   all of the above.

   e.   only b and c above.

___ 9. The HR guideline which typically allows for no discretion in its application is a

   a.   rule.

   b.   policy.

   c.   procedure.

   d.   guideline.

___ 10. Employment-at-will is a common law doctrine stating employers have the right to hire or fire whomever they choose unless

   a.   the employer is a federal government contractor.

   b.   there is a law to the contrary.

   c.   there is a contract to the contrary.

   d.   all of the above.

   e.   only b and c above.

___ 11.   The courts generally have conceded that unionized workers cannot pursue EAW action as at-will employees can because
      a.   they are covered by the grievance arbitration procedure.
      b.   unions tend to discriminate in the hiring of their own employees.
      c.   of due process protection under civil service regulations.
      d.   ali of the above.

___ 12.   With regard to off-the-job behavior, employers can generally
      a.   forbid smoking or alcohol use.
      b.   forbid an employee from dating an employee of a rival firm.
      c.   dismiss employees if the behavior causes an adverse effect on employer-employee relationship.
      d.   differentiate in health-care premiums for off-the-job smoking.
      e.   only a and d above.

___ 13.   The goal of _____ is to heighten employee awareness of organizational policies and rules.
      a.   self-discipline
      b.   preventive discipline
      c.   positive reinforcement
      d.   punishment
      e.   progressive discipline

___ 14.   Progressive discipline incorporates more _____ into the training and shaping of employee behavior.
      a.   counselling
      b.   positive reinforcement
      c.   behavior modification
      d.   whistle-blowing

___ 15.   The federal government requires a 60-day notice before massive layoff or plant closing involving more than 50 people. The Worker Adjustment and Retraining Notification Act requires
      a.   exemptions for bankrupted companies.
      b.   severe fines for employers if notice is not given.
      c.   state governments to set up retraining programs for workers who have been laid off.
      d.   all of the above
      e.   a and c only.

Essay Questions

1.   Discuss the following statement:

     "Employment-at-will is the right of every employer and this doctrine must not be infringed by the legislature or the courts."

2.   What should be included in an employee handbook? What legal precautions would you take?

3.   Do employees have a right to privacy with regard to drug testing? In what situations would you recommend for and against the use of drug testing?

4.   Describe how the correct use of a progressive discipline procedure can protect the employer in the event of a wrongful discharge law suit.

5.   Discuss the concept of "employment as a reciprocal agreement."

6.   How are alternative dispute resolution methods useful in avoiding lawsuits?

ANSWER KEY

Matching

1. c	2. j	3. a	4. l	5. i
6. b	7. k	8. d	9. e	10. m
11. n	12. h	13. o	14. g	15. f

True/False

1. T	2. F	3. F	4. F	5. F
6. T	7. F	8. T	9. F	10. T
11. T	12. F	13. T	14. T	15. F
16. T	17. F	18. F	19. T	20. T

Idea Completion

1. rights affecting the employment agreement
    employee privacy rights
    other employee rights

2. eliminate controversial phrases
    use disclaimers
    keep the handbook current

3. job title
    dates of employment
    ending salary

4. verbal caution
    written reprimand
    suspension
    demotion
    dismissal

5.   arbitration
      peer review panels
      mediation

Multiple Choice

1.	a	2.	d	3.	b	4.	a	5.	d
6.	c	7.	c	8.	b	9.	a	10.	e
11.	a	12.	d	13.	b	14.	c	15.	b

AFFAIRS OF THE HEART AND WORK

International Computers Inc. (ICI) demands, and gets, a high degree of loyalty from its employees. A person who joins ICI soon learns that joining the company is equivalent to getting married. Job candidates are carefully screened not only for the technical job qualifications, but also for character and lifestyle qualifications. A candidate who admits to casual drug use in college will not get hired. And just to make sure, the firm conducts an extensive pre-hiring analysis, requiring all candidates to submit to urinalysis testing, honesty tests, and background investigations.

Once hired, new employees are welcomed with elaborate ceremony. Employees soon learn that joining ICI is an act calling for absolute fidelity to the company in matters big and small. And just in case an ICI employee isn't a self-starter in the loyalty department, the company has a training regimen geared to instilling it. In brief, this consists of supervising new trainees closely, grading them, repeatedly setting new goals for them, and rewarding them amply for achievement. Suffused in work and pressure to conform, employees often develop a camaraderie, an esprit de corps.

What it all amounts to is a kind of ICI culture, a set of attitudes and approaches shared to a greater or lesser degree by ICIers everywhere. People who leave ICI speak of their departure as if it were a divorce.

Margaret Anne Kelly was once an ICI person who went through a painful divorce. A self-described "ICI person," she got into trouble when her interpretation of ICI's largely unwritten rules clashed with that of her superiors. Unlike most separations from ICI - quiet resignations to pursue other interests - hers was a messy divorce that ended up in court.

Ms. Kelly joined ICI as a receptionist in Los Angeles eighteen years ago at age 22. She had just graduated from a midwestern university with a bachelor's degree in organizational communication. After fourteen years, five transfers, and numerous stints in ICI training schools, Margaret Anne Kelly became a division marketing manager located in Dallas, supervising salesmen who sold personal computers to small businesses and community colleges in the southwest.

On a steamy August day, Margaret Anne Kelly abruptly turned in her keys and her plastic ICI identification card and fled ICI, after her boss confronted her about her relationship with Bryan Matthews. Mr. Matthews was once an ICI super-salesman who left ICI the previous December and was now manager of a competing office products company. Ms. Kelly had made no attempt to hide her involvement with Mr. Matthews, and had in fact invited him to escort her to the ICI summer picnic. It was obvious that they spent much of their social life together.

In an emotionally charged interview, her boss said she was being given a non-management position at the same salary. To Margaret Anne Kelly, steeped in ICI's fast track culture, this was tantamount to being released, so she quit. She sued, claiming constructive discharge.

At the trial, ICI conceded that Ms. Kelly was a loyal employee with an outstanding record and that there was no indication she had ever passed company secrets to her boyfriend. But, it argued, the mere existence of a relationship between business rivals was a conflict. ICI claimed that she clearly cared for Mr. Matthews' success, and as such had a conflict of interest.

Ms. Kelly's lawyers argued that what really worried ICI was the possibility she would defect to Matthews' company, encouraging other ICI salesmen to defect as well.

Margaret Anne Kelly claimed that the company couldn't dictate an employee's off-the-job behavior.

Questions

1. Describe ICI's culture. How do they achieve it? Are their hiring procedures legal? Ethical?

2. Did Margaret Anne Kelly have an obligation to ICI that transcended any formal legal contract?

3. Did ICI have any alternatives to transferring or dismissing Ms. Kelly? Is ICI in violation of any law in transferring her to the non-management position?

4. Assume that you are a member of the jury in *Kelly v. International Computers Inc*. What would be your decision? Explain.

SUBSTANCE ABUSE POLICIES

The substance abuse policies of three different organizations are printed on the following pages. Evaluate each of the policies for legality, practicality, and comprehensiveness.

Assignment

1.   What would you add to, or delete from, each policy?

2.   Are there alternatives to writing and communicating policies such as these?

3.   What impact are substance-abuse policies likely to have on employee behavior, responsibility, and morale?

A CONSTRUCTION FIRM

1.   All contractors, subcontractors, and employees will sign the policy in acknowledgment that they have read it.

2.   Anyone will be denied access to the property if there are reasonable grounds to believe that he or she is under the influence of alcohol or other substances, or is exchanging or selling such substances.

3.   If there are reasonable grounds to believe that a violation has taken place, then the person will submit a blood or urine sample.

A DEFENSE CONTRACTOR

1. Any person who uses or is in possession of drugs on the job or during work hours will be terminated.

2. Employees who use or are in possession of alcoholic beverages during work hours could be subject to disciplinary action, including termination.

3. Any person who observes another in possession of drugs or alcohol, including use on the job, must report this to supervision or security, or be subject to disciplinary action.

4. If a supervisor has reason to believe that an employee is unfit for duty as a result of alcohol or drugs, a blood test will be administered, and the employee will remain off the job until the results are available.

    Those who are directly involved in operations, maintenance, construction, security, personnel protection, or operation of company vehicles or equipment are subject to random drug testing.

    If an employee shows drugs or alcohol in his or her urine or blood as a result of the test, disciplinary action will result - up to and including termination.

5. An employee may submit a challenge specimen to a company approved lab within two calendar days of notification of the positive test results.

6. Any employee who has a problem with drugs or alcohol will be encouraged to use the employee assistance program (EAP). Use of the program will not require a drug screening. Use of the EAP will not shield an employee from discipline.

A PRIVATE UNIVERSITY

1.   An "overview" of the HR policy states the university's concern about alcohol and drug abuse as they undermine the work environment, job performance, and the public's confidence in the university.

      The university will take action against employees who use, distribute, or possess controlled substances on or off the job, and who violate university rules in reference to possession of alcohol on the job.

2.   All employees must report to work in a fit condition for duty. Being under the influence of alcohol and drugs is prohibited.

3.   Alcoholism and drug abuse are recognized as illnesses or disorders. The university accepts responsibility to seek help.

      If the employee seeks help prior to discovery, then confidentiality, job security, and promotional opportunities will be protected.

      If the employee doesn't seek help, and the problem in some way comes to the attention of the administration, disciplinary action will result.

4.   Employees who use or distribute illegal drugs on the job will be discharged. Any drugs will be turned over to local law enforcement authorities.

5.   If an employee is arrested off the job for drug involvement, the university will consider various circumstances surrounding the arrest before taking disciplinary action.

6.   If an employee is under treatment with a drug that could alter his or her ability to do the job, the employee could be subject to job reassignment.

7.   Each employee is required to sign this policy statement.

Chapter 18

Union/Management Relations

CHAPTER OBJECTIVES

1. Describe what a union is and discuss why employees join unions.

2. Explain reasons for the decline in the percentage of U.S. workers represented by unions.

3. Explain the acts that compose the National Labor Code.

4. Identify and discuss the stages in the unionization process.

5. Define *decertification* and explain how it occurs.

SUMMARY OF THE CHAPTER

A *union* is a formal association of workers that promotes the interests of its members through collective action. When employees choose a union to represent them, formal collective bargaining over certain issues between management and union representatives must occur. When these issues are resolved into a labor contract, management and union representatives must work together to manage the contract and prevent grievances.

Unions in the U.S. serve two major purposes. Their primary purpose has been on the collective pursuit of the basic economic issues such as helping workers obtain higher wages, shorter working hours, job security, and safe working conditions. In order to do some of these things it has been necessary for unions to become politically active to assist in getting laws passed to facilitate obtaining these economic issues. In recent years, political activity has spread into the broader area of social issues where unions have been at the forefront of pushing for such items as mandatory parental leaves, child-care tax credits, and universal health insurance. Unions in the United States have been undergoing numerous changes in recent years. Increases in the number of white collar workers, part-time workers, and women in the workforce have contributed to the decline in unions membership. To counter these declines, unions have broadened their agenda to include such issues as pay equity, career ladders, child care, job training, and flexible work arrangements.

Today two basic types of unions exist reflecting the different roots of their founding. *Craft unions* represent workers who do one type of work, often using specialized skills and training, while *industrial unions* represent persons working in the same industry or company, regardless of the type of job held.

American unions today are organized in an hierarchical structure with multiple levels. At the bottom of the hierarchy, local unions may be centered around a particular employer organization at a particular geographic location. Officers in local unions are elected by the membership. Intermediate union organizational units coordinate the activities of a number of local unions. National or international unions determine broad union policy and provide services to local union units. At the top level, the AFL-CIO is a loose confederation of national unions.

Although unions existed as early as 1794 in the U.S., major growth in unionism did not occur until after the Civil War when rapid industrial growth began. The first major labor organization was the Knights of Labor, a large single national union which attempted to represent all workers. After their peak in 1885, the Knights faded from the labor scene, and were replaced by the formation of the American Federation of Labor (AFL). The AFL was a federation of a number of different independent national unions, each representing a particular group of skilled craft workers such as carpenters, plumbers, etc. Although the AFL was effective in representing skilled craft workers, they were unsuccessful in representing the unskilled or semiskilled factory workers. Thus in 1938 the Congress for Industrial Organizations (CIO) was formed to represent these types of workers.

Over the years, the federal government has taken action that has both hindered and protected the union movement. The *Sherman Antitrust Act* in 1890 forbade monopolies and efforts to legally restrain trade - including union boycotts. In 1926 the *Railway Labor Act* was passed which gave railroad employees the right to organize and bargain collectively through representatives of their own choosing. In 1936 airline employees were added to those covered under this act and both these industries are still covered by this act instead of by others passed later. The *Norris-LaGuardia Act*, passed in 1932, freed union activity from court interferences and made the "yellow dog" contract illegal.

Three significant acts collectively form the **National Labor Code**: the *Wagner Act* (1935), the *Taft-Hartley Act* (1947), and the *Landrum-Griffin Act* (1959). Together these acts establish the workers' right to organize, define unfair labor practices of management, forbid a series of unfair labor practices by unions, outlawed the closed shop, permit states to pass right-to-work laws, and protected individual union members. A fourth law, the *Federal Service Labor-Management Statute* of 1978, provides U.S. governmental employees and their unions coverage similar to that provided private sector employees under the National Labor Code.

The unionization process begins either at the initiative of a particular union which believes it can successfully organize a given group of employees, or as a result of individual workers in an organization contacting the union to indicate a desire to be unionized. Once the unionization efforts begin, the typical stages of the process include:

1.   organizing campaign,
2.   authorization cards,
3.   representation elections,
4.   certification, and
5.   contract negotiation.

Employees who no longer wish to be represented by a union can use a similar election process, called decertification, to remove the union.

STUDY QUESTIONS

Matching Questions

Match the key term from the list below with its most appropriate definition.

a.   Union

b.   Wagner Act

c.   AFL-CIO

d.   Business agents

e.   Union stewards

f.   Sherman Antitrust Act

g.   Craft union

h.   Federal Service Labor-
Management Relations Act

i.   Right-to-work

j.   Taft-Hartley Act

k.   Landrum-Griffin Act

l.   Handbilling

m.   Authorization cards

n.   Representation election

o.   Decertification

p.   Closed shop

____   1.   Provides U.S. governmental employees and their unions coverage similar to that provided private sector employees by the National Labor Code.

____   2.   Full-time union officials usually elected.

____   3.   The Magna Carta of labor, which helped union growth.

____   4.   An act aimed at protecting individual union members.

____   5.   Practice by unions of giving written publicity to employees which tries to convince them to sign authorization cards.

____   6.   The American Federation of Labor and the Congress of Industrial Organizations.

____   7.   The pro-management segment of the National Labor Code.

___ 8. A formal association of workers that promotes the interests of its members through collective action.

___ 9. Forbade monopolies and efforts to restrain trade illegally.

___ 10. Represent the lowest elected officer in the local union.

___ 11. Provision that outlaws the closed shop.

___ 12. An election to determine if a union will represent the employees.

___ 13. A type of union whose members do one type of work using specialized skills and training.

___ 14. Process whereby a union is removed as the representative of a group of employees.

___ 15. Indicates employees' desire to vote on having a union.

___ 16. Requires individuals to join a union before they can be hired.

True/False Questions

___ 1. Certification means that the NLRB approves the contract negotiated by union and management representatives.

___ 2. The ratio of union members to the total work force in the U.S. has decreased in recent years.

___ 3. The Taft-Hartley Act outlaws the closed shop, which requires individuals to join a union before they can be hired.

___ 4. Shop stewards are usually appointed by the business agent for the local.

___ 5. Right-to-work laws have outlawed unions in some states.

___ 6. The Wagner Act was more pro-union than pro-management.

___ 7. The Wagner Act allowed an employer to contribute to and support a labor organization.

___ 8. Corrupt union practices are covered by the Wagner Act.

___ 9. U.S. unions have followed the international union trend to be at the forefront of nationwide political trends.

___ 10. A majority of the firm's total non-management employees must vote for a union if a union is to be certified.

___ 11. American unionism focuses primarily on wages, working hours, and working conditions.

___ 12. A bargaining unit consists of all the employees in a given work unit.

___ 13. Industrial unions were formed before craft unions.

___ 14. The Clayton Act ultimately had a significant impact on the state of unionism in the U.S.

___ 15. Right-to-work laws are state laws that prohibit both closed and union shops.

___ 16. The major area of potential union growth is among white-collar groups and government employees.

Idea Completion Questions

1. Union structure consists of _____ unions at the bottom,
    _____ _____ unions in the middle,
    and the _____ at the top.

2. _____ unions represent members doing one type of work using specialized skills and
    training, while _____ unions represent persons working in the same industry or
    company regardless of the type of job held.

3. The three laws that make up the National Labor Code are:
    _____, _____, and_____.

4. The five steps in the typical unionization process are:
    _____, _____, _____,
    _____, and _____.

5. The right-to-work provision of the Taft-Hartley Act outlaws
    _____,
    and allows _____.

Multiple Choice Questions

___   1.   In the representation election process, if 300 employees are the identified unit and 200 of those persons vote in the election, the number of votes necessary for the union to win the election is
a.   300.
b.   200.
c.   151.
d.   101.

___   2.   The National Labor Relations Board was established by
a.   the Clayton Act.
b.   the Railway Labor Act.
c.   the Wagner Act.
d.   the Taft-Hartley Act.

___   3.   Which of the following acts is pro-management?
a.   the Wagner Act
b.   the National Industrial Recovery Act
c.   the Taft-Hartley Act
d.   all are pro-union

___   4.   The act dealing with internal union democracy and the rights of individual union members is the
a.   Clayton Act.
b.   Landrum-Griffin Act.
c.   Hoffa-Kennedy Act.
d.   the Norris-LaGuardia Act.

___   5.   Congress passes the Norris-LaGuardia Act to
a.   make the "yellow dog" contract illegal.
b.   establish union grievance procedures.
c.   free union activity from court interference.
d.   encourage management/union bargaining.
e.   only a and c above.

___   6.   The primary philosophy of unions in the U.S. has been
           a.   job-centered emphasis.
           b.   political solidarity.
           c.   class consciousness.
           d.   worker participation in decision making.
           e.   all of the above.

___   7.   A major emphasis of the Knights of Labor was
           a.   to create several big unions for various trade workers.
           b.   to emphasize political reform and establish work comparatives.
           c.   to be concerned only with the traditional "bread and butter" issues.
           d.   to ensure the individuality of the worker.

___   8.   Which is not a part of the National Labor Code?
           a.   the Railway Labor Act
           b.   the Taft-Hartley Act
           c.   the Landrum-Griffin Act
           d.   the Wagner Act

___   9.   A closed shop
           a.   prohibits unions from organizing at the plant.
           b.   requires individuals to join a union before they can be hired.
           c.   was permitted by the National Labor Code.
           d.   requires that an employee join the union after being hired.

___   10.   The percentage of employees who must sign authorization cards in order to call a representation election is
           a.   100.
           b.   60.
           c.   50.
           d.   30.

___   11.   Union membership trends indicate that
    a.   union membership as a percent of the total work force has been declining.
    b.   blue collar unionism is declining.
    c.   unionism is becoming somewhat successful in the public sector.
    d.   all of the above are true.
    e.   only a and b above are true.

___   12.   Which of the following tactics would be identified as an unfair practice by management?
    a.   tell employees the high cost of union dues
    b.   promise employees pay increases if they vote against the union
    c.   forbid distribution of union literature during work hours in work areas
    d.   show employees negative articles about unions
    e.   all of the above are unfair labor practices

___   13.   The right-to-work provision is a part of the
    a.   Taft-Hartley Act.
    b.   Wagner Act.
    c.   Landrum-Griffin Act.
    d.   Clayton Act.

___   14.   Reasons why union membership has dropped significantly include
    a.   the decline of manufacturing jobs which traditionally had the highest percentage of union members.
    b.   an increase in white collar workers in the workforce.
    c.   an increase in women in the workforce.
    d.   all of the above.
    e.   only a and c above.

___   15.   In the labor relations interface, the HR unit typically would do all of the following except
    a.   deal with union organizing attempts.
    b.   help negotiate labor agreements.
    c.   provide detailed knowledge of labor legislation.
    d.   administer the labor agreement on a daily basis.

___   16.   Unions have difficulty in organizing white collar workers because
      a.   unions are seen as not in touch with concerns of a more educated work force.
      b.   professionals define fairness differently than traditional unions do.
      c.   unions are perceived as being resistant to change.
      d.   all of the above.

Essay Questions

1.   Discuss the concept of "right-to-work" and explain the impact of right-to-work laws on the closed shop, the union shop, and the agency shop.

2.   Discuss the basic intent and provisions of the following acts:

      a.   Railway Labor Act,

      b.   Wagner Act,

      c.   Taft-Hartley Act,

      d.   Landrum-Griffin Act,

      e.   Federal Service Labor-Management Statute.

3.   Explain past and present trends in unionism regarding white collar workers, women, and public sector employees.

4.   What tactics can management legally use to try to defeat a unionization effort?

5.   List in order and briefly discuss the steps involved in employees becoming unionized.

ANSWER KEY

Matching

1. h	2. d	3. b	4. k	5. l
6. c	7. j	8. a	9. f	10. e
11. i	12. n	13. g	14. o	15. m
16. p				

True/False

1. F	2. T	3. T	4. F	5. F
6. T	7. F	8. F	9. F	10. F
11. T	12. F	13. F	14. F	15. T
16. T				

Idea Completion

1. local
   national
   AFL-CIO federation

2. craft
   industrial

3. the Wagner Act
   the Taft-Hartley Act
   the Landrum-Griffin Act

4. organizing campaign
   authorization cards
   representation election
   certification
   contract negotiation

5.   the closed shop
      states to pass right-to-work laws

Multiple Choice

1.	d	2.	c	3.	c	4.	b	5.	a
6.	a	7.	b	8.	a	9.	b	10.	d
11.	d	12.	b	13.	a	14.	d	15.	d
16.	d								

POWER STRUGGLE AT RECYCLE SERVICES

Three years into his company's labor dispute, a bitter Zach Brummett wonders if his business will survive. Sales at the company he founded and runs, Recycle Services Inc., have slipped so much from over $9 million in 1990 that "I'll be lucky if I do $2 million this year," he says. And no one can put a price tag on the emotional toll.

A deteriorating labor situation at Recycle Services culminated in a strike. It left Jose Catalan, a former welder at the company, finding only day-to-day work and separated from his wife and children. At home, "little problems would become big problems" he laments. Mr. Brummett became so angered by picketing workers shouting obscene comments and making lewd gestures at his wife that he grabbed a worker's union picket sign and burned it in the parking lot.

Certainly this was not the message President Clinton was promoting at a Chicago conference in the summer of 1993 to boost labor-management cooperation. Companies in this country must know "that you can grow and prosper by treating workers as indispensable partners," the president told a group of 400 corporate executives, union leaders, and academics. "This is an opportunity we have to seize."

But many small businesses think such concepts as worker-management teams are a big company's game. Indeed, at small companies, the democracy Mr. Clinton was urging can run smack into autocracy. Owners often say "it's my business. I own it. I created it. No one is going to tell me how to run it."

Labor Secretary Robert Reich acknowledges the difficulty of shifting U.S. companies to a new level of teamwork. "Managers got to where they are because they were good at controlling. It's a little scary to give up that control. There's a lot of distrust between workers and managers out there."

The labor conflict at Recycle Services shows what can go wrong when a proud, independent owner faces workers making demands on that independence.

Zach Brummett started Recycle Services in the San Diego area in 1979 with $300. He hired one employee and together they started making large trash dumpsters which were divided into three, four, or five sections. Mr. Brummett was something of a pioneer in the recycling industry. Before recycling become fashionable, he saw the need for dumpsters and trash cans to facilitate sorting recyclable trash.

But Mr. Brummett wasn't an easy man to work for. "He would scream at you every day," recalls Javier Spinosa, who joined Recycle Services in 1980 as a welder. Mr. Spinosa, who later became chairman of the union-bargaining committee, says Mr. Brummett would force welders to work in the rain, and safety inspectors cited Recycle Services for a string of violations in the mid-1980s. Mr. Brummett countered that the inspectors came in only after a "drunk" worker cut off three fingers in a machine.

Mr. Brummett acknowledges morale problems at the plant, but says they stemmed mostly from workers comparing pay checks. The 41 year old entrepreneur says he likes to give raises to the employees who work hardest. For the others, he says: "I told you to hustle more. You make me more money, you'll make more money. I'm not going to give raises to people who tell me to pay them more money or they won't work hard. That's not American."

Despite the working environment, or perhaps because of it, Recycle Services grew into a successful small manufacturing business. By 1990, it had hired a full-time salesman, two foremen, and a plant manager. Eighty-two workers reported to them. The company had a backlog of more than ten weeks, remarkable in an industry where customers want their products yesterday. But trouble was brewing. The mix of Mr. Brummett's cantankerous personality, workers' discontent over pay, and two strong external forces - the union and the slowing California economy - would soon prove too much.

It wasn't just Mr. Brummett's fault. Workers, who often don't see what it takes to run the business, meet a payroll, or accept risk, simply viewed his success as an opportunity to get a share. At larger companies a phalanx of trained managers and HR professionals schooled in the science of labor disputes would intervene. But at smaller companies, like Recycle Services, which don't have the training resources or know-how, the clash can be devastating.

In the summer of 1990, Javier Spinosa and another employee stepped into Recycle Services' cinder block office building and told the plant manager that the workers wanted more pay and an extra week of vacation. The plant manager told them to put their request in writing.

But workers apparently took that as a rejection. A week later, the company received a letter from a national union saying that workers had signed cards seeking a vote on representation from the union. Within weeks, the workers, hoping for higher pay, benefits, and relief from workplace pressure, voted the union in, 39-25.

With the third party involved in ensuing contract negotiations, relations between Recycle Services and its workers deteriorated quickly. Mr. Spinosa says that in a meeting with workers, Mr. Brummett told them that "the [expletive] union will never tell me what to do in my plant. How would you like it if I told you what to do in your homes?"

Mr. Brummett's resistance led to a string of miscalculations by the union. Frustrated by a lack of progress on a contract, the union, hoping to improve workers' leverage, got strike authorization. That move was never meant to result in a walkout.

But Mr. Brummett, seeing his 11-year-old creation slip into outsiders' hands, presented a "final" offer, and called workers in to argue that the union was a bad idea. Some workers said that he gave selected employees raises to win their backing. As Mr. Brummett fought back, the union, worried that its support was dwindling, turned its threat into reality. On January 8, 1991, the workers called a strike.

Neither side expected more than a two-week impasse. At $100 a week in strike pay from the union, it would be tough for the workers to live. The union felt that it couldn't show weakness lest it demonstrate to other business owners that a hard line would soften it.

Fifty-eight workers stayed out that first week, most walking the picket line in front of the plant. By the second week, seventeen workers returned to work. As the strike dragged on for weeks and then months, morale decayed. Gradually, the number of pickets shrank to 22, with many workers walking away to find other jobs.

Mr. Brummett's business began to suffer, too. Customers coming to the gate had to wait until strikers moved off the driveway. Eventually, they declined to come. Truck drivers were prodded to keep away. Many did.

As Recycle Services' backlog dwindled, even employees who had returned started to lose work. New orders weren't coming in. The salesmen, frustrated, left, taking customers with them.

For the strikers and Mr. Brummett, emotions began to take over. For example, one morning a truck driver came to the gate to pick up some dumpsters the company had made. But he refused to cross the picket line. So, Mr. Brummett, who wanted the $2,300 sale, agreed to bring the steel dumpsters out to the street. He began driving a forklift towards the gate. Five strikers walked across the driveway. Mr. Brummett kept driving slowly, eventually hitting the strikers and forcing them out of the way.

In November 1991, the 22 remaining strikers, broke and disillusioned, offered to return unconditionally. Only three have been hired back. The two sides continue to wage a legal battle as Recycle Services' business remains depressed.

The company's workforce has dropped to about twenty from more than eighty. The union local has spent far more than it can ever hope to recoup in union dues. There are no winners - unless one counts lawyers and competitors.

Questions

1.   What prompted the employees of Recycle Services Inc. to seek union representation?

2.   What benefits have the employees at Recycle Services gained as a result of their union membership? Did they have any alternative to organizing?

3.   Examine Zach Brummett's attitude towards the union. Were his actions justified? Did he overreact? What has he gained by his actions?

4.   Could the strike have been avoided? How?

5.   If the NLRB investigates the situation at Recycle Services, would they find cause for citing Mr. Brummett and/or the union for unfair labor practices?

UNION BUSTING?

You are Vice President of Human Resources at Imperial Grocery Stores. The company owns 35 supermarkets throughout the northwest and two distribution centers. The company employs over 1,000 cashiers, warehouse workers, and support staff. With the exception of the store managers and the head office clerical staff, all the employees are represented by the Grocery Workers Union (GWU).

Yesterday, while you were on a routine visit to a store in Bellingham, Washington, Wanda Neville, a cashier, expressed her dissatisfaction with the union. She told you, confidentially, that all the staff at her store hated the union and resented paying union dues. She asked for your assistance in "getting rid of" the union. You advised her that you would much prefer to deal with the employees one-on-one, without the interference of the union bosses, and agreed to help her.

You are now back in your office, and reflect on your conversation with Wanda Neville. Prepare a list of the actions you can and cannot take to assist Ms. Neville. Then write a memo to Ms. Neville advising her of what steps she can take to secure the decertification of GWU.

Chapter 19

Collective Bargaining and Grievance Management

CHAPTER OBJECTIVES

1. Define *collective bargaining* and identify at least four bargaining relationships and structures.

2. Explain the three categories of collective bargaining issues.

3. Identify and describe a typical collective bargaining process.

4. Discuss how union/management cooperation has been affected by NLRB rulings.

5. Define *grievance* and describe the importance and extent of grievance procedures.

6. Explain the basic steps in a grievance procedure.

SUMMARY OF THE CHAPTER

This chapter continues the discussion of the labor relations topic by looking at the processes of collective bargaining, contract administration and grievances. *Collective Bargaining* is the process whereby representatives of management and workers negotiate over wages, hours, and other terms and conditions of employment. It is a give-and-take process between the representatives of two organizations for the benefit of both. The most significant aspect of collective bargaining is that it is an ongoing relationship that does not end immediately after an agreement is reached.

Union/management relationships in collective bargaining can follow one of several patterns including conflict, armed truce, power bargaining, accommodation, cooperation, or collusion. Regardless of the approach to bargaining, the process may be structured in any one of the following ways:

1.   One employer, one union.
2.   One employer, multiplant.
3.   One employer, multiunion.
4.   Multiemployer, one union.
5.   Multiemployer, multiunion.

A wide range of issues can be subject to collective bargaining. The Wagner Act identified three broad categories of issues including illegal issues, mandatory issues, and permissive issues. Most labor contracts include a wide array of items most of which fall within the mandatory issues categories. A typical contract will include clauses covering management rights, union security, wages, benefits, working conditions, work rules, and other necessary legal conditions.

In a typical bargaining process, both labor and management representatives would spend a considerable amount of time preparing for negotiations. At this time management may be required to provide the union with necessary company information. The process would then continue with an initial presentation of expectations (called "demands") by both sides. Once the opening positions have been taken, each side attempts to determine what the other values highly so the best bargain can be struck. Each side then begins to trade off demands in order to get comparable concessions from the other side. This process continues until a final contract is negotiated.

During the negotiations, both management and labor may use a computerized mathematical modeling system to quickly evaluate the cost of changes in wages, benefits and other economic items. Four sets of factors impact the bargaining power of management and the union including economic factors, the organizational/institutional context of the bargaining situation, sociodemographic factors, and the legal environment. In the collective bargaining process the behavior of negotiators is critical. Representatives can exhibit any of four behavior subprocesses including distributive bargaining, integrative bargaining, attitudinal structuring, or intraorganizational bargaining.

Ratification occurs when the union members vote to accept the terms of a negotiated labor agreement. During the 1980s and early 1990s the need to reduce costs caused many organizations to drastically reduce labor costs. This clearly changed the collective bargaining environment and made unions realize they had to be more concerned with plant closings, force reductions, and productivity issues than with traditional wage and benefits issues. Both sides realized that without change there will be no companies and no jobs. Thus, the notable changes and trends evolving out of this situation are union/management cooperation, concessionary bargaining, bankruptcy and plant closings, and striker replacement.

If the two sides cannot reach an agreement a bargaining deadlock exists, which could result in either a union strike or a management lockout. Types of strikes which might occur are economic strikes, unfair labor practice strikes, wildcat strikes, jurisdictional strikes, and sympathy strikes. To forestall such drastic action, conciliation/mediation or arbitration may be used.

Once a collective bargaining contract has been negotiated and signed, it becomes the document that governs union/management relations. If an employee feels that any of his or her rights under the contract has been violated, the individual can file a grievance. A *grievance* is an alleged misinterpretation, misapplication, or violation of a provision in a union/management agreement. A *complaint* is an indication of employee dissatisfaction which has not taken the formal grievance settlement route. A complaint is, however, a good indicator of potential workforce problems.

Grievance procedures are almost always included in labor/management contracts and are designed to settle a grievance as soon as possible after the problem arises. A typical grievance procedure has several steps through which it can progress, if necessary, until agreement is reached. Grievance procedures also are becoming more common in non-unionized firms as managements are becoming concerned about protecting employee rights and providing employees due process.

Grievance arbitration, the final step in the grievance process, removes the solution from the two parties involved and places it with an impartial third party whose decision (award) becomes binding on both parties. The arbitrator is basically being asked to make an interpretation of the meaning of the contract language. Arbitration has been criticized as too costly, too legalistic, and too time consuming. An alternative is mediation where neutral parties act as counselors to reopen communication, clarify problems, and find areas where the two parties can agree.

STUDY QUESTIONS

Matching Questions

Match the key term from the list below with its most appropriate definition.

a.	Collective bargaining	f.	Mediation
b.	Lockout	g.	Arbitration
c.	Pattern bargaining	h.	Grievance
d.	Two-tier wage structure	i.	Grievance procedure
e.	Distributive bargaining	j.	Ratification

____ 1. Using the contract negotiated with one company as a model for contracts with other firms in the industry.

____ 2. Occurs when an outside individual attempts to help two deadlocked parties continue negotiations and arrive at a solution.

____ 3. A formal channel of communication used to resolve formal complaints.

____ 4. Process whereby representatives of management and workers negotiate over wages, hours, and other terms and conditions of employment.

____ 5. A specific, formal notice of employee dissatisfaction expressed through an identified procedure.

____ 6. A situation in which new union members receive lower wages and fewer benefits than existing members performing similar jobs.

____ 7. Management shuts down company operations to prevent union members from working.

____ 8. A means of settling a dispute whereby an impartial individual determines the relative merits of each argument and makes the final decision.

____ 9. A bargaining behavior occurring when one party must win and the other lose over a conflicting issue.

____ 10. Occurs when union members vote to accept the terms of a negotiated labor agreement.

True/False Questions

____ 1. An individual worker who believes his or her union did not properly pursue a grievance can sue the union in a federal court.

____ 2. Sympathy strikes occur when a union tries to force an employer to assign work to its members instead of to another union.

____ 3. The legal approach to grievance resolution is more interested in settlement than in symptoms, unlike the behavioral approach.

____ 4. Based on the Wagner Act many of the employee involvement programs set up in recent years may be illegal.

____ 5. Unions favor concession bargaining because it improves the credibility of union leaders.

____ 6. In an economic strike an employer is free to replace the striking workers.

____ 7. Executive Order 12954 prohibits firms that hire permanent striker replacements from receiving government contracts at $100,000 or more.

____ 8. An "open-door" policy is not a sufficient substitute for a formal grievance procedure.

____ 9. Bargaining trends for the 1990s will likely move away from the cooperative union/ management stance of the 1980s.

____ 10. A grievance procedure can be useful in providing employees with job security.

____ 11. Collective bargaining is an ongoing process, and does not cease when a contract is ratified.

____ 12. Some employers bargain with more than one union at the same time.

____ 13. Conciliation and arbitration are basically different terms for the same concept.

____ 14. A mediator makes a decision after considering the relative merits of the positions of both parties.

____ 15. Most labor contracts contain grievance procedure provisions.

____ 16. A collective bargaining trend of the 1990s is union ownership of the firm.

Idea Completion Questions

1.   Collective Bargaining is the process whereby representatives of management and workers negotiate
over _____, _____, and_____.

2.   Six types of bargaining relationships are:
_____, _____, _____,
_____, _____, and _____.

3.   A _____ is a specific formal dissatisfaction expressed through an identified procedure,
whereas a _____ is merely an indication of employee dissatisfaction.

4.   "Good faith" bargaining occurs when _____
_____.

5.   Some shortcomings of arbitration are:
_____, _____, and_____.

6.   Three types of bargaining issues identified in the Wagner Act are:
_____, _____, and_____.

Multiple Choice Questions

_____ 1. When the union agrees to reduce wages, benefits, or other factors during collective bargaining it is referred to as
   a.   two-tier bargaining.
   b.   good faith bargaining.
   c.   concessionary bargaining.
   d.   distributive bargaining.

_____ 2. As a result of recent NLRB decisions such as the Electromation and DuPont decisions it is likely that future labor/management efforts at cooperation will
   a.   continue as they have been set up.
   b.   become more formalized.
   c.   feature less involvement by managers.
   d.   both b and c above are likely.

_____ 3. In a(n) _____ strike, workers who want their jobs back at the end of the strike must be reinstated.
   a.   economic
   b.   unfair-labor-practice
   c.   wildcat
   d.   all of the above

_____ 4. Taking the position that "the only good union is a dead union" would typify the which bargaining strategy?
   a.   conflict
   b.   power
   c.   accommodation
   d.   collusion

_____ 5. "Management and the union learn to adjust to each other and attempt to minimize conflict, to conciliate whenever necessary, and to tolerate each other" describes
   a.   cooperation.
   b.   collusion.
   c.   power bargaining.
   d.   accommodation.

___   6.   In the _____ strategy, union and management engage in labor price fixing designed to inflate wages and profits at the expense of the general public.
        a.   collusion
        b.   armed truce
        c.   power bargaining
        d.   conflict

___   7.   Normally the first step in a grievance procedure is for the employee to discuss the grievance with
        a.   the HR department representative.
        b.   the union grievance committee.
        c.   the plant manager.
        d.   his or her immediate supervisor.

___   8.   _____ occurs when union members vote to accept the terms of a negotiated labor agreement.
        a.   Settlement
        b.   Ratification
        c.   Mediation
        d.   Two-tier wage bargaining

___   9.   Which of the following union security measures can be negotiated in right-to-work states?
        a.   union shop
        b.   agency shop
        c.   maintenance of membership
        d.   dues checkoff
        e.   all of the above

___   10.   The shortcomings of the arbitration process include which of the following?
        a.   it is non-legalistic
        b.   it is difficult to select an arbitrator since there are so many to choose from
        c.   it is too costly
        d.   all of the above are shortcomings
        e.   only a and b are shortcomings

___ 11. Recognizing that a grievance may be a symptom of an underlying problem that management should investigate, represents taking a(n) _____ approach to the resolution of grievances.
   a. legal
   b. arbitration
   c. integrative
   d. behavioral

___ 12. The one employer, multiunion bargaining structure is the common model in which of the following industries?
   a. coal mining industry
   b. construction industry
   c. auto industry
   d. garment industry

___ 13. A win-lose approach to bargaining would characterize which bargaining behavior?
   a. distributive bargaining
   b. integrative bargaining
   c. attitudinal structuring
   d. intra-organizational bargaining

___ 14. When management shuts down company operations to prevent union members from working, it is referred to as a
   a. lack of "good faith."
   b. strike.
   c. lockout.
   d. picket line.

___ 15. Having an impartial third party make a binding decision on a grievance is called
   a. conciliation.
   b. mediation.
   c. arbitration.
   d. negotiation.

____ 16.   In the grievance interface, the HR unit typically would do all of the following except:
a.   acts as management's representative in the first step of the grievance procedure.
b.   assists in designing the grievance procedure.
c.   monitors trends in grievance rates for the organization.
d.   may assist preparation of grievance cases for arbitration.

Essay Questions

1.   List and explain four types of bargaining relationships and two types of bargaining structures.

2.   Explain what a grievance is, and outline the typical steps in a grievance procedure.

3.   Discuss the use of both arbitration and mediation in resolving union/management disputes.

4.   Define a bargaining impasse and describe the two types of outcomes which can result.

5.   Describe the typical process used to reach a collective bargaining agreement.

6.   Discuss the collective bargaining trends in the latter 1990s and into the 21st century.

ANSWER KEY

Matching

1. c	2. f	3. i	4. a	5. h
6. d	7. b	8. g	9. e	10. j

True/False

1. T	2. F	3. T	4. T	5. F
6. T	7. T	8. T	9. F	10. T
11. T	12. T	13. F	14. F	15. T
16. T				

Idea Completion

1. wages
   hours
   other terms and conditions of employment

2. conflict
   armed truce
   power bargaining
   accommodation
   cooperation
   collusion

3. grievance
   complaint

4. the parties agree to send negotiators who are in a position to bargain and make decisions

5. too costly
   too legalistic
   too time-consuming

6.   illegal
      mandatory
      permissive

Multiple Choice

1.	c	2.	d	3.	b	4.	a	5.	d
6.	a	7.	d	8.	b	9.	d	10.	c
11.	d	12.	b	13.	a	14.	c	15.	c
16.	a								

BILLY BOB'S GRIEVANCE

Billy Bob Murphy is a construction worker employed by a construction firm in Pittsburgh, and is a member of the Teamsters Union. He has filed a grievance against his employer, Thompson Construction, claiming that he was unjustly disciplined for leaving his job. His version of the incident was quite different from his employer's.

Management said that Murphy left his job and went home at 12 noon instead of the usual 4:00 pm quitting time on the Friday before Labor Day weekend. (The company closes down on Labor Day, and the employees get a paid holiday as provided for in their union contract.) Murphy was suspended for three days without pay as a disciplinary action for this behavior. The relevant part of the union contract states that:

"No employee shall leave his or her work position to clock out except:

1.   at quitting time;
2.   if the employee's immediate supervisor gives written approval; or
3.   on the approval of the company nurse in the case of illness."

Murphy claims he visited the nurse at about 11:30 on the morning in question with a migraine headache, and she confirmed his opinion that he should go home immediately. He remembers a large number of employees in the nurse's office at the time, and said he reminded the nurse of the need to log him in and record the fact that he was sent home. She assured him she would do this.

Management invoked the suspension because they could find no supervisory approval for the early departure nor could they find any record of Murphy having visited the nurse that day. The nurse didn't remember his coming in either, although she claimed she logged in more people than average on the Fridays preceding holiday weekends. She remembers having had a terrible headache herself that day and would have surely remembered a similar complaint if an employee had made one.

Murphy has filed lots of grievances before and has a reputation of being a complainer, always questioning the supervisor's authority and challenging various company policies. The company is determined not to back down.

Murphy really felt strongly about this case, and was determined to "fight it all the way." The union had processed the grievance through the first five internal steps of the grievance procedure but had not resolved the controversy. So now the case is set to go to arbitration.

Questions

1.   How should Thompson Construction go about preparing its case for arbitration?

2.   Prepare the union's presentation of its position in behalf of Billy Bob Murphy.

3.   Assume the role of arbitrator. What factors would you consider? What factors in the case should you **not** allow to influence your decision?

4.   What award would you render for the case? What is the rationale for your decision?

TOY CONTRACTS

Specialty Toy Manufacturing Inc. (STM) produces "up-market" specialty toys in a small New England town for distribution nationwide. STM employs about three hundred production workers. It is much smaller than its competitors since STM is not diversified in its operations. It has been able to meet its competition by emphasizing high production quality and personalized marketing techniques. It has the best reputation in the industry for quality.

For many years, the production workers have been organized by the Wood Workers of America (WWA), and union/management relations have been good. No time has ever been lost due to a work stoppage or strike. In 1996, one of STM's largest competitors dropped its specialty toy operations to concentrate on mass produced items. This gave STM a tremendous opportunity to increase its market share from 40 to 70 percent. Management is excited about the possibilities and wants to increase its production as soon as possible.

The current union contract expires next week. Representatives from management and the union have been negotiating the new contract for several weeks, but no agreements have been reached.

Instructions

1. Divide into an even number of groups of four to six members. Half of the groups are to play the role of union negotiators and the other half are company negotiators.

2. Study the following:

    a. Selected Labor/Management Agreements in New England,
    b. Rules for Negotiation,
    c. Bargaining Issues.

3. The union and management groups prepare for negotiation.

4. Two opposing groups can begin negotiations whenever they choose. Keep track of the time it takes to reach agreement.

5. The present contract expires thirty minutes after the negotiating groups begin their preparations.

SELECTED LABOR/MANAGEMENT AGREEMENTS IN NEW ENGLAND

Bargaining Issue	Firm #1	Firm #2	Firm #3	New England
Hourly Wage Rate	$9.20	$9.00	$9.60	$9.40
Third Shift Differential	$1.00	None	$1.10	$0.50
Health Insurance/ Company Contributions	25%	50%	100%	50%
Vacation Benefits	2 wks	1 wk	2 wks	2 wks
Child Care Subsidy	50%	100%	None	100%

RULES FOR NEGOTIATION

1. Any tactic is acceptable, within the "good faith" concept. Time is important. If a contract is not approved in thirty minutes, a strike occurs. A strike will cost STM $50,000 a day in lost production, and WWA membership $21,600 per day in lost wages. (5 minutes = 1 day).

2. Record the agreements as they are reached on the form below.

3. Once agreement on an issue has been reached, it cannot be renegotiated.

BARGAINING ISSUES

1. Hourly Wage Rate

```
        Current contract    $9.00 per hour
        STM offer           $9.20 per hour (20 cents increase)
        WWA demand          $9.80 per hour (80 cents increase)
```

Per Hour Increases

```
          .20              .40              .60              .80
STM   <------------------------------------------------------> WWA
        $124,800         $249,600         $374,400         $499,200
```

2. Third Shift Differential

```
        Current contract    No shift differential
        STM offer           No shift differential
        WWA demand          $1.00 per hour shift differential
```

Per Hour Differentials

```
        0      .25      .50       .75      $1.00
STM   <------------------------------------------> WWA
       $0    $5,000   $10,000   $15,000   $20,000
```

3. Medical Insurance/Company Contributions

```
        Current contract    STM paid 25%, and employees paid 75%
                            of premiums at group rates
        STM offer           No change (employee should pay 75%)
        WWA demand          STM should pay full cost
```

Company Contribution

```
        25%           50%           75%           100%
STM   <------------------------------------------------> WWA
        $0         $100,000      $200,000      $300,000
```

4.   **Vacation Benefits**

Current contract   1 week for first and second year,
                       2 weeks after two years service
STM offer   No change
WWA demand   2 weeks for all employees

Weeks of Vacation

```
        2 after         2 after                   2 for
        2 years         1 year                    all
STM  <─────────────────────────────────────────────────>  WWA
        $0              $20,000                   $45,000
```

5.   **Child Care Subsidy**
Current contract   STM paid 50% of child care costs.
                       Employee paid the balance
STM offer   No change (employee should pay 50%)
WWA demand   STM should pay full cost

Company Subsidy

```
        50%             75%                       100%
STM  <─────────────────────────────────────────────────>  WWA
        $0              $80,000                   $160,000
```

FINAL AGREEMENT

Hourly Wage Rate _____

Third Shift Differential _____

Health Insurance/Company Contribution _____

Vacation Benefits _____

Child Care Subsidy _____

Questions for Analysis and Discussion

1. How much does the final agreement cost Specialty Toy Manufacturing Inc. per year?

2. What was the most difficult item to reach agreement on?

3. How much did the competitors' agreements influence your negotiations?

4. Did you consider STM's ability to pay the additional costs?

5. Would you recommend that the Wood Workers of America call a strike if an agreement could not be reached before the old contract expired?

6. How could a mediator or an arbitrator have helped you during negotiations?

Chapter 20

Assessing Human Resource Effectiveness

CHAPTER OBJECTIVES

1. Identify three general areas in which HR departments should set goals.

2. Discuss three major reasons why HR records are necessary.

3. Identify several uses of a human resource information system (HRIS).

4. Differentiate between primary and secondary research, and identify four methods for researching HR problems.

5. Discuss why assessing HR effectiveness is important, and identify two approaches for doing so.

6. Identify an HR audit and describe how one is conducted.

SUMMARY OF THE CHAPTER

As in other areas of the organization, it is important for HR activities to be assessed for effectiveness. There are several reasons why assessment of HR effectiveness and efficiency has been difficult and deficient. However, it is important that HR departments collect measurement data on what it does and communicate that information to the rest of the organization.

The sources of information for measuring HR effectiveness are HR Records. *HR record-keeping* is necessary for three major reasons:

1. **Government compliance** - Federal, state, and local laws require that numerous records be kept on employees. For compliance with the Fair Labor Standards Act, records should be kept on all covered employees with regard to wages, employment, work schedules, performance appraisals, merit and seniority systems, and affirmative action programs. Other records may be required on issues relating to EEO, OSHA, the Age Discrimination Act, and ADA.

2. **Documentation** - HR records serve as important documentation should legal challenges be brought. Disciplinary actions, past performance appraisals, and other documents may provide the necessary "proof" that employers need to defend their actions as job-related and non-discriminatory.

3. **Assessment of HR effectiveness** - HR records also provide an excellent source of information for research. They help the organization audit or assess the effectiveness of any unit, and provide the basis for research into possible causes of HR problems.

Given the vast amount of data to be kept and the large number of uses to which the information may be put, the major problem presented by HR record-keeping is the inability to retrieve information without major difficulties. The solution to this problem may be a *human resource information system* (HRIS), which is an integrated system to provide information used in HR decision making. An HRIS serves two major purposes: to improve the efficiency of HR activities and to provide HR information more rapidly. An HRIS is used primarily in the areas of payroll, benefits administration, and EEO/affirmative action tracking.

HR research analyzes past and present HR practices by using collected data and records. HR research can be used in four main ways:

> monitoring current HR activities,
> identifying HR problem areas and possible solutions,
> forecasting trends and their impact on HR management, and
> evaluating the costs and benefits of future HR activities.

Primary research is the method by which data are gathered directly on problems and issues. *Secondary research* utilizes research done by others and reported in articles in professional journals and books.

A number of different methods can be used when doing HR Research. Experiments and pilot projects can provide useful HR insights. An experiment involves studying how some factors respond when changes are made in one or more variables. Another research method uses employee questionnaires that give employees an opportunity to voice their opinions about specific HR activities. A specific type of questionnaire is an attitude survey that focuses on feelings and beliefs that underlie opinions. A third research method is the interview which may focus on a wide variety of problems. Research also can be conducted using other organizations.

One approach to assessing HR effectiveness is *benchmarking* which compares specific measures of performance against data on those measures in "best practice" organizations. To do benchmarking requires planning, establishing evaluation methods, and identifying best practices.

HR specialists can gain new insight and learn about best practices from managers and specialists in other organizations by participating in professional groups.

The transfer of information is another important HR role. *Communication* affects the management of people. Through communications efforts, new policies are explained, changes are implemented, and instructions are given. Organizations also need to develop means for employees to communicate upward so that data and information from them are obtained. The advent of electronic communication (e-mail), a computerized system to send and receive messages, make individual and organizational communication almost immediate. It also often results in by-passing the formal organizational structure and channels. HR information can be formally communicated up and down an organization through internal publications and media, audiovisual media, and suggestion systems.

A number of methodologies have been suggested for assessing HR effectiveness. They include:

> HR audits,
> ratio analyses,
> return on investment (ROI) and economic value added (EVA), and
> utility or cost/benefit analyses.

STUDY QUESTIONS

Matching Questions

Match the key term from the list below with its most appropriate definition.

a.	Experiment		f.	Attitude surveys
b.	HR audit		g.	e-mail
c.	Primary research		h.	Secondary research
d.	HRIS		i.	Grapevine
e.	HR research		j.	Benchmarking

____   1.   Informal communication channels in an organization.

____   2.   The method by which data is gathered directly on problems and issues.

____   3.   Utilizes research done by others and reported in articles in professional journals and books.

____   4.   Studying how a factor responds when changes are made in one or more variables and conditions.

____   5.   An integrated system designed to provide information used in HR decision making.

____   6.   A formal research effort to evaluate the current state of HR management in an organization.

____   7.   A computerized system to send and receive messages for individuals and organizations.

____   8.   Focuses on employees' feelings and beliefs that underlie their opinions about their jobs and the organization.

____   9.   The analysis of data from HR records to determine the effectiveness of past and present HR practices.

____   10.   Comparing specific measures of performance against data on those measures in "best practice" organizations.

True/False Questions

____   1.   The government does not require organizations to keep records on employees.

____   2.   The best defence in a discrimination suit is for the organization to have no records on its employees.

____   3.   The use of e-mail often results in by-passing the formal organizational structure and channels.

____   4.   An advantage of an HRIS is that many HR activities can be performed more efficiently and with less paperwork.

____   5.   A firm's net operating profit after the cost of capital is deducted is known as return on investment (ROI).

____   6.   The "grapevine" is a formal communication channel in organizations.

____   7.   Formal communications must allow information to flow both up and down in the organization.

____   8.   A suggestion system is a formal way to move information upward through an organization.

____   9.   Searching professional journals for articles on research done by others is a common method of primary research.

____   10.   A study into the relationship of a pre-employment physical exam to workers' compensation claims would be an example of secondary research.

____   11.   Attitude surveys provide a composite view of the characteristics of an organization as seen by its employees.

____   12.   An HR audit, similar to a financial audit, conducts a survey of the salaries paid by comparable organizations in the local area.

____   13.   An exit interview asks those leaving the organization to identify the reasons for their departure.

____   14.   HR assessment activities utilize both direct and indirect measurement methods.

Idea Completion Questions

1. Gathering and maintaining records on a variety of HR related activities is useful in three major ways:
    _____, _____, and_____.

2. Comparing specific measures of performance against data on those measures in "best practices" organizations is known as _____.

3. In _____ research, data are gathered directly on problems of concern, while _____ research utilizes research done by others and reported in professional journal articles and books.

4. Major methods for assessing HR effectiveness include:
    _____, _____, _____, and _____.

5. A _____ is a formal method of obtaining employee input and upward communication.

Multiple Choice Questions

___   1.   In _____ economic or other statistical models are built to identify the costs and benefits associated with specific HR activities.
   a.   utility analysis
   b.   an HR audit
   c.   human resource accounting
   d.   selection analysis

___   2.   HR records are necessary for which of the following reasons?
   a.   government compliance
   b.   documentation
   c.   HR assessment and research
   d.   all of the above
   e.   a and b only

___   3.   The major advantages of a human resource information system is that:
   a.   small companies also can use the system.
   b.   information can be retrieved and analyzed more easily.
   c.   more accurate information is kept.
   d.   all of the above.

___   4.   Which of the following information about employees should <u>not</u> be included in most HRIS?
   a.   race, marital status, gender
   b.   skill profile
   c.   salary and benefits
   d.   name, address, and phone number
   e.   none of these should be excluded

___   5.   Establishing an HRIS entails which of the following?
   a.   system design and implementation
   b.   user training
   c.   controlling for security and privacy
   d.   all of the above
   e.   only a and b above

___   6.   Which of the following is <u>not</u> an example of formal HR communication?
     a.   company magazine
     b.   bulletin boards
     c.   suggestion system
     d.   grapevine
     e.   all of the above are examples of formal HR communication

___   7.   Comparing specific measures of performance against data on those measures in "best practice" organizations is known as
     a.   utility analysis.
     b.   HR auditing.
     c.   performance surveying.
     d.   benchmarking.

___   8.   Which of the following would <u>not</u> be classified as HR research?
     a.   conducting a flexitime experiment
     b.   discussing selection problems with a management consulting firm
     c.   contacting a local employers' council for area pay statistics
     d.   reading *HR Magazine*
     e.   all are methods of HR research

___   9.   HR Research data are useful for which of the following?
     a.   monitoring current HR activities
     b.   identifying HR problem areas and possible solutions
     c.   forecasting trends and their impact on HR management
     d.   projecting the costs and benefits of future HR activities
     e.   all of the above

___   10.   The exit interview often does not divulge the real reasons for leaving, because resigning employees
     a.   do not want to "burn any bridges."
     b.   fear candid responses will hinder receiving favorable references.
     c.   never want to admit they are leaving for more pay.
     d.   all of the above.
     e.   a and b only.

___ 11.   Calculations showing the value of expenditures for HR activities and how long it will take for activities to pay for themselves is known as
   a.   economic value added.
   b.   utility analyses.
   c.   cost benefit analyses.
   d.   return on investment.

___ 12.   _____ is a formal research effort to evaluate the current state of HR management in an organization
   a.   Human asset accounting.
   b.   An HR audit
   c.   An employee questionnaire
   d.   An HR experiment

___ 13.   More accurate responses to an employee questionnaire can be obtained if
   a.   the questionnaires are distributed and collected by supervisors.
   b.   the questionnaires are mailed to the employees' homes.
   c.   the employees can return the questionnaires anonymously.
   d.   the questionnaires are given out with employee paychecks.

___ 14.   Which of the following is (are) important in designing and conducting attitude surveys?
   a.   Insuring validity and reliability of the questions.
   b.   Insuring anonymity of respondents.
   c.   Providing feedback to respondents.
   d.   All of the above are important.
   e.   Only a and b above are important

Essay Questions

1.   Prepare a proposal arguing for the installation of a computer-based human resource information system at a medium sized manufacturing company.

2.   Describe the usefulness and limitations of each the following means of HR communication:

   a.   employee handbook,

   b.   suggestion system,

   c.   grapevine,

   d.   e-mail.

3.   Why is HR research important?

4.   Design and describe an experiment for testing the relationship(s) between employee satisfaction and absenteeism.

5.   Is it possible to measure HR costs and benefits? Explain.

ANSWER KEY

Matching

1. i	2. c	3. h	4. a	5. d
6. b	7. g	8. f	9. e	10. j

True/False

1. F	2. F	3. T	4. T	5. F
6. F	7. T	8. T	9. F	10. F
11. F	12. F	13. T	14. T	

Idea Completion

1. government compliance
    documentation
    assessment of HR effectiveness

2. benchmarking

3. primary; secondary

4. HR audits
    ratio analyses
    ROI and EVA
    utility or cost/benefit analyses

5. suggestion system

Multiple Choice

1. a	2. d	3. b	4. e	5. d
6. d	7. d	8. e	9. e	10. e
11. d	12. b	13. c	14. d	

THE VALUE OF DOCUMENTATION

February started out as a special month for Leo Catsavis. To celebrate their twenty-fifth wedding anniversary, Leo and his wife took a three-week second honeymoon trip to Europe culminating with a Mediterranean cruise. When Leo returned to work as the Senior Partner for Human Resources at the regional office of a national accounting firm, he found three letters of inquiry from the district office of the Equal Employment Opportunity Commission. The letters advised him of complaints filed against his firm, and sought his response.

Catsavis was upset. A naturalized American who spoke with a heavy accent, Leo tried to comply with all civil rights and labor law requirements. He was especially sensitive to the needs of minorities having encountered discrimination himself in the early stages of his career.

Trained as an accountant, Catsavis always keeps detailed records on HR activities. As he prepares to answer these complaints, he hopes that his records will help the firm and not the complainants.

COMPLAINT #1: Meredith Olsen

Meredith Olsen was a December graduate of City University with a major in accounting. She had a 3.82 GPA and had served as president of her university's chapter of the Accounting Honor Society.

Ms. Olsen is forty-two, having returned to college following a divorce. Last summer she scheduled an interview with Leo Catsavis to apply for a position as staff accountant (the standard entry-level position for new accounting graduates.) At the time Catsavis informed her that the firm already had hired its quota of new graduates, but to contact him again following graduation. In November, just prior to graduation, Ms. Olsen wrote to Catsavis enclosing an updated copy of her resume. In a letter of reply, Catsavis thanked Ms. Olsen for her letter, but regretted that the firm had no vacancies at that time. He advised her that he would keep her resume on file.

Referring to the Age Discrimination Act, Meredith Olsen complained to the EEOC that the firm failed to hire her because of her age.

COMPLAINT #2: Tonya King

About a year and a half ago, Tonya King was hired as a secretary in the business office of the firm. After six months, she received her first performance review which appraised her work as "above average" and recommended that her probationary employment be made permanent.

Soon after that, however, Leo Catsavis began to receive complaints concerning her lack of responsibility. She was often late for work, took extended lunch breaks, and regularly left the office early in the evenings. One year after she was hired, she was given her annual performance appraisal. Her supervisor drew attention to her tardiness, and warned her that if this behavior continued, she would be terminated. Two months later, there had been no improvement, and Mr. Catsavis received a request to dismiss Tonya. Almost immediately, Tonya announced that she was pregnant and was taking three months leave of absence. Following the birth of her child, Tonya returned to work, only to be told that she was fired. She was given one month's severance pay.

Miss King filed a complaint with the EEOC claiming that the accounting firm had a policy that permitted medical leaves of absence, and which guaranteed employees a job of at least the same level and pay following the leave. She cited the Family and Medical Leave Act of 1993, claiming that she was denied a medical leave due to her pregnancy.

COMPLAINT #3: William Valentine

Leo Catsavis was not surprised to learn of Bill Valentine's complaint. An African American who had joined the firm as a staff accountant following graduation, Valentine had gained a reputation as a chronic complainer. Last summer, after two years with the firm, Valentine had been denied a promotion. He was advised at the time that his performance was below expectations, and that his record of absenteeism and tardiness was causing some concern.

Valentine filed an official charge of discrimination with the Equal Employment Opportunity Commission. He listed the following allegations:

1. William Valentine stated that he had a severe allergy to cigarette smoke. Since several of the accountants smoked in their offices, he regularly suffered headaches and respiratory problems. When he complained to his manager, he was told to buy a fan and to ask his doctor for an allergy medication.

2. Although the firm had denied his promotion request in part because of excessive absenteeism, a white employee in the office, with as many absences as he had, was recently promoted.

3. A white employee was given less demanding assignments and this enabled him to earn better performance appraisals.

4. He was restricted by his manager from having conversations with members of the secretarial staff, who were the only other African Americans employed in the office. When he discussed this problem with the HR Partner, the partner did not seem to understand the problem and failed to correct it.

Questions

1.   From the information provided, do you think these complaints have merit?

2.   Do the complaints suggest a pattern of unlawful discrimination at the accounting firm?

3.   What records will Leo Catsavis require as he prepares a response to each of the complaints?

4.   What records might the EEOC request as they investigate the complaints?

5.   How can an HRIS assist Leo Catsavis to avoid complaints such as these in the future?

KEEPING IT IN THE FAMILY

Gerstner Boyd Enterprises has been unusually successful in the competitive fast food industry. Claire Gerstner and her brother, Jeremy Boyd, decided to invest their joint inheritance in a hamburger restaurant in suburban Seattle in 1983. Their restaurant was part of a national franchise operation. After two years they built a second restaurant, then a third, and by the end of 1993 they owned eighteen fast food restaurants in the northwest. Actually, it was Claire Gerstner who operated the business. Her brother, a human resource manager working in Phoenix, was content to let her run the business and to reinvest most of the profits.

At each restaurant, Claire Gerstner employed a manager and an assistant manager, one of whom was on duty whenever the restaurant was open. The managers, in turn, employed approximately 30 part-time workers, primarily teenagers and semi-retired people, at each restaurant. Claire Gerstner had one strict personnel policy: "No relatives." She firmly believed that a business was courting trouble if it hired spouses, siblings, children, or even girl or boy friends of current employees. The restaurants operated smoothly with little evidence of employee dissatisfaction.

In mid-1993, Gerstner Boyd purchased the OWI Corporation which owned and operated six motels in Washington. Claire explained to Jeremy Boyd that this was a natural diversification of their business within the service sector.

The motels also employed a small number of managers together with many part-time, semi-skilled workers. However, Claire Gerstner soon became aware that OWI gave preference to relatives of current employees when it came to hiring. Two of the motels were managed by husband and wife teams, and most of the housekeepers and janitors had at least one family member also employed at the same motel.

Claire Gerstner explained the former owner's hiring policy to her brother. Jeremy advised her that: "Nepotism is alive and well. Many small businesses cite hiring family members of employees as one of their secrets of success." He suggested that she obtain details of a 1993 survey conducted by the Society for Human Resource Management. This survey found that 88% of small businesses employ relatives and 84% have no policy prohibiting employment of spouses. In fact nearly three-quarters of the 432 firms surveyed disagreed with the statement that the employment of family members should be discouraged.

They both agreed that Gerstner Boyd Enterprises needed to have a consistent policy regarding hiring family members - either ban it at the motels, despite the fact that it could affect employee morale, or else lift the ban at the restaurants. Claire Gerstner wanted her decision to be based on hard facts not anecdotes or her own limited experience.

So she decided to do some research.

Instructions

1. Outline the steps Gerstner Boyd Enterprises should take to use secondary sources in researching the question of hiring family members.

2. Design an employee survey that Claire Gerstner can use to obtain the opinions of her restaurant employees regarding the employment of relatives.

3. Adapt the questionnaire to survey the motel employees as to their opinions about hiring family members.

4. Design an experiment to study the impact of hiring family members on the recruitment, turnover, satisfaction, and performance of employees.